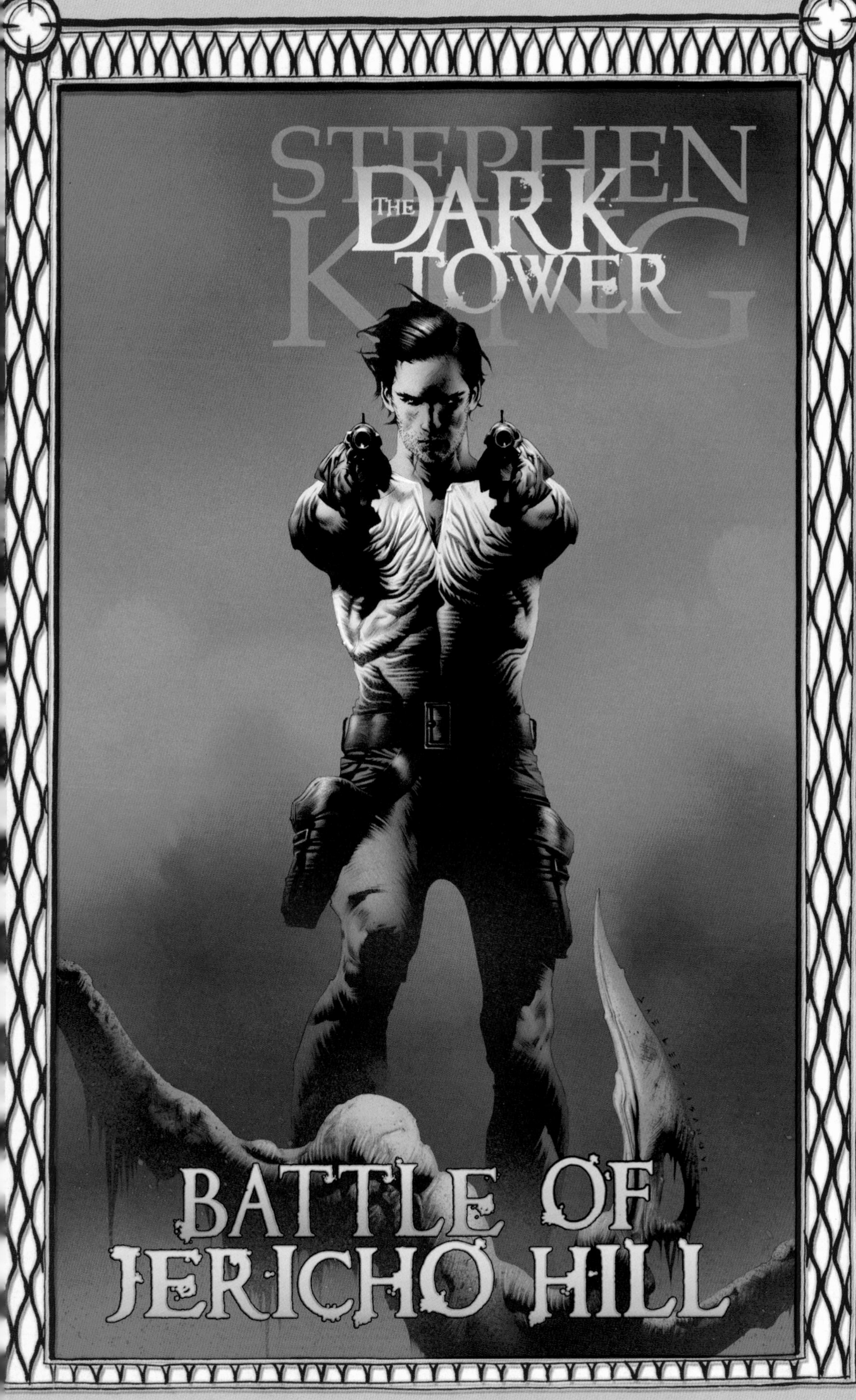
STEPHEN KING
THE DARK TOWER
BATTLE OF JERICHO HILL

THE DARK TOWER

BATTLE OF JERICHO HILL

CREATIVE DIRECTOR AND EXECUTIVE DIRECTOR
STEPHEN KING

PLOTTING AND CONSULTATION
ROBIN FURTH

SCRIPT
PETER DAVID

ART
JAE LEE & RICHARD ISANOVE

LETTERING
CHRIS ELIOPOULOS WITH RUS WOOTON

ASSISTANT EDITORS
MICHAEL HORWITZ & CHARLIE BECKERMAN

SENIOR EDITOR
RALPH MACCHIO

COVER ART
JAE LEE & RICHARD ISANOVE

DARK TOWER: BATTLE OF JERICHO HILL. Contains material originally published in magazine form as DARK TOWER: THE BATTLE OF JERICHO HILL #1-5. First printing 2010. ISBN# 978-0-78
2953-0. Published by MARVEL WORLDWIDE, INC., a subsidiary of MARVEL ENTERTAINMENT, LLC. OFFICE OF PUBLICATION: 417 5th Avenue, New York, NY 10016. Copyright © 2009 and 2010 Step
King. All rights reserved. $24.99 per copy in the U.S. and $27.99 in Canada (GST #R127032852); Canadian Agreement #40668537. All characters featured in this publication and the distinc
names and likenesses thereof, and all related indicia are trademarks of Stephen King. No similarity between any of the names, characters, persons, and/or institutions in this magazine with th
of any living or dead person or institution is intended, and any such similarity which may exist is purely coincidental. Marvel and its logos are TM & © Marvel Characters, Inc. **Printed in the U.**
ALAN FINE, EVP - Office of the President, Marvel Worldwide, Inc. and EVP & CMO Marvel Characters B.V.; DAN BUCKLEY, Chief Executive Officer and Publisher - Print, Animation & Digital Media;
SOKOLOWSKI, Chief Operating Officer; DAVID GABRIEL, SVP of Publishing Sales & Circulation; DAVID BOGART, SVP of Business Affairs & Talent Management; MICHAEL PASCIULLO, VP Merchandi
& Communications; JIM O'KEEFE, VP of Operations & Logistics; DAN CARR, Executive Director of Publishing Technology; JUSTIN F. GABRIE, Director of Publishing & Editorial Operations; SU
CRESPI, Editorial Operations Manager; ALEX MORALES, Publishing Operations Manager; STAN LEE, Chairman Emeritus. For information regarding advertising in Marvel Comics or on Marvel.co
please contact Ron Stern, VP of Business Development, at rstern@marvel.com. For Marvel subscription inquiries, please call 800-217-9158. **Manufactured between 5/31/10 and 6/30/10 by**
DONNELLEY, INC., SALEM, VA, USA.

10 9 8 7 6 5 4 3 2 1

COLLECTION EDITOR
MARK D. BEAZLEY

EDITORIAL ASSISTANTS
JOE HOCHSTEIN & JAMES EMMETT

ASSISTANT EDITOR
ALEX STARBUCK

ASSOCIATE EDITOR
JOHN DENNING

EDITOR, SPECIAL PROJECTS
JENNIFER GRÜNWALD

SENIOR EDITOR, SPECIAL PROJECTS
JEFF YOUNGQUIST

SENIOR VICE PRESIDENT OF SALES
DAVID GABRIEL

SENIOR VICE PRESIDENT OF STRATEGIC DEVELOPMENT
RUWAN JAYATILLEKE

BOOK DESIGN
SPRING HOTELING AND PATRICK McGRATH

EDITOR IN CHIEF
JOE QUESADA

PUBLISHER
DAN BUCKLEY

SPECIAL THANKS TO CHUCK VERRILL, MARSHA DEFILIPPO,
RALPH VICINANZA, BARBARA ANN MCINTYRE, BRIAN STARK,
JIM NAUSEDAS, JIM MCCANN, ARUNE SINGH, JEFF SUTER,
JOHN BARBER & LAUREN SANKOVITCH

FOR MORE INFORMATION ON DARK TOWER COMICS, VISIT MARVEL.COM/DARKTOWER.
TO FIND MARVEL COMICS AT A LOCAL COMIC SHOP, CALL 1-888-COMICBOOK.

INTRODUCTION

The journey has been long and satisfying. Five years ago members of Marvel Editorial, including Publisher Dan Buckley and Editor in Chief Joe Quesada met with Stephen King and his top men including Chuck Verrill to discuss the possibility of Marvel's acquisition of the Dark Tower property to publish as a comic book. It was at this fabled gathering that Mr. King intoned the phrase that set the stage for what was to come: A man's quest begins with a boy's test. That line perfectly encapsulates the direction we've pursued. Thus, the great wheel of Ka turned, and with the invaluable guidance and input of Dark Tower expert supreme Robin Furth, we conceived the first of our many story arcs: The Gunslinger Born.

In this strange, misty realm called Mid-World, Roland Deschain became the youngest gunslinger in history at age fourteen. He and his ka-tet set out on a series of adventures that took them far from the familiar walls of their home barony Gilead. Roland met his one true love, Susan Delgado, and watched her die aflame, tied to a stake. His spirit was transported to the court of ultimate evil, the Crimson King himself. Inadvertently, he had slain his own mother and later found his father's murdered body in his bed chamber. He failed to prevent the destruction of Gilead by the forces of Walter O'Dim and the Good Man John Farson, and thus was driven from his homeland. What an extraordinary series of events for someone of that age—or any age—to have experienced.

Now, years later, he finds himself still in exile. The world he had known since birth is crumbling before his eyes in so many ways. But this young gunslinger is not a man to be underestimated as you will see in the stories that follow. He is the last of the exalted line of Arthur Eld, and he will not slip quietly into the good night. On that you can bet your pearl-handled six shooters.

Someone else we can't let slip quietly away is our peerless penciler, Jae Lee. Along with the equally titanic talent of colorist Richard Isanove, they established the look of the Dark Tower universe over this past half decade. Sweeping landscapes, incredible architecture and terrifying images of hell-spawned entities all characterized the Lee/Isanove era. Jae conceived the very iconography of Mid-World and its environs, giving it a unique and palpable atmosphere of both strangeness and familiarity. It has been a privilege to work with such a singular talent.

While Jae's stay in the Dark Tower has concluded, an exciting array of new pencilers will continue to deliver a visual tour de force month after month, with their work exquisitely enhanced by the stunning colors of Richard Isanove. New realms of wonderment await.

Now it is time once again to step across the threshold to a world that has moved on. Time to reacquaint ourselves with a young protagonist who may hold the very future of reality itself in his calloused hands. But first he has to attend to a little matter up at a place called Jericho Hill. Let's join him...

—Ralph Macchio

Ralph Macchio

May 2010

In a world that has moved on...

Despite the best defenses erected in the ancient times by the fabled Arthur Eld, the city of Gilead has fallen. The once rich barony trembled before the forces of the Good Man, John Farson, sworn enemy of the Affiliation once led by the late gunslinger, Steven Deschain.

Following Steven's death, his gunslinger son, young Roland, took control of the city and faced down Farson's army in a losing, final battle.

Several years have passed, and having been routed from Gilead, Roland and his companions, his ka-tet, have been driven into hiding.

That status is about to change...

STEPHEN KING

THE DARK TOWER

BATTLE OF JERICHO HILL

CHAPTER ONE

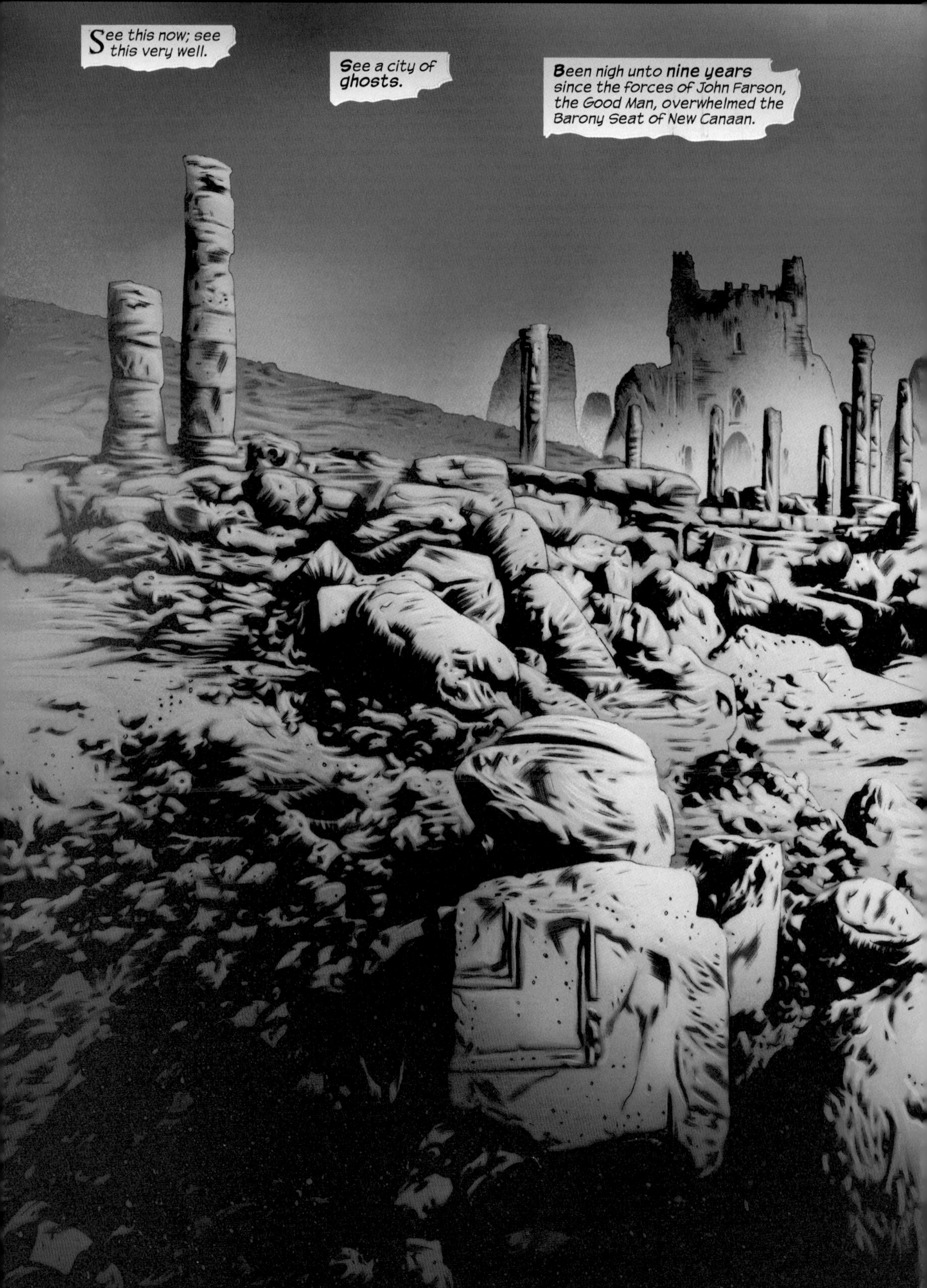
See this now; see this very well.
See a city of ghosts.
Been nigh unto nine years since the forces of John Farson, the Good Man, overwhelmed the Barony Seat of New Canaan.

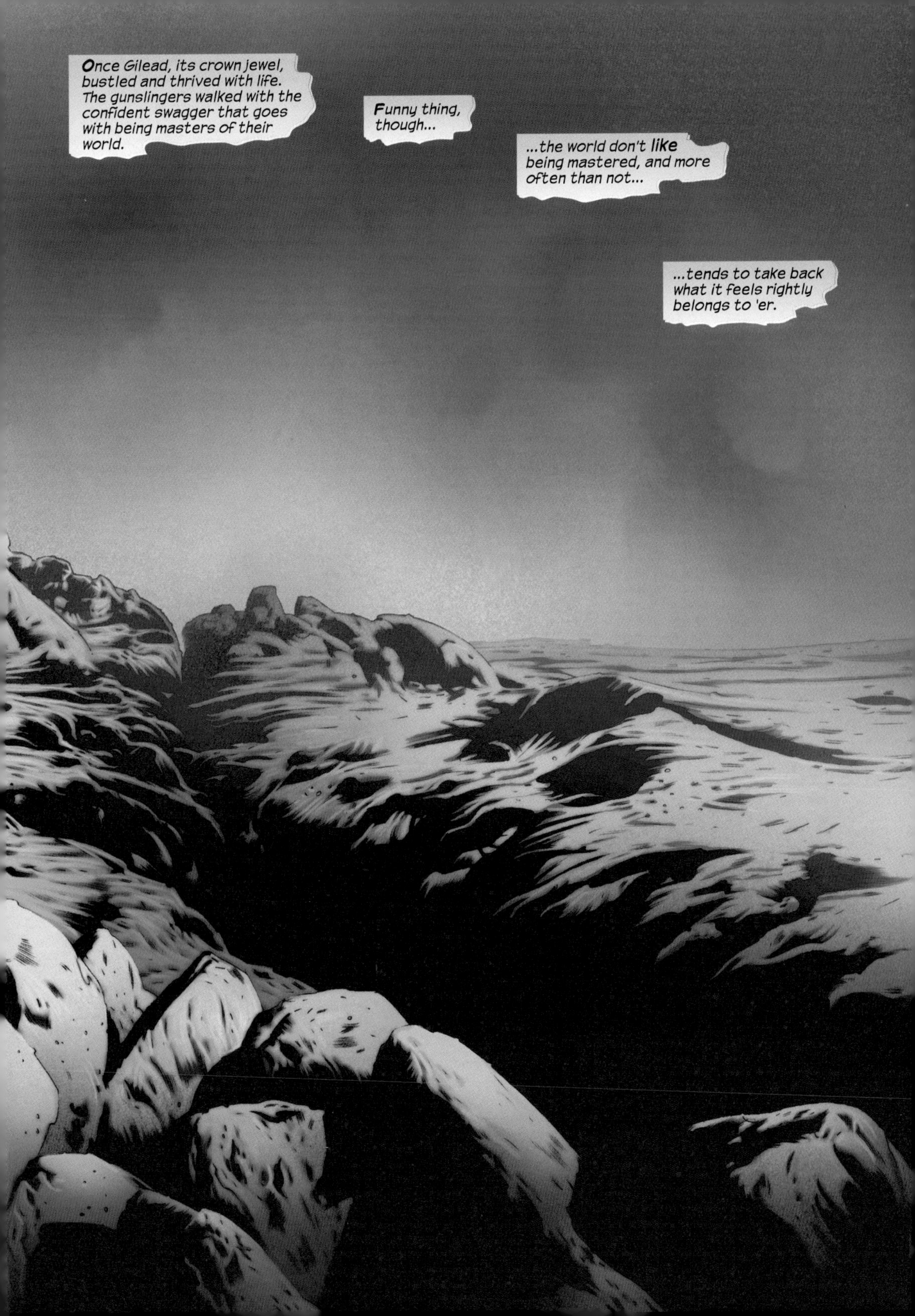
Once Gilead, its crown jewel, bustled and thrived with life. The gunslingers walked with the confident swagger that goes with being masters of their world.
Funny thing, though...
...the world don't like being mastered, and more often than not...
...tends to take back what it feels rightly belongs to 'er.

...as subject to crumbling and overgrowth as are the mountains of Mid-World. **Moreso**, in fact.

...in the air.

The only noise, aside from birds and the skittering of vermin...

...is the low moaning and snarling of **Slow Mutants**...

...sustaining themselves on the flesh of occasional vagabonds unfortunate enough to pass through hoping for salvage...

...and washing it down with once-good wine now turned to **vinegar**.

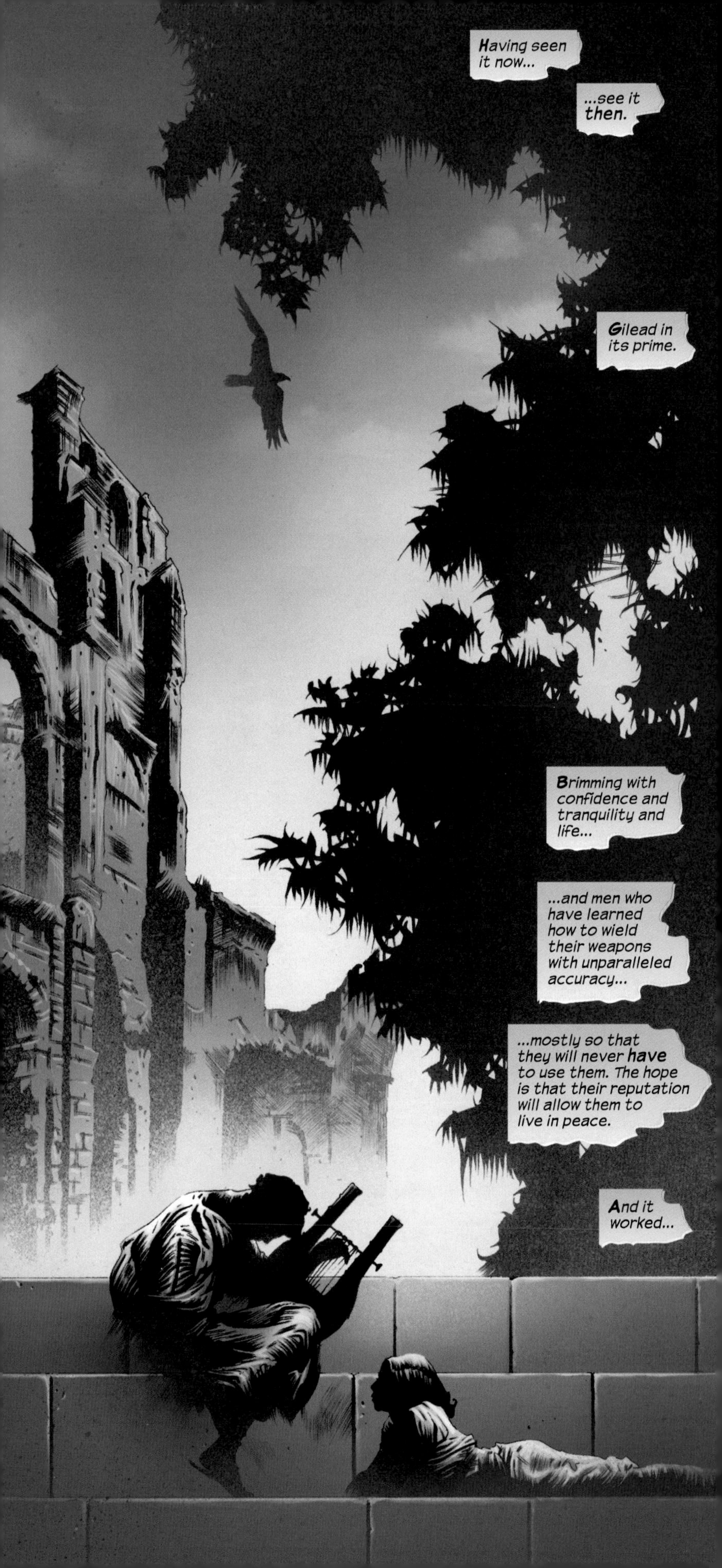
Having seen it now...
...see it then.
Gilead in its prime.
Brimming with confidence and tranquility and life...
...and men who have learned how to wield their weapons with unparalleled accuracy...
...mostly so that they will never have to use them. The hope is that their reputation will allow them to live in peace.
And it worked...

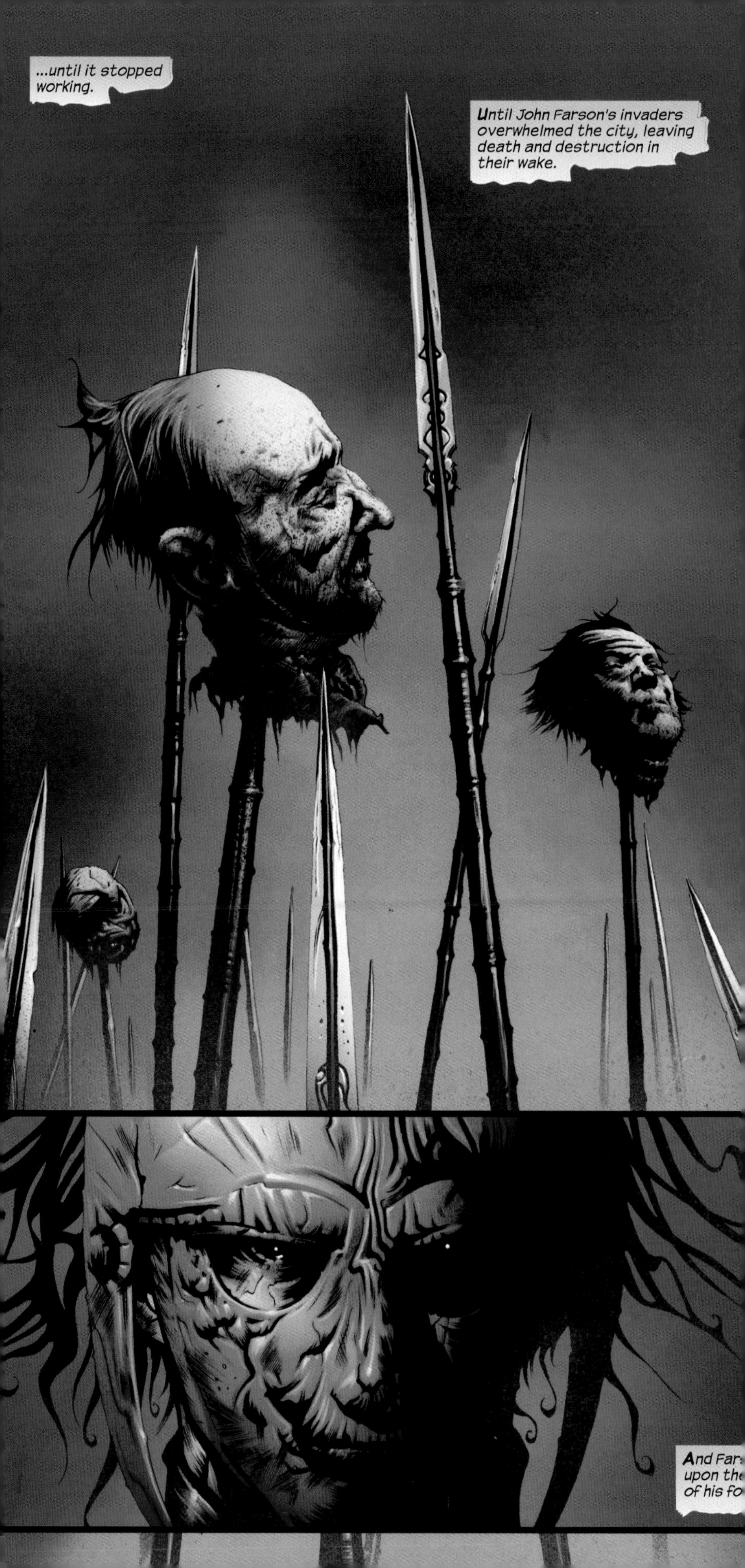

...until it stopped working.
Until John Farson's invaders overwhelmed the city, leaving death and destruction in their wake.
And Fars
upon the
of his fo

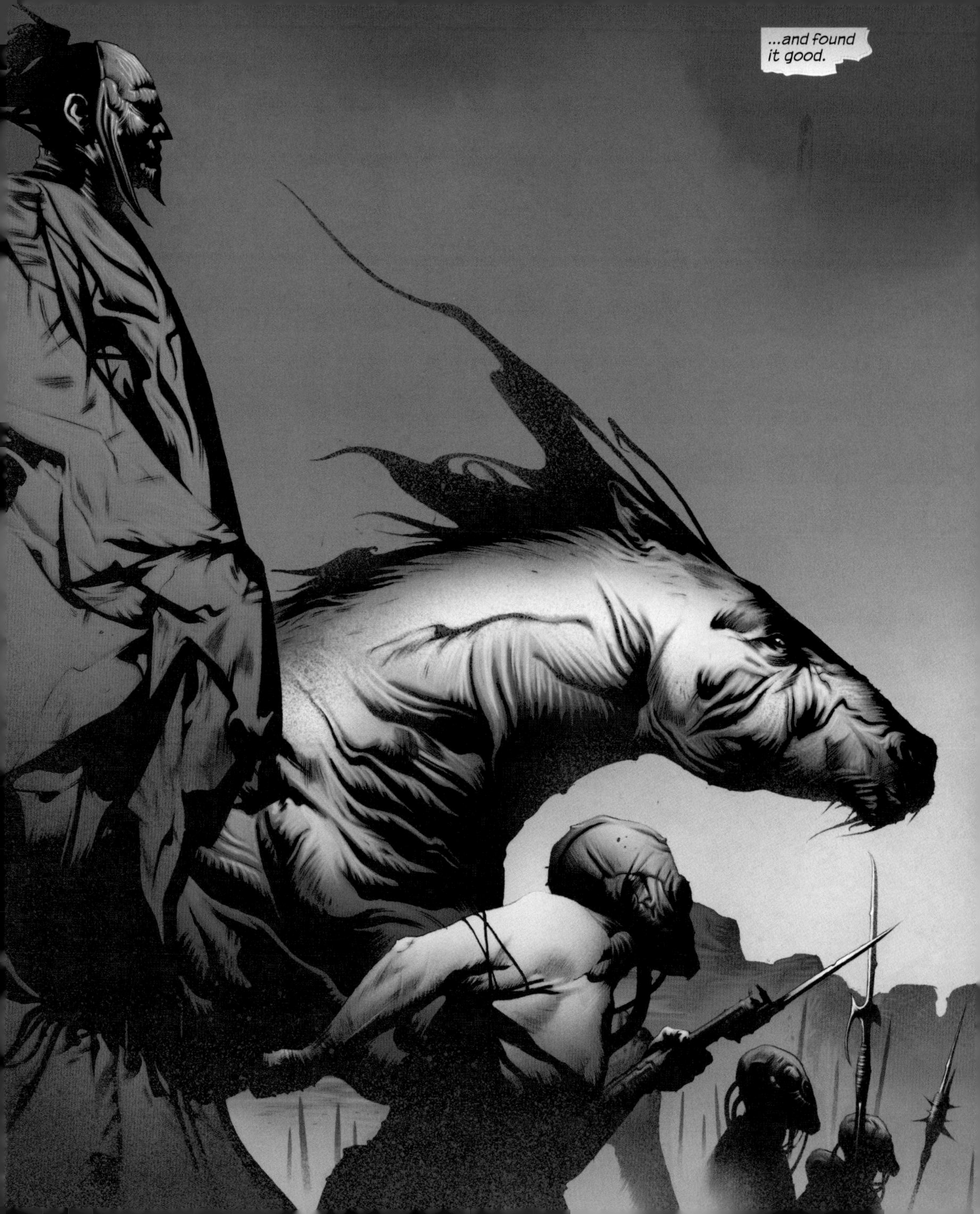
...and found
it good.

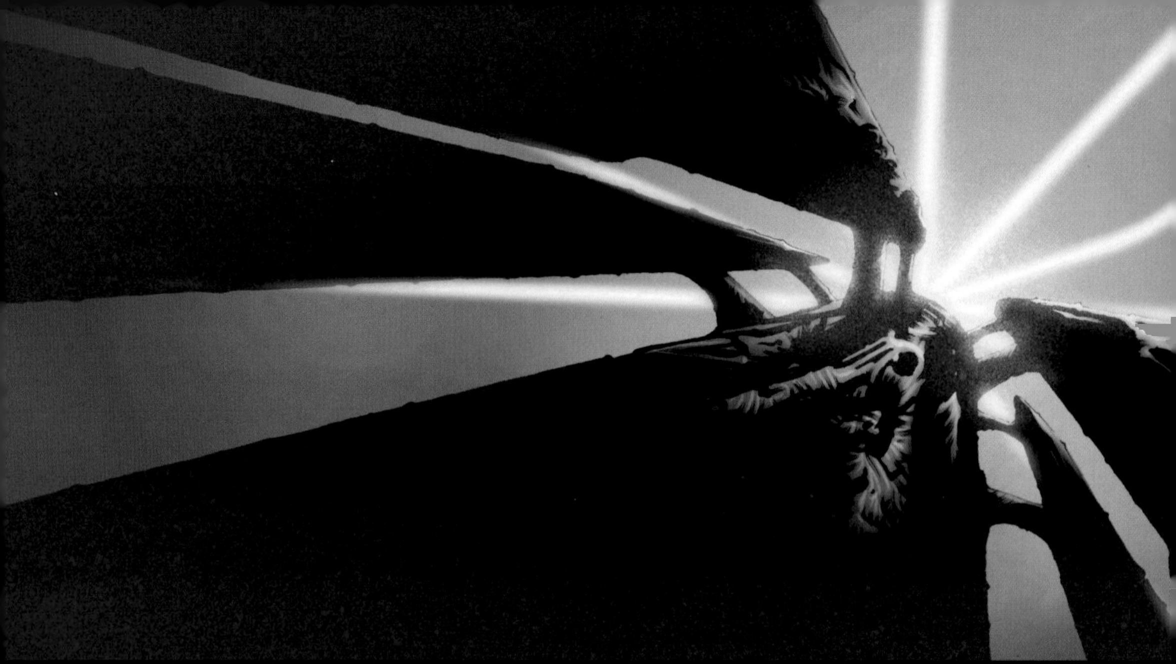

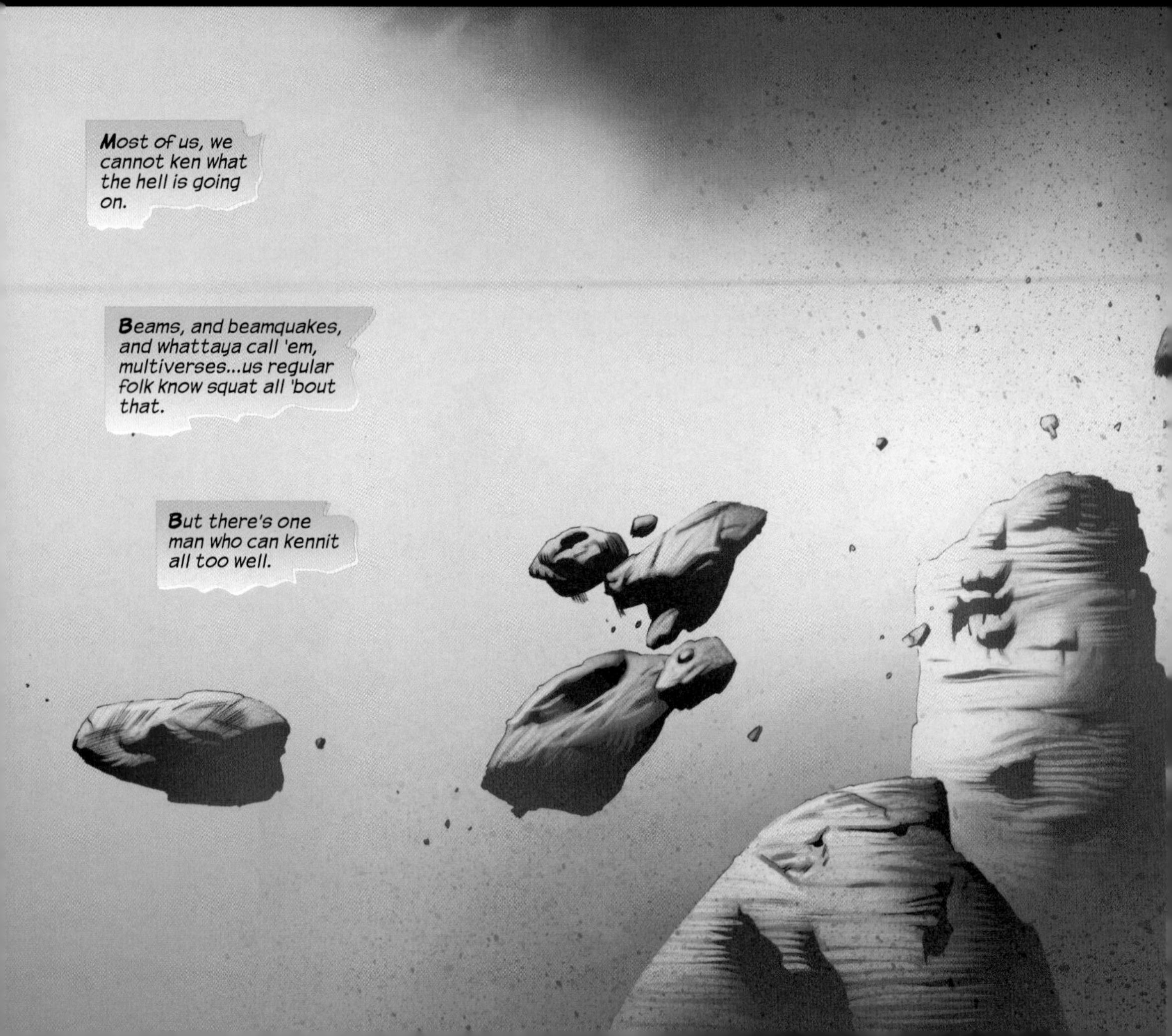
Most of us, we cannot ken what the hell is going on.
Beams, and beamquakes, and whattaya call 'em, multiverses...us regular folk know squat all 'bout that.
But there's one man who can kennit all too well.

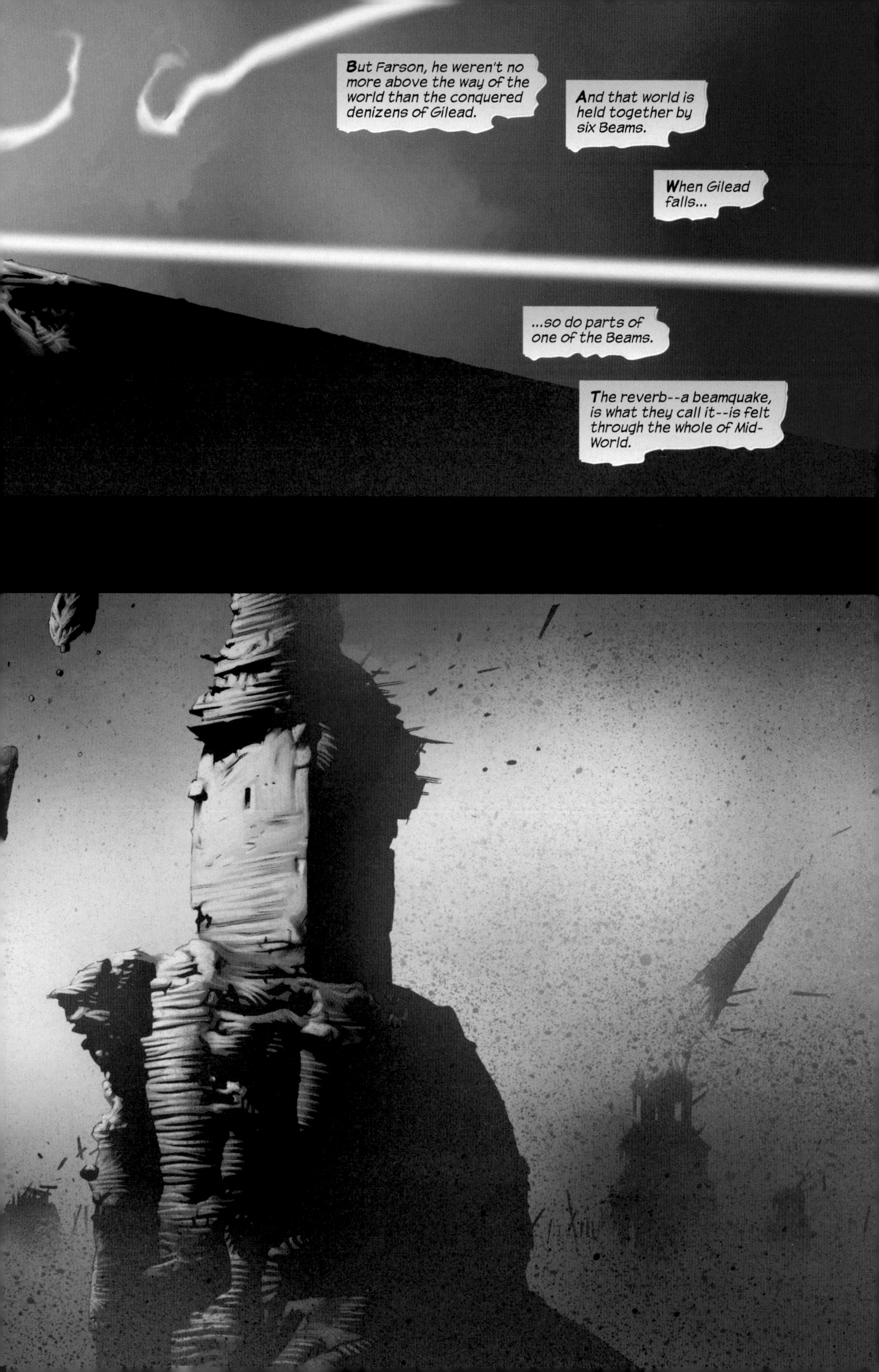
But Farson, he weren't no more above the way of the world than the conquered denizens of Gilead.
And that world is held together by six Beams.
When Gilead falls...
...so do parts of one of the Beams.
The reverb--a beamquake, is what they call it--is felt through the whole of Mid-World.

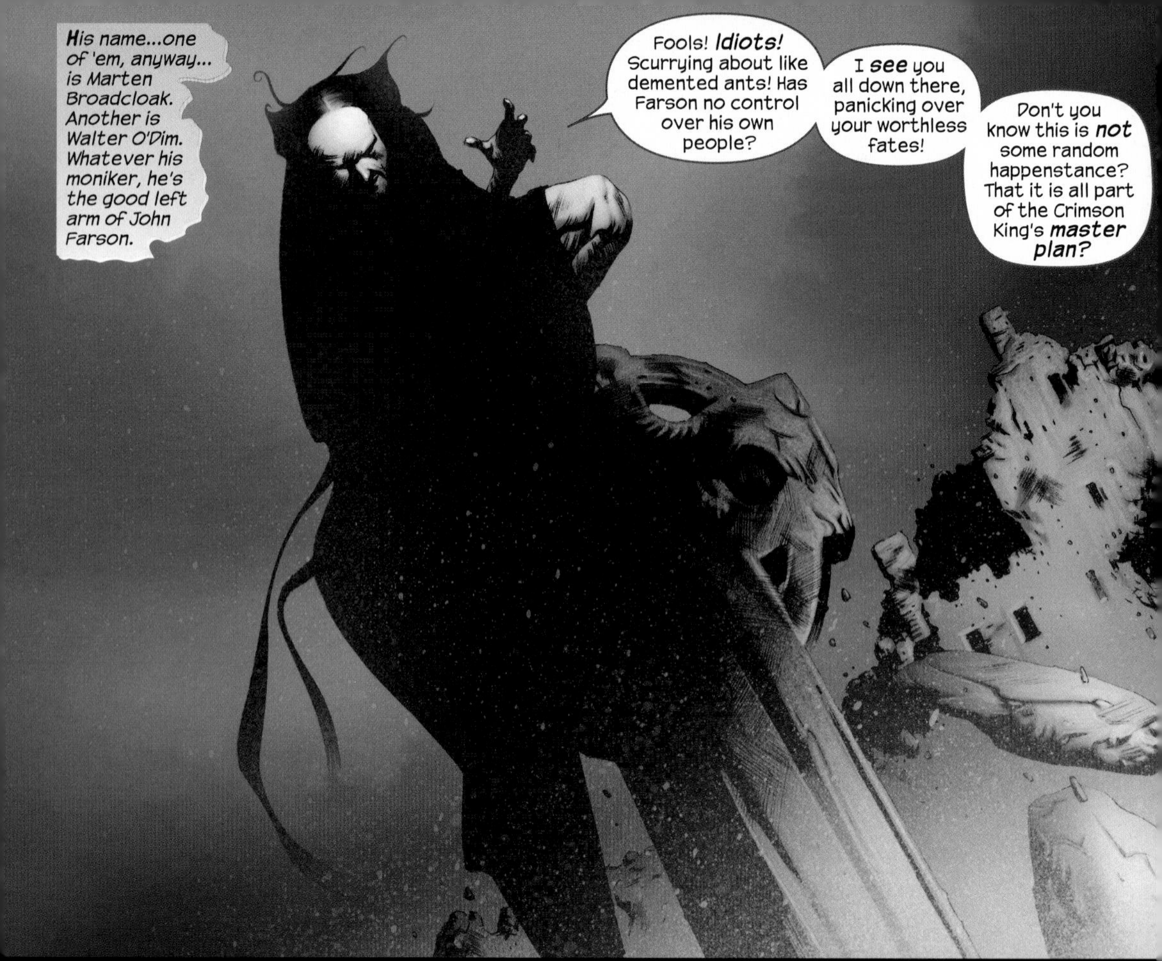
His name...one of 'em, anyway... is Marten Broadcloak. Another is Walter O'Dim. Whatever his moniker, he's the good left arm of John Farson.
Fools! Idiots! Scurrying about like demented ants! Has Farson no control over his own people?
I see you all down there, panicking over your worthless fates!
Don't you know this is not some random happenstance? That it is all part of the Crimson King's master plan?

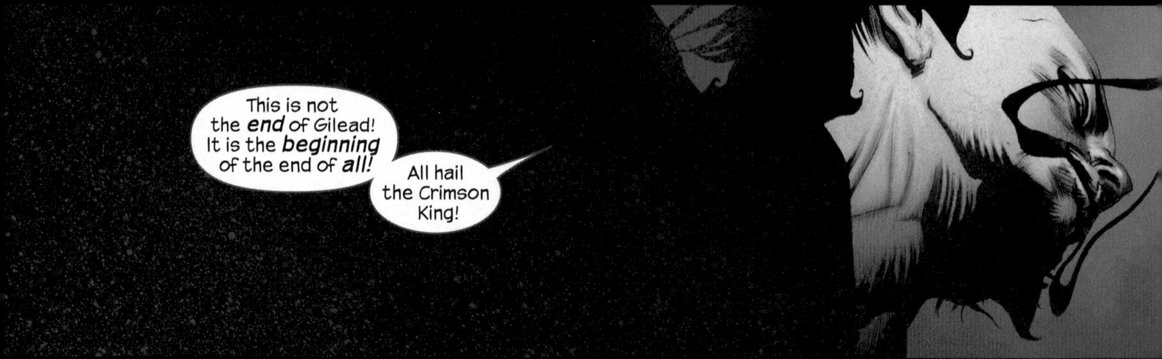
This is not the end of Gilead! It is the beginning of the end of all!
All hail the Crimson King!

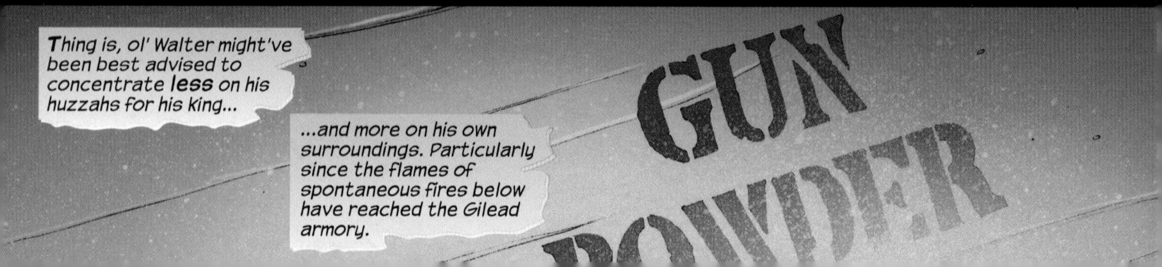
Thing is, ol' Walter might've been best advised to concentrate less on his huzzahs for his king...
...and more on his own surroundings. Particularly since the flames of spontaneous fires below have reached the Gilead armory.
GUN
POWDER

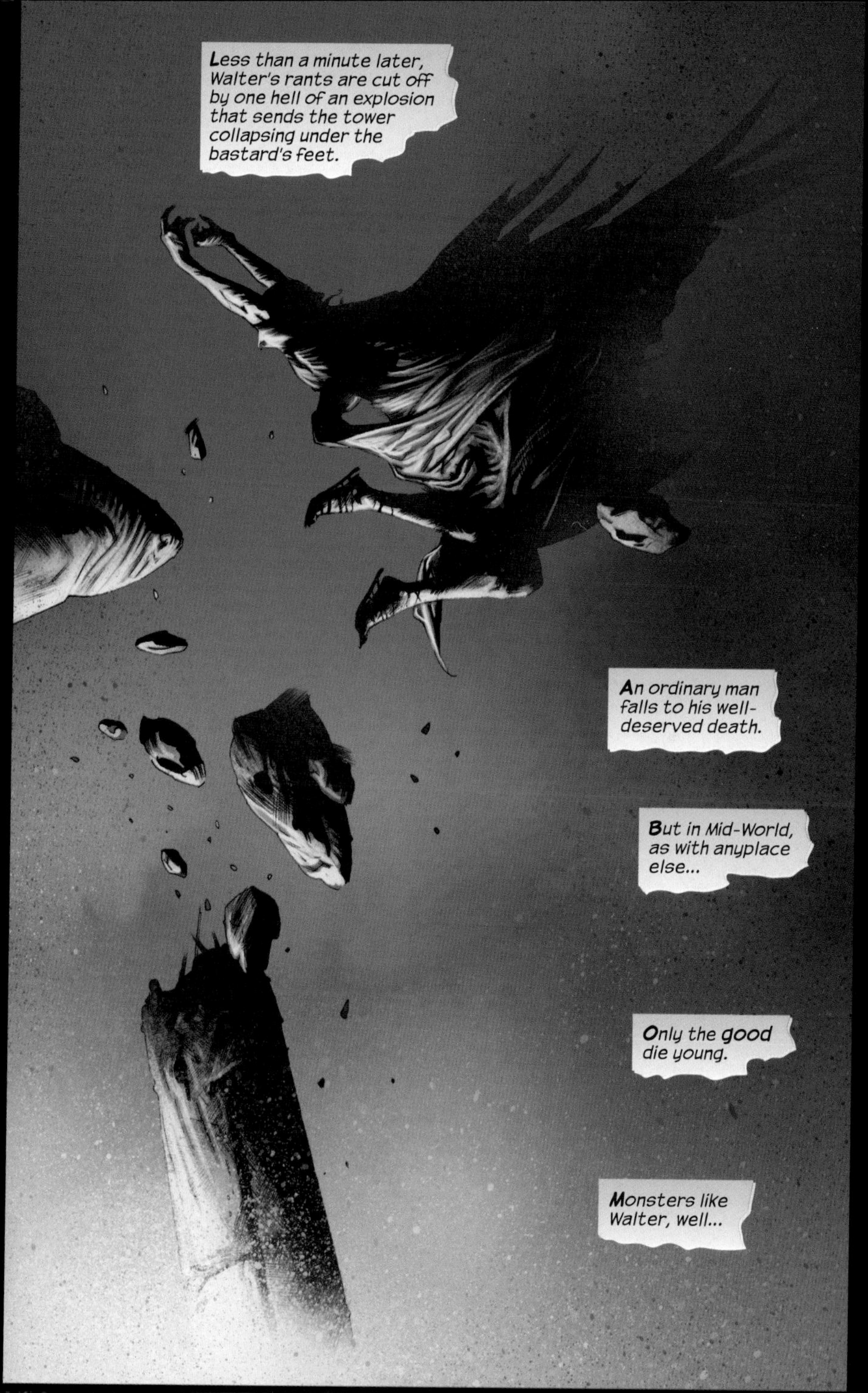
Less than a minute later, Walter's rants are cut off by one hell of an explosion that sends the tower collapsing under the bastard's feet.
An ordinary man falls to his well-deserved death.
But in Mid-World, as with anyplace else...
Only the good die young.
Monsters like Walter, well...

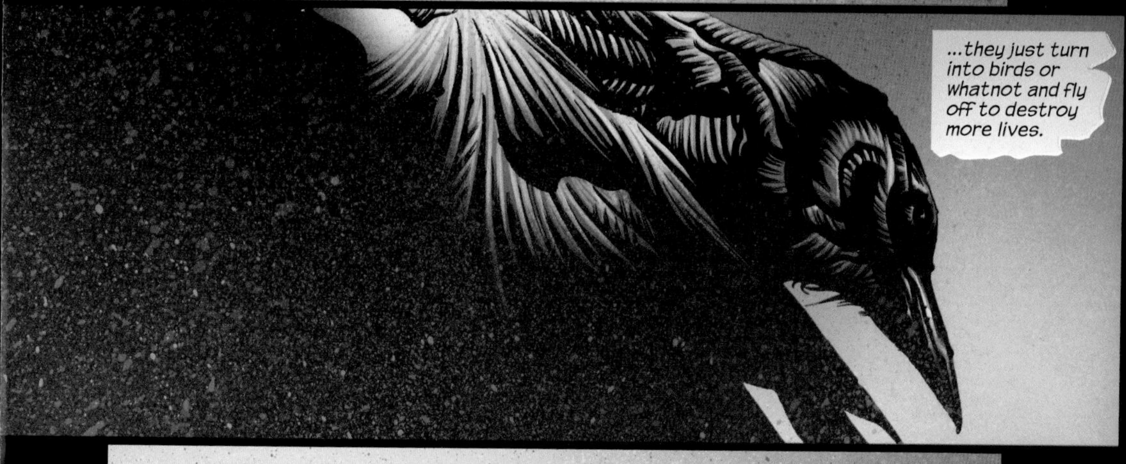
...they just turn into birds or whatnot and fly off to destroy more lives.

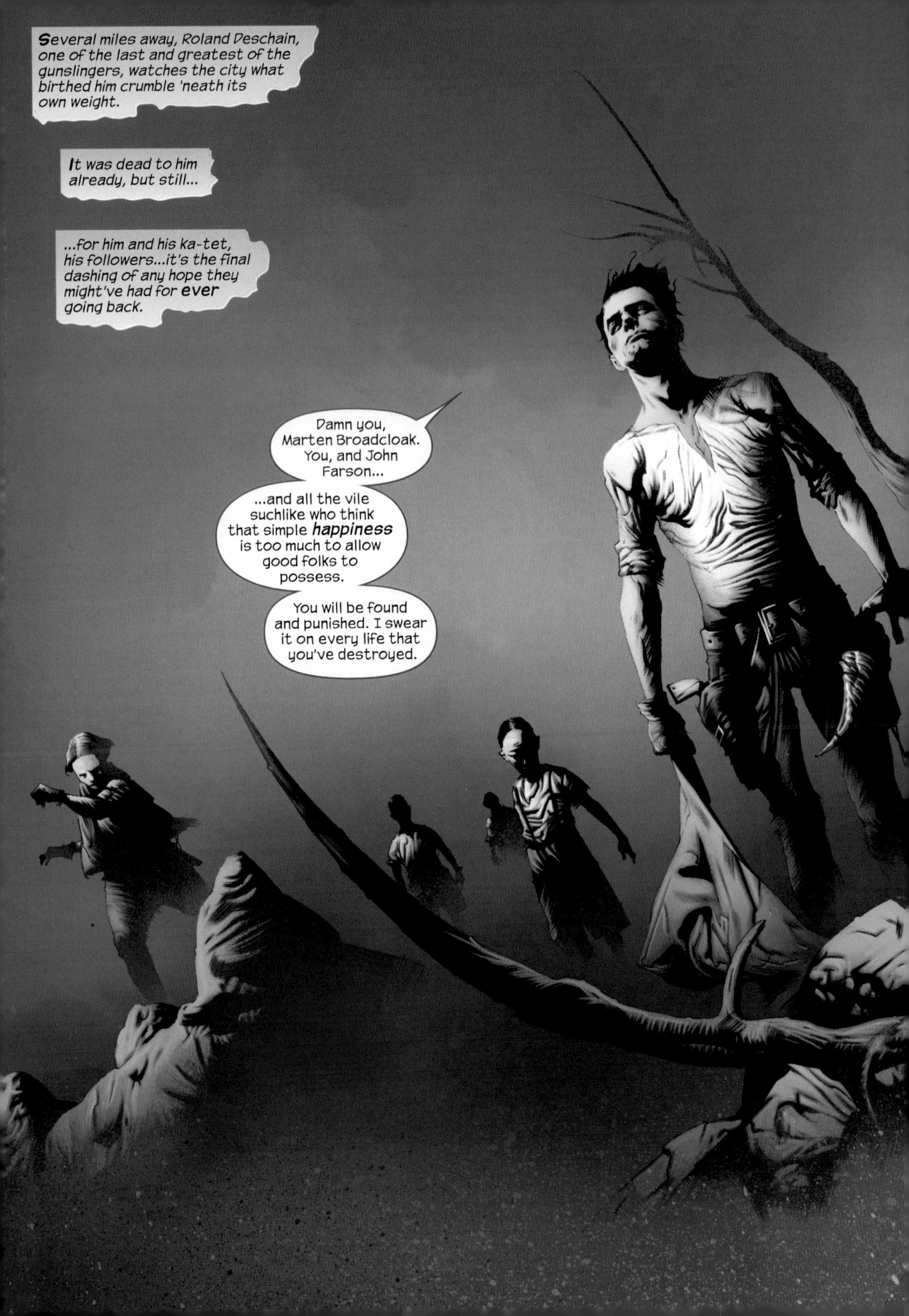
Several miles away, Roland Deschain, one of the last and greatest of the gunslingers, watches the city what birthed him crumble 'neath its own weight.
It was dead to him already, but still...
...for him and his ka-tet, his followers...it's the final dashing of any hope they might've had for **ever** going back.
Damn you, Marten Broadcloak. You, and John Farson...
...and all the vile suchlike who think that simple *happiness* is too much to allow good folks to possess.
You will be found and punished. I swear it on every life that you've destroyed.

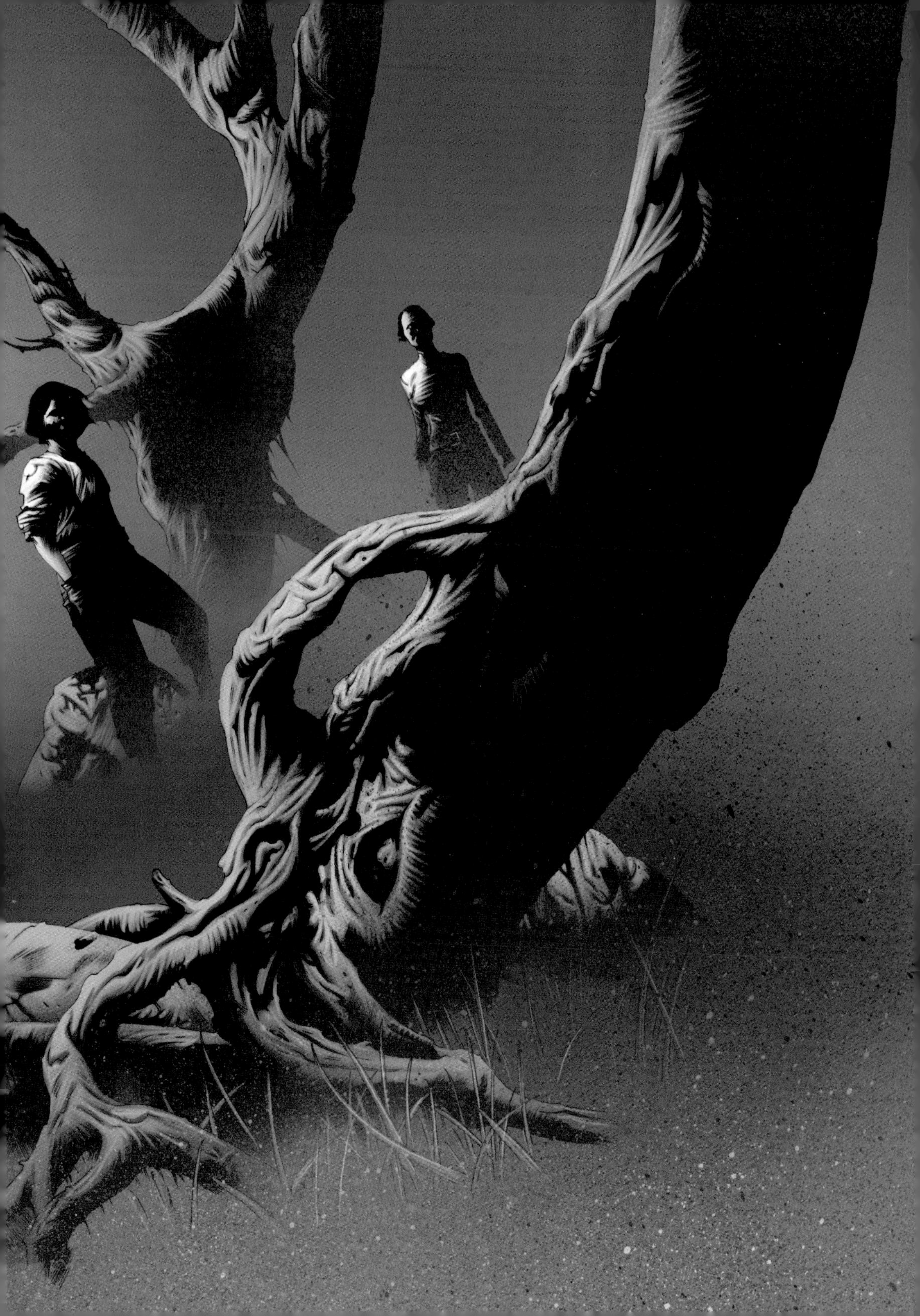

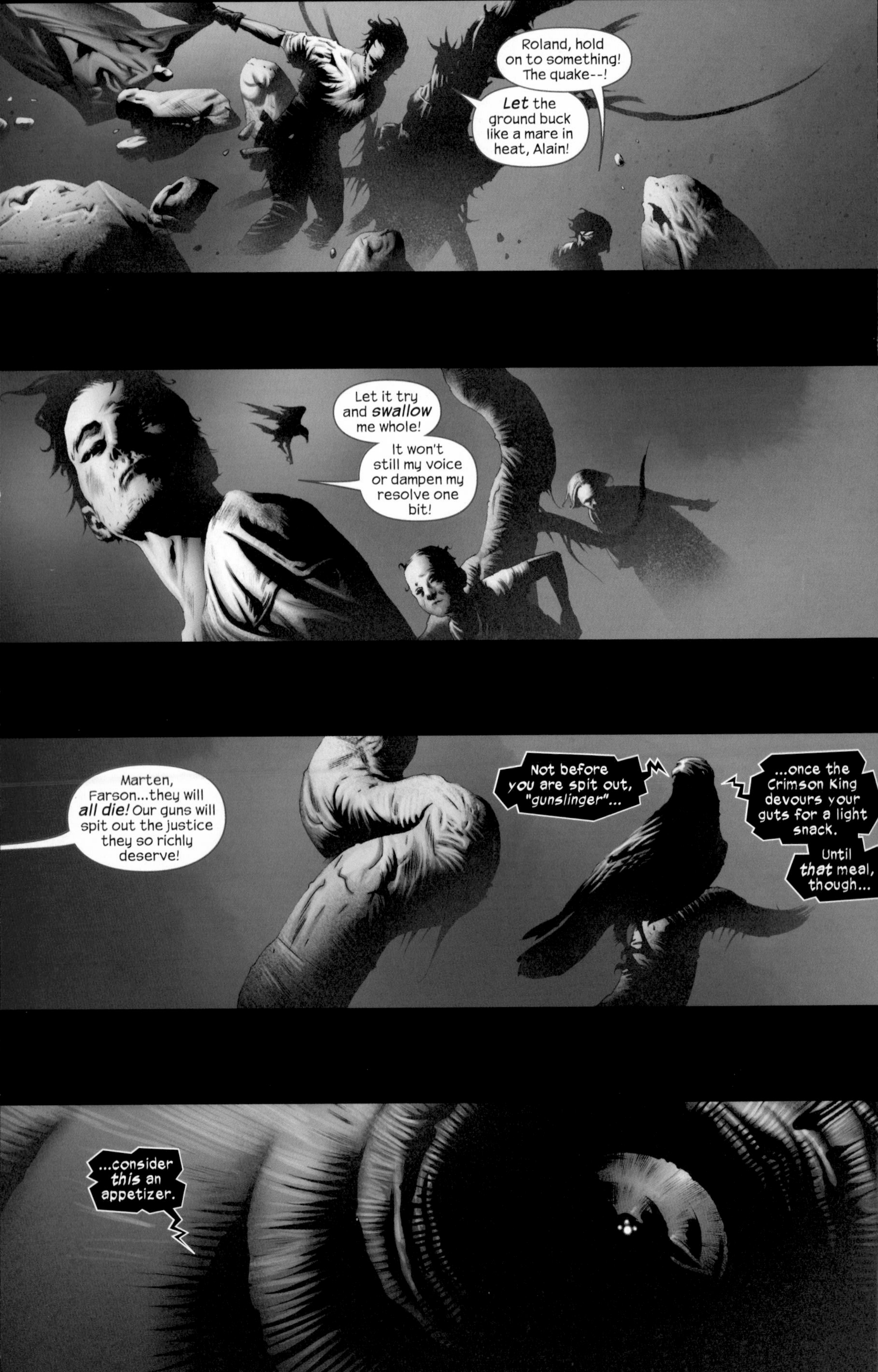
Roland, hold on to something! The quake--!
Let the ground buck like a mare in heat, Alain!
Let it try and swallow me whole!
It won't still my voice or dampen my resolve one bit!
Marten, Farson...they will all die! Our guns will spit out the justice they so richly deserve!
Not before you are spit out, "gunslinger"...
...once the Crimson King devours your guts for a light snack.
Until that meal, though...
...consider this an appetizer.

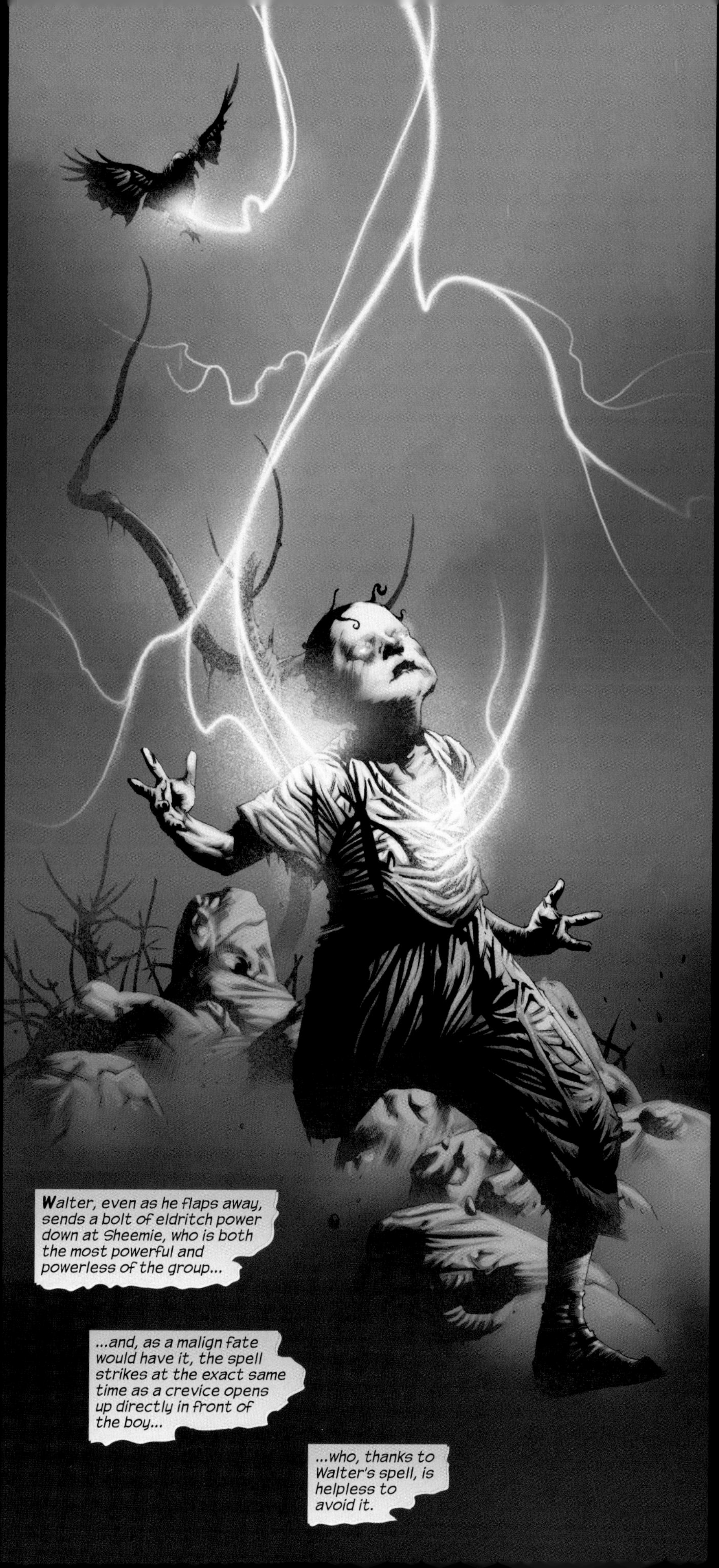
Walter, even as he flaps away, sends a bolt of eldritch power down at Sheemie, who is both the most powerful and powerless of the group...
...and, as a malign fate would have it, the spell strikes at the exact same time as a crevice opens up directly in front of the boy...
...who, thanks to Walter's spell, is helpless to avoid it.

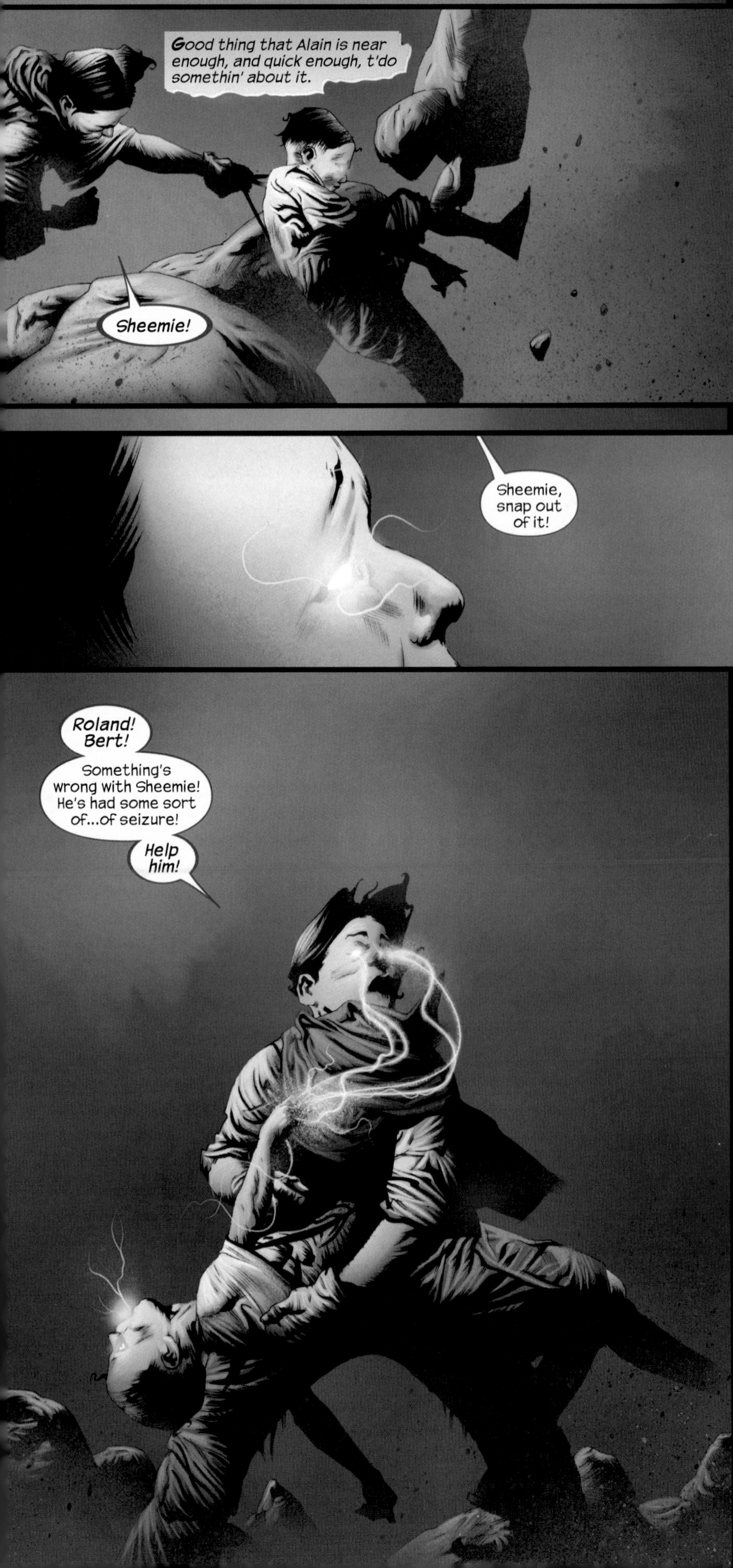
Good thing that Alain is near enough, and quick enough, t'do somethin' about it.
Sheemie!
Sheemie, snap out of it!
Roland! Bert!
Something's wrong with Sheemie! He's had some sort of...of seizure!
Help him!

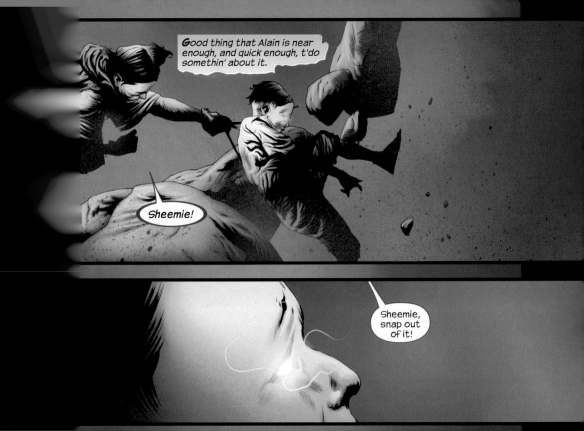

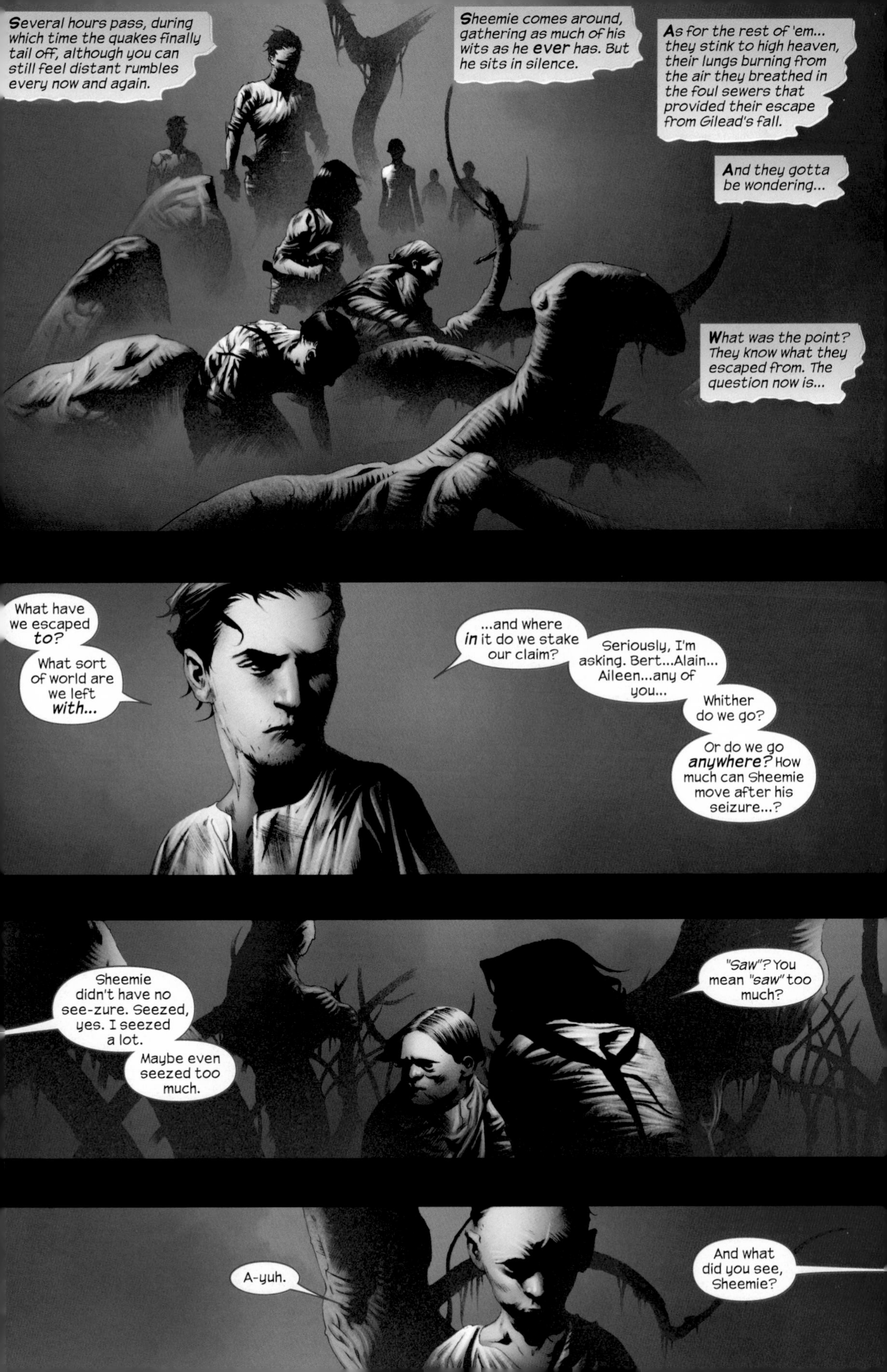

Several hours pass, during which time the quakes finally tail off, although you can still feel distant rumbles every now and again.
Sheemie comes around, gathering as much of his wits as he ever has. But he sits in silence.
As for the rest of 'em... they stink to high heaven, their lungs burning from the air they breathed in the foul sewers that provided their escape from Gilead's fall.
And they gotta be wondering...
What was the point? They know what they escaped from. The question now is...
What have we escaped to?
What sort of world are we left with...
...and where in it do we stake our claim?
Seriously, I'm asking. Bert...Alain... Aileen...any of you...
Whither do we go?
Or do we go anywhere? How much can Sheemie move after his seizure...?
Sheemie didn't have no see-zure. Seezed, yes. I seezed a lot.
Maybe even seezed too much.
"Saw"? You mean "saw" too much?
A-yuh.
And what did you see, Sheemie?

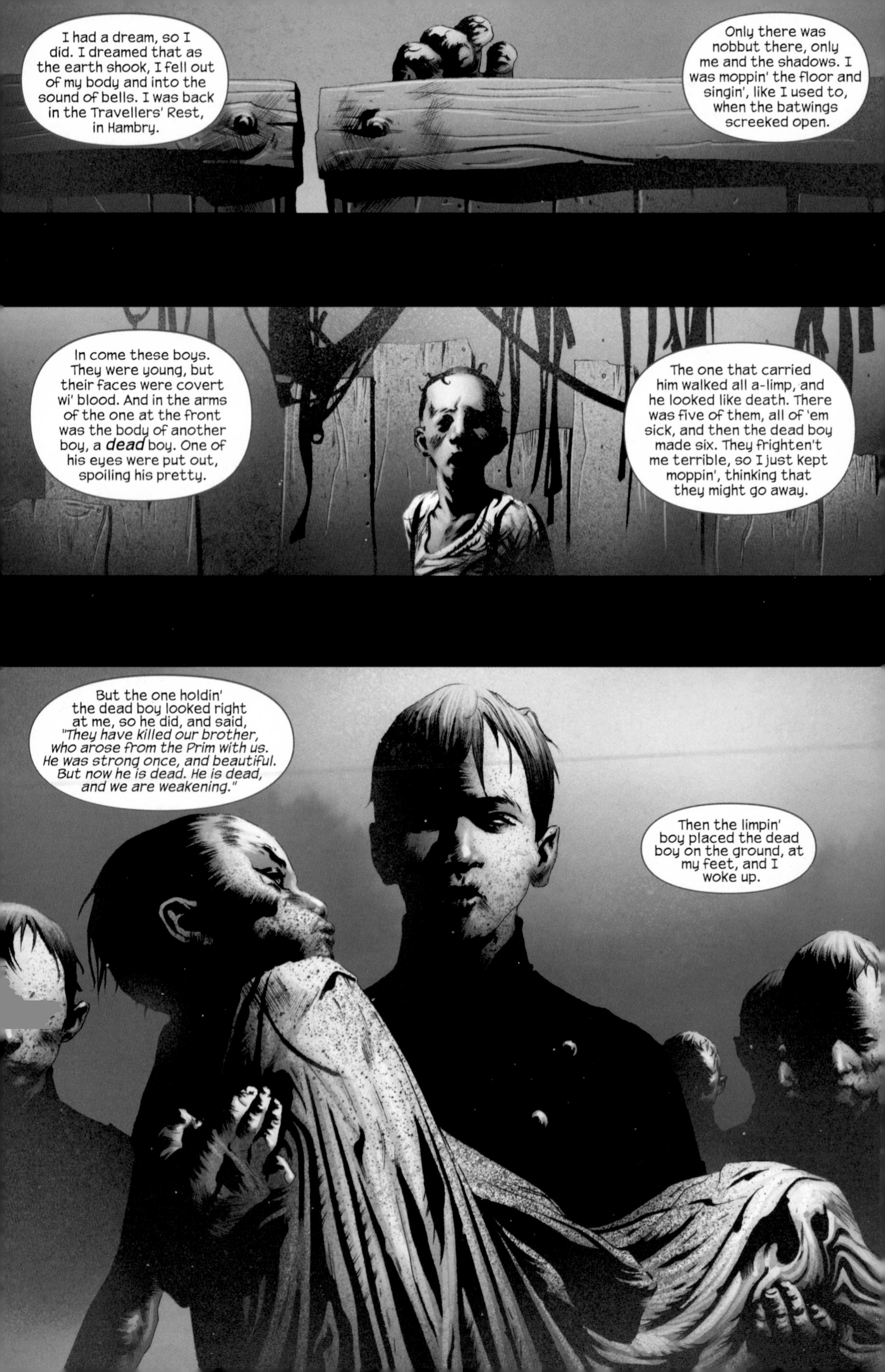
I had a dream, so I did. I dreamed that as the earth shook, I fell out of my body and into the sound of bells. I was back in the Travellers' Rest, in Hambry.
Only there was nobbut there, only me and the shadows. I was moppin' the floor and singin', like I used to, when the batwings screeked open.
In come these boys. They were young, but their faces were covert wi' blood. And in the arms of the one at the front was the body of another boy, a *dead* boy. One of his eyes were put out, spoiling his pretty.
The one that carried him walked all a-limp, and he looked like death. There was five of them, all of 'em sick, and then the dead boy made six. They frighten't me terrible, so I just kept moppin', thinking that they might go away.
But the one holdin' the dead boy looked right at me, so he did, and said, *"They have killed our brother, who arose from the Prim with us. He was strong once, and beautiful. But now he is dead. He is dead, and we are weakening."*
Then the limpin' boy placed the dead boy on the ground, at my feet, and I woke up.

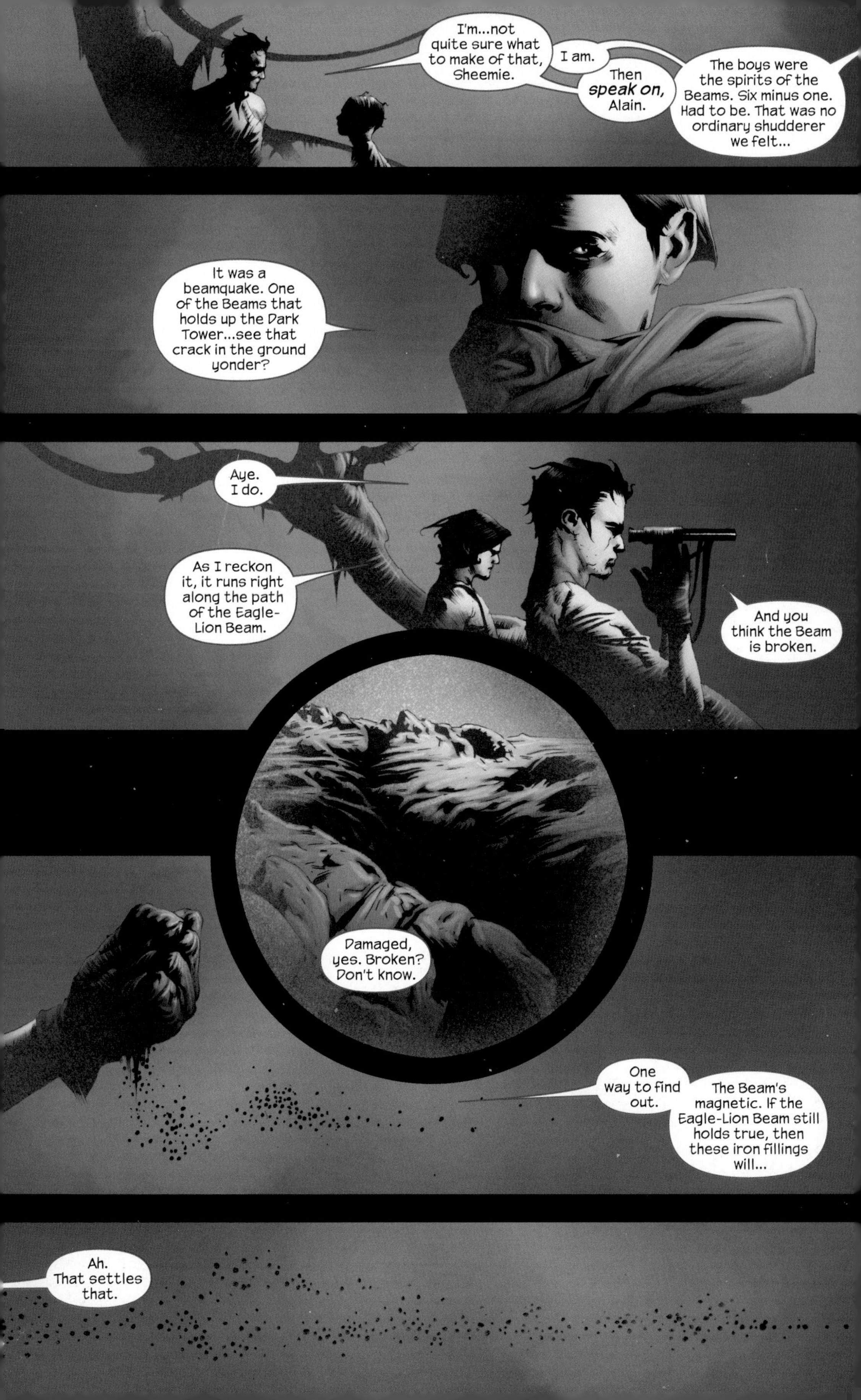
I'm...not quite sure what to make of that, Sheemie.
I am.
Then speak on, Alain.
The boys were the spirits of the Beams. Six minus one. Had to be. That was no ordinary shudderer we felt...
It was a beamquake. One of the Beams that holds up the Dark Tower...see that crack in the ground yonder?
Aye. I do.
As I reckon it, it runs right along the path of the Eagle-Lion Beam.
And you think the Beam is broken.
Damaged, yes. Broken? Don't know.
One way to find out.
The Beam's magnetic. If the Eagle-Lion Beam still holds true, then these iron fillings will...
Ah. That settles that.

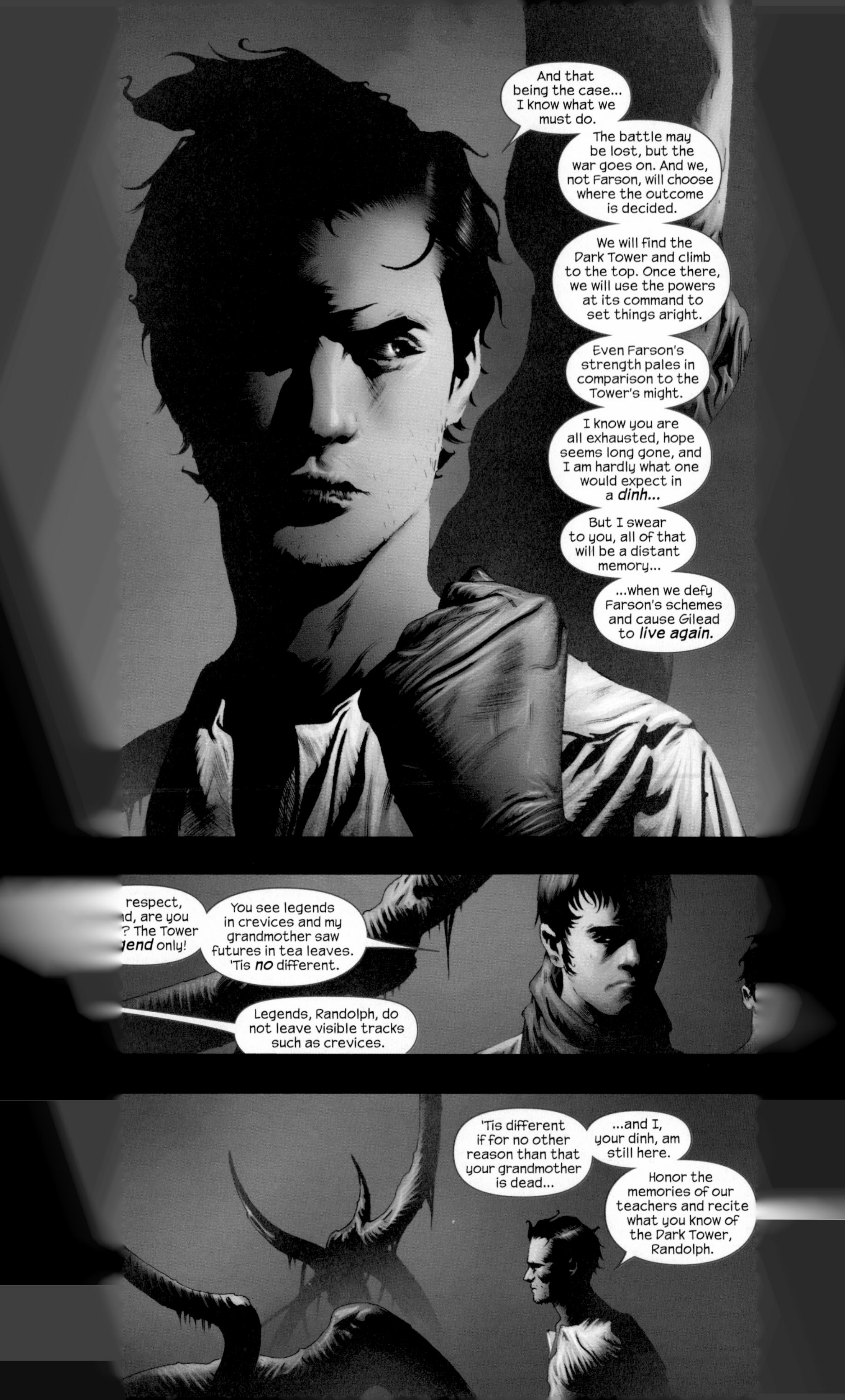

And that being the case... I know what we must do.
The battle may be lost, but the war goes on. And we, not Farson, will choose where the outcome is decided.
We will find the Dark Tower and climb to the top. Once there, we will use the powers at its command to set things aright.
Even Farson's strength pales in comparison to the Tower's might.
I know you are all exhausted, hope seems long gone, and I am hardly what one would expect in a *dinh...*
But I swear to you, all of that will be a distant memory...
...when we defy Farson's schemes and cause Gilead to *live again.*
respect, ... are you ... The Tower ... only!
You see legends in crevices and my grandmother saw futures in tea leaves. 'Tis *no* different.
Legends, Randolph, do not leave visible tracks such as crevices.
'Tis different if for no other reason than that your grandmother is dead...
...and I, your dinh, am still here.
Honor the memories of our teachers and recite what you know of the Dark Tower, Randolph.

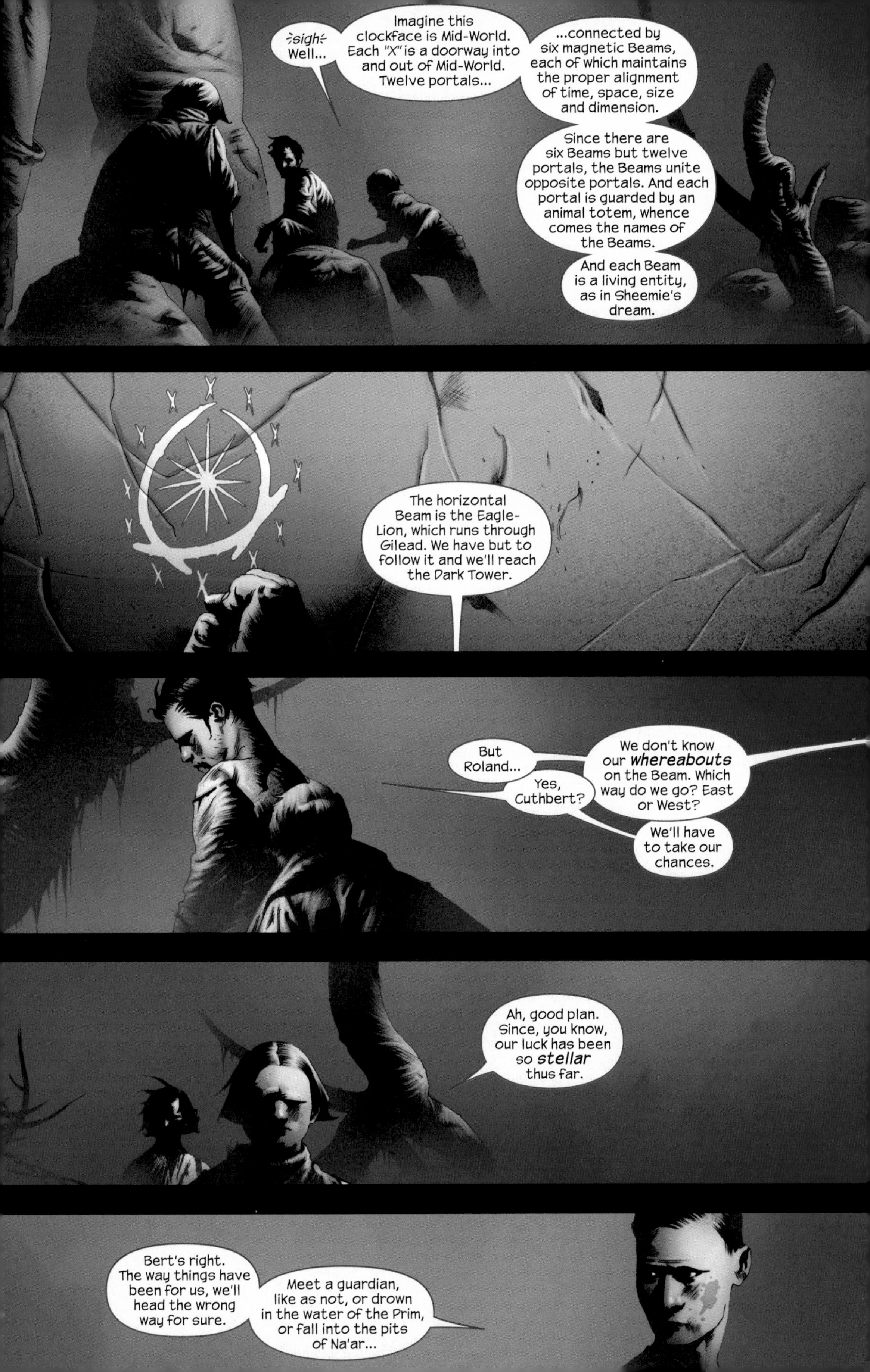

sigh Well...
Imagine this clockface is Mid-World. Each "X" is a doorway into and out of Mid-World. Twelve portals...
...connected by six magnetic Beams, each of which maintains the proper alignment of time, space, size and dimension.
Since there are six Beams but twelve portals, the Beams unite opposite portals. And each portal is guarded by an animal totem, whence comes the names of the Beams.
And each Beam is a living entity, as in Sheemie's dream.
The horizontal Beam is the Eagle-Lion, which runs through Gilead. We have but to follow it and we'll reach the Dark Tower.
But Roland...
Yes, Cuthbert?
We don't know our ***whereabouts*** on the Beam. Which way do we go? East or West?
We'll have to take our chances.
Ah, good plan. Since, you know, our luck has been so ***stellar*** thus far.
Bert's right. The way things have been for us, we'll head the wrong way for sure.
Meet a guardian, like as not, or drown in the water of the Prim, or fall into the pits of Na'ar...

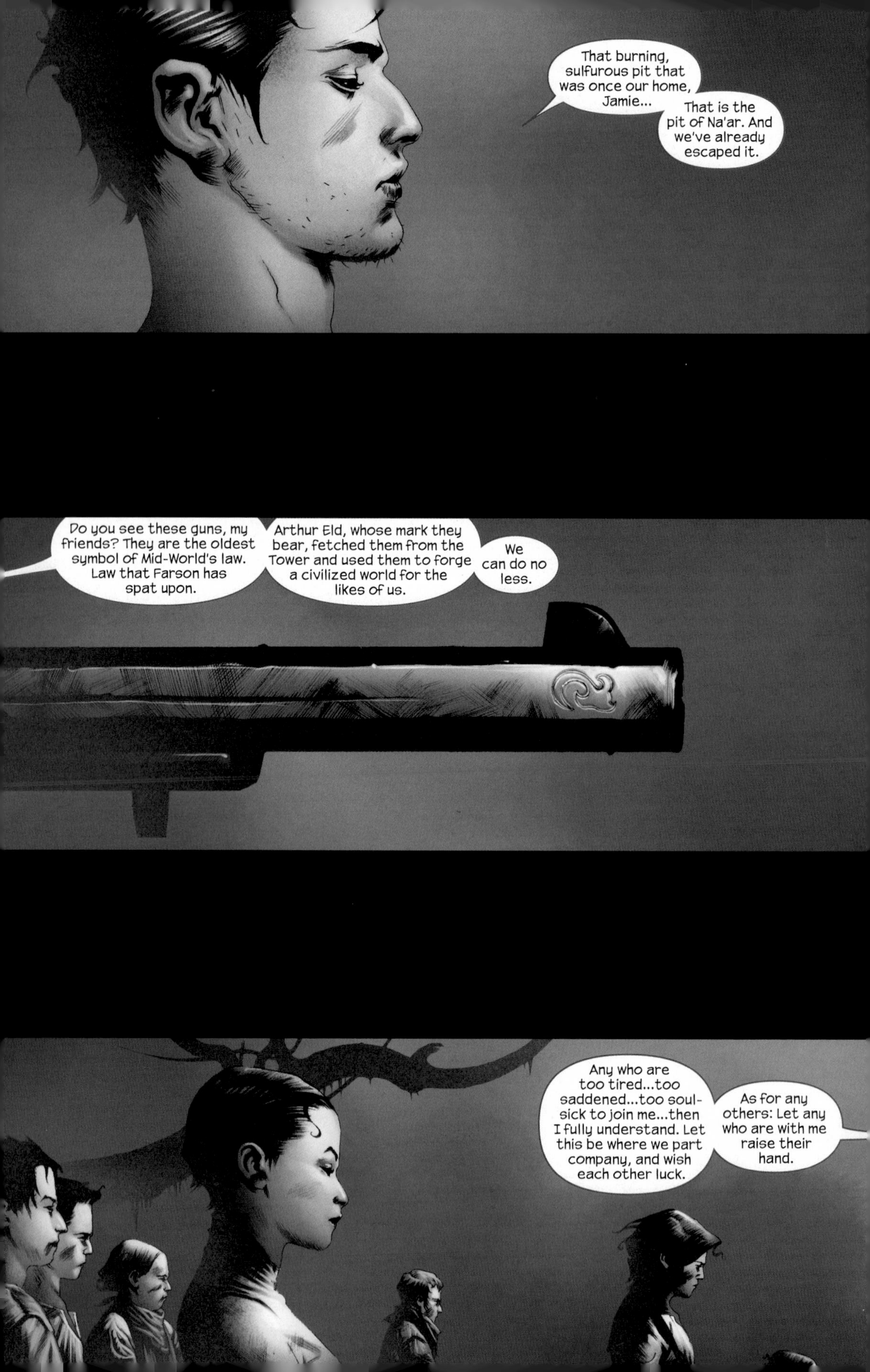
That burning, sulfurous pit that was once our home, Jamie...
That is the pit of Na'ar. And we've already escaped it.
Do you see these guns, my friends? They are the oldest symbol of Mid-World's law. Law that Farson has spat upon.
Arthur Eld, whose mark they bear, fetched them from the Tower and used them to forge a civilized world for the likes of us.
We can do no less.
Any who are too tired...too saddened...too soul-sick to join me...then I fully understand. Let this be where we part company, and wish each other luck.
As for any others: Let any who are with me raise their hand.

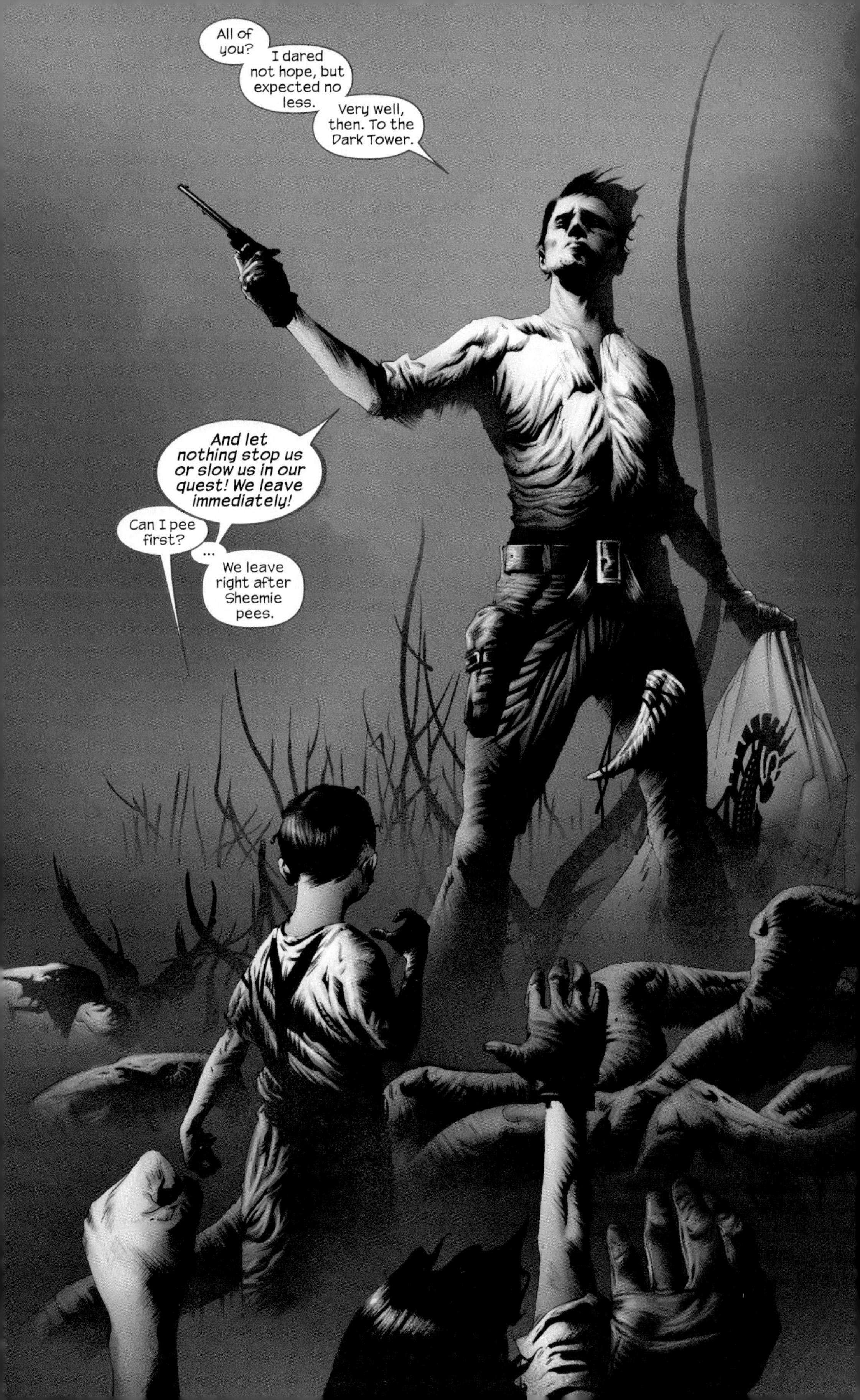

All of you?
I dared not hope, but expected no less.
Very well, then. To the Dark Tower.
And let nothing stop us or slow us in our quest! We leave immediately!
Can I pee first?
...
We leave right after Sheemie pees.

STEPHEN KING
THE DARK TOWER

BATTLE OF JERICHO HILL
CHAPTER TWO

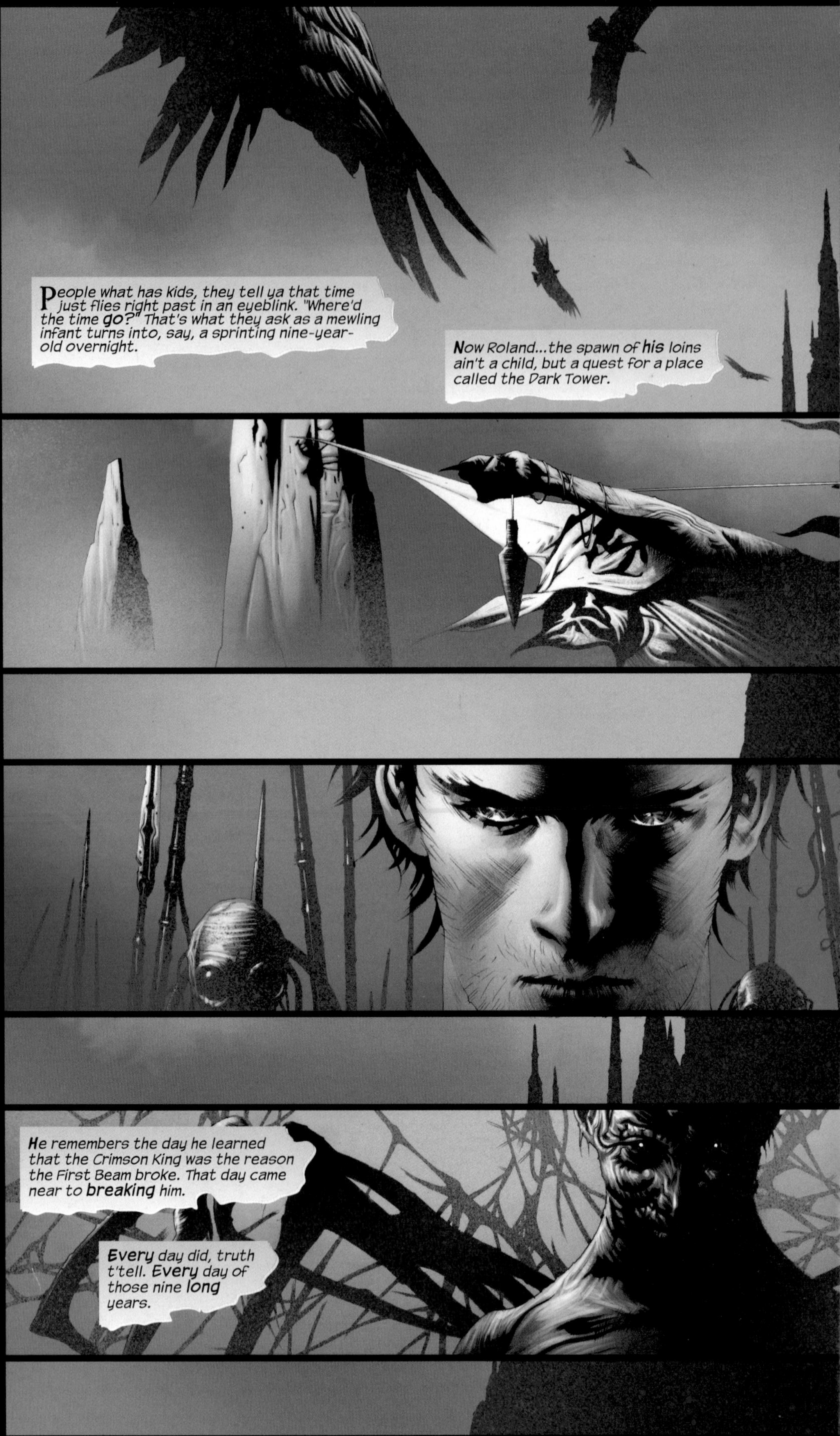
People what has kids, they tell ya that time just flies right past in an eyeblink. "Where'd the time go?" That's what they ask as a mewling infant turns into, say, a sprinting nine-year-old overnight.
Now Roland...the spawn of his loins ain't a child, but a quest for a place called the Dark Tower.
He remembers the day he learned that the Crimson King was the reason the First Beam broke. That day came near to breaking him.
Every day did, truth t'tell. Every day of those nine long years.

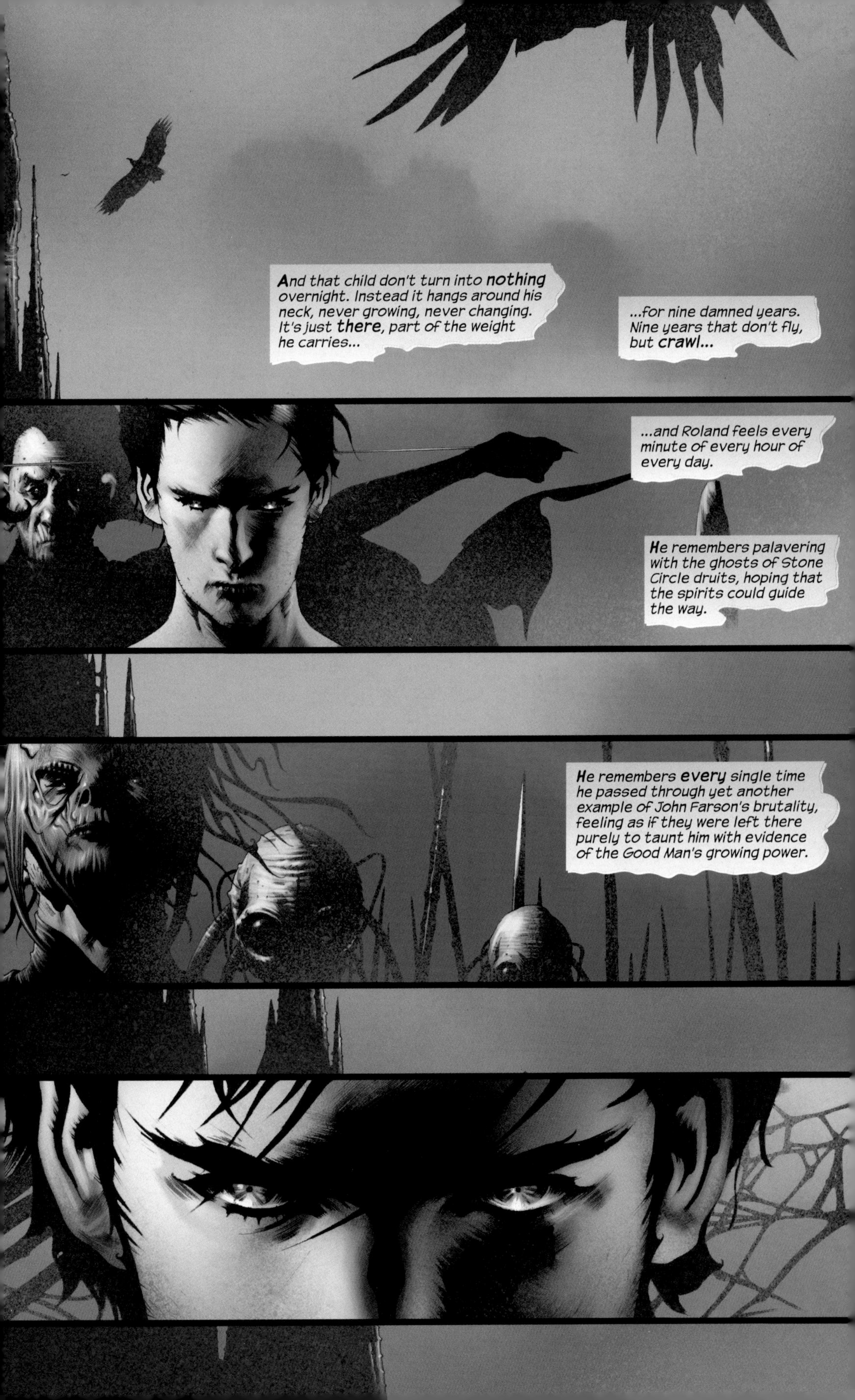
And that child don't turn into **nothing** overnight. Instead it hangs around his neck, never growing, never changing. It's just **there**, part of the weight he carries...
...for nine damned years. Nine years that don't fly, but **crawl...**
...and Roland feels every minute of every hour of every day.
He remembers palavering with the ghosts of Stone Circle druits, hoping that the spirits could guide the way.
He remembers **every** single time he passed through yet another example of John Farson's brutality, feeling as if they were left there purely to taunt him with evidence of the Good Man's growing power.

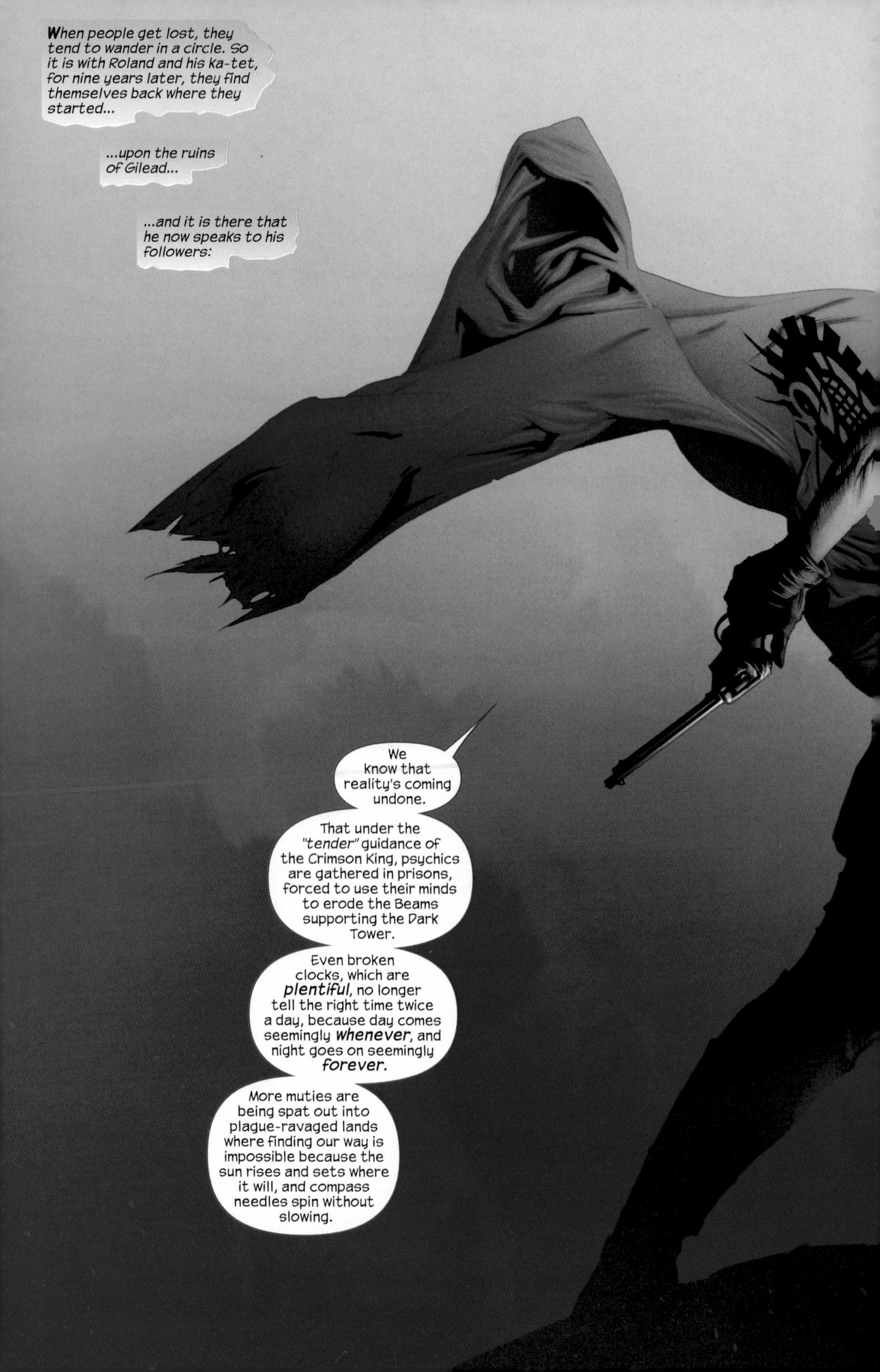
When people get lost, they tend to wander in a circle. So it is with Roland and his ka-tet, for nine years later, they find themselves back where they started...
...upon the ruins of Gilead...
...and it is there that he now speaks to his followers:
We know that reality's coming undone.
That under the "tender" guidance of the Crimson King, psychics are gathered in prisons, forced to use their minds to erode the Beams supporting the Dark Tower.
Even broken clocks, which are plentiful, no longer tell the right time twice a day, because day comes seemingly whenever, and night goes on seemingly forever.
More muties are being spat out into plague-ravaged lands where finding our way is impossible because the sun rises and sets where it will, and compass needles spin without slowing.

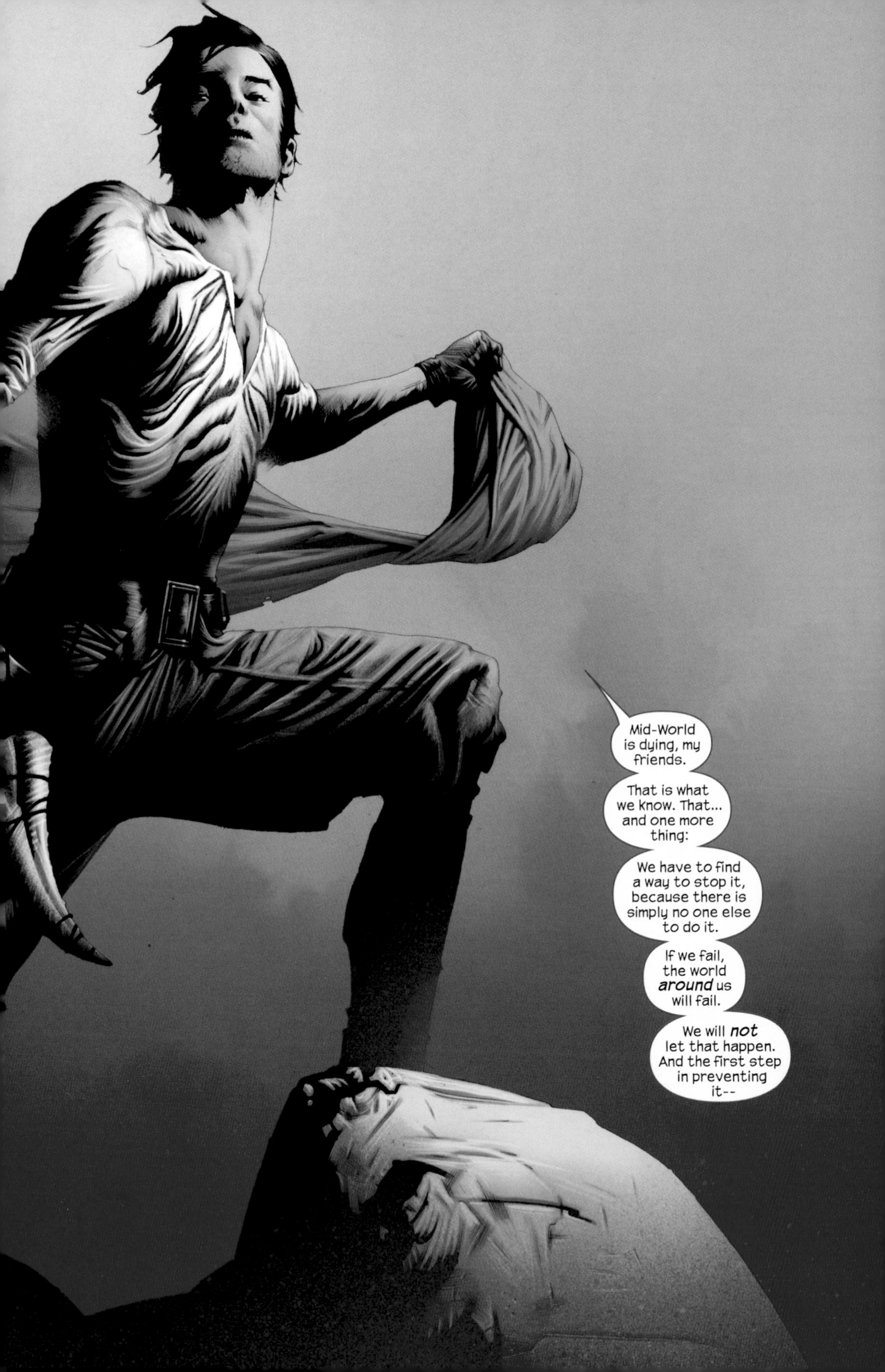
Mid-World is dying, my friends.
That is what we know. That... and one more thing:
We have to find a way to stop it, because there is simply no one else to do it.
If we fail, the world *around* us will fail.
We will *not* let that happen. And the first step in preventing it--

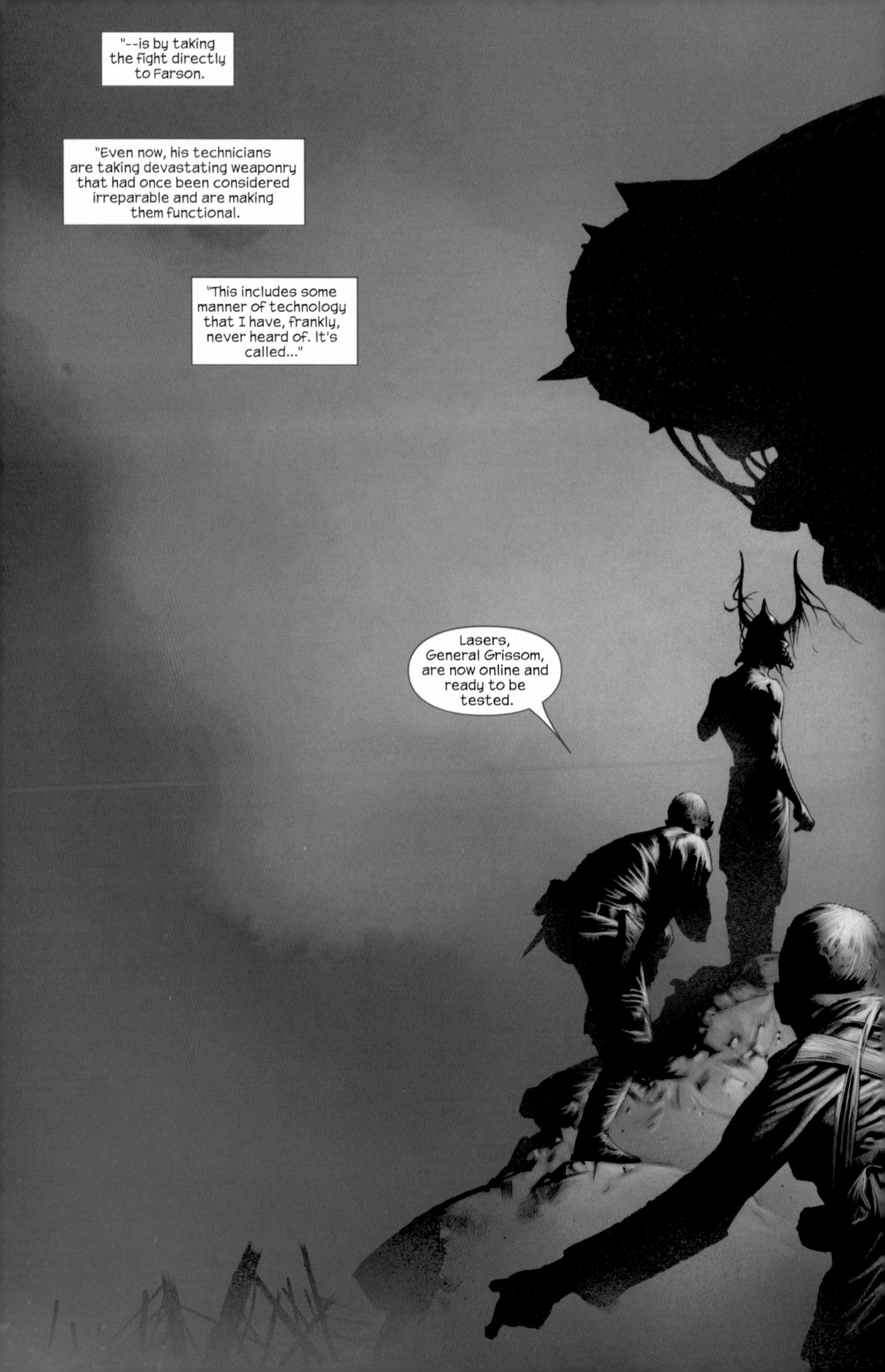
"--is by taking the fight directly to Farson.
"Even now, his technicians are taking devastating weaponry that had once been considered irreparable and are making them functional.
"This includes some manner of technology that I have, frankly, never heard of. It's called..."
Lasers, General Grissom, are now online and ready to be tested.

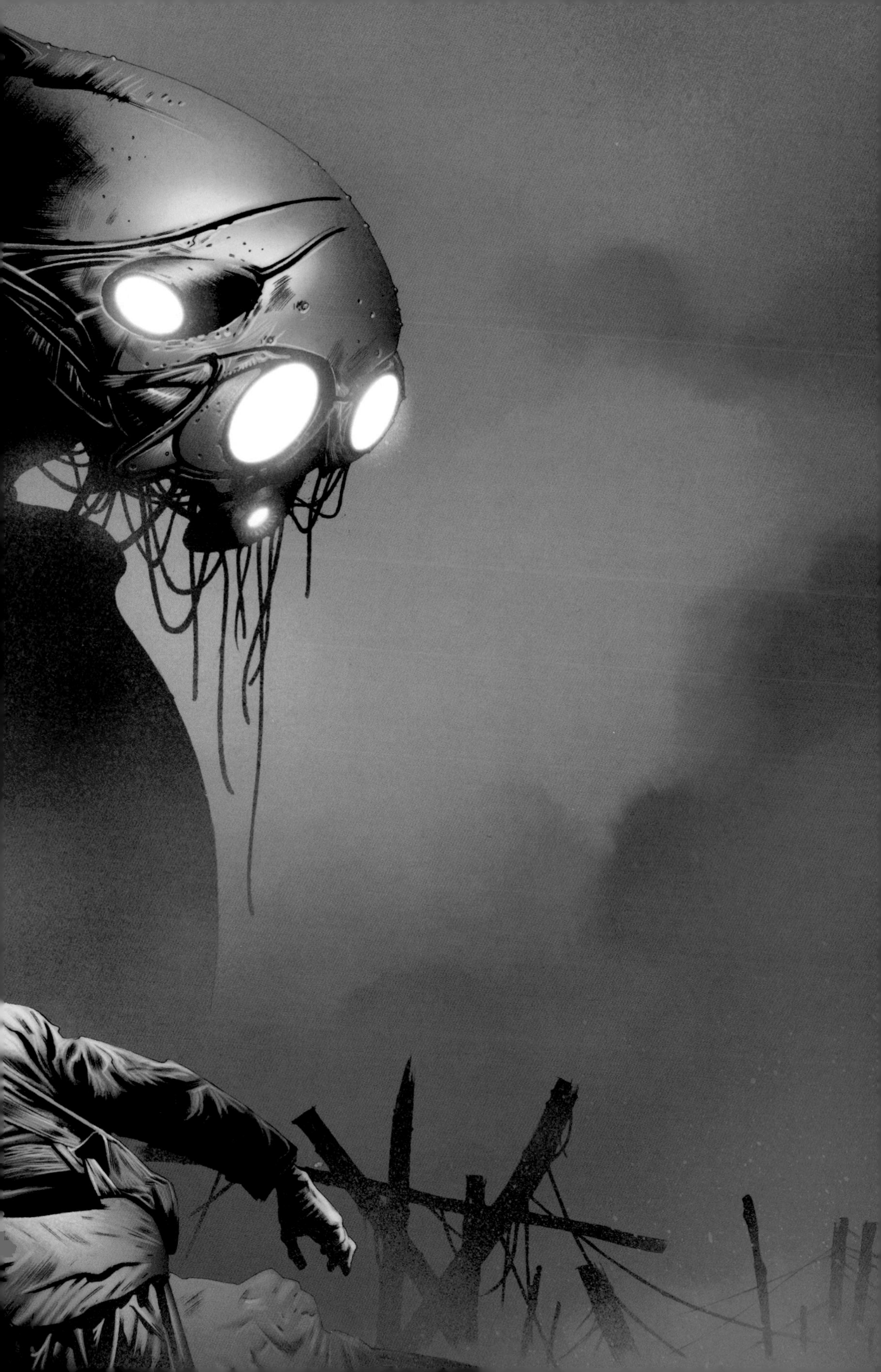

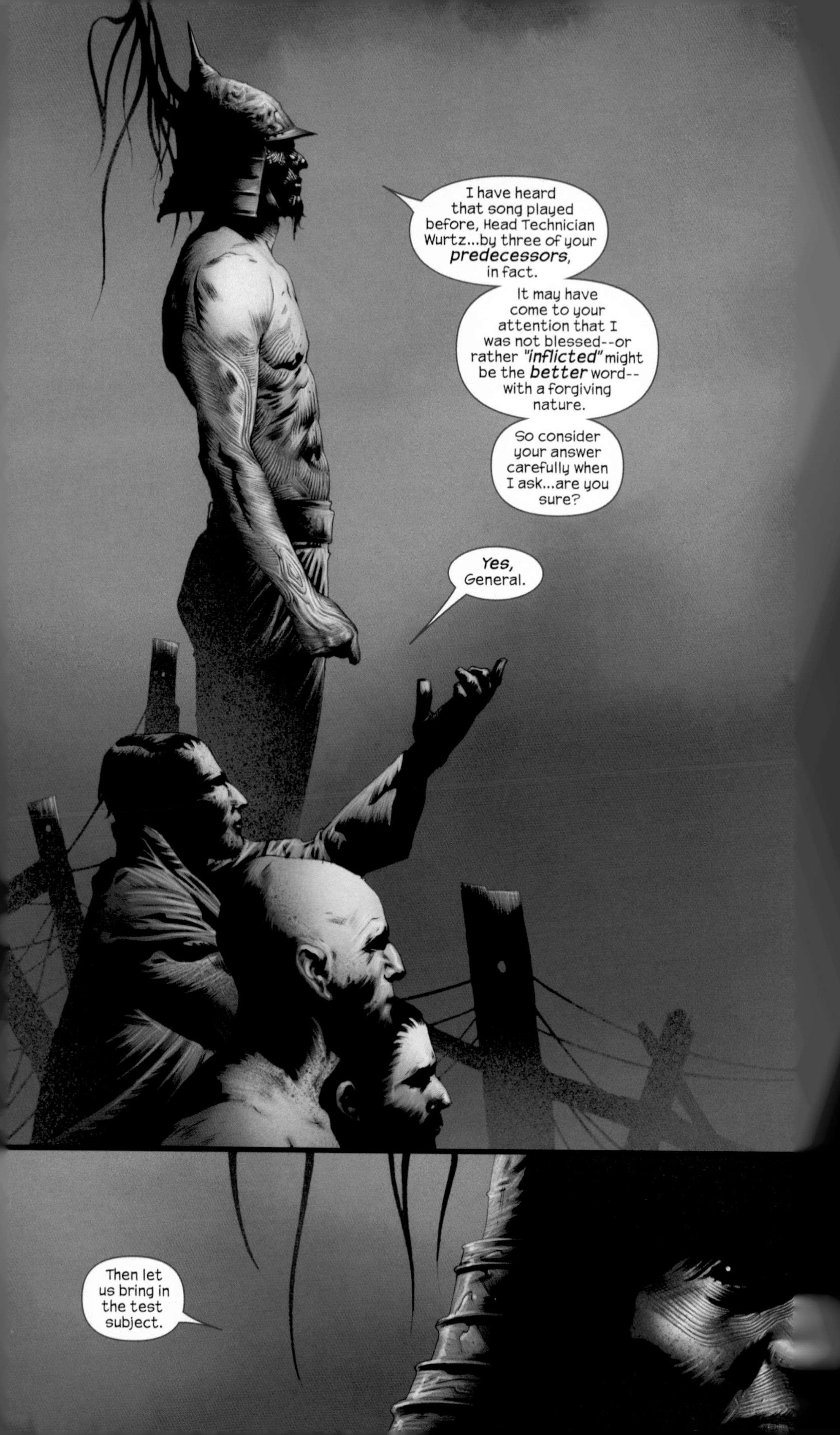
I have heard that song played before, Head Technician Wurtz...by three of your *predecessors*, in fact.
It may have come to your attention that I was not blessed--or rather *"inflicted"* might be the *better* word--with a forgiving nature.
So consider your answer carefully when I ask...are you sure?
Yes, General.
Then let us bring in the test subject.

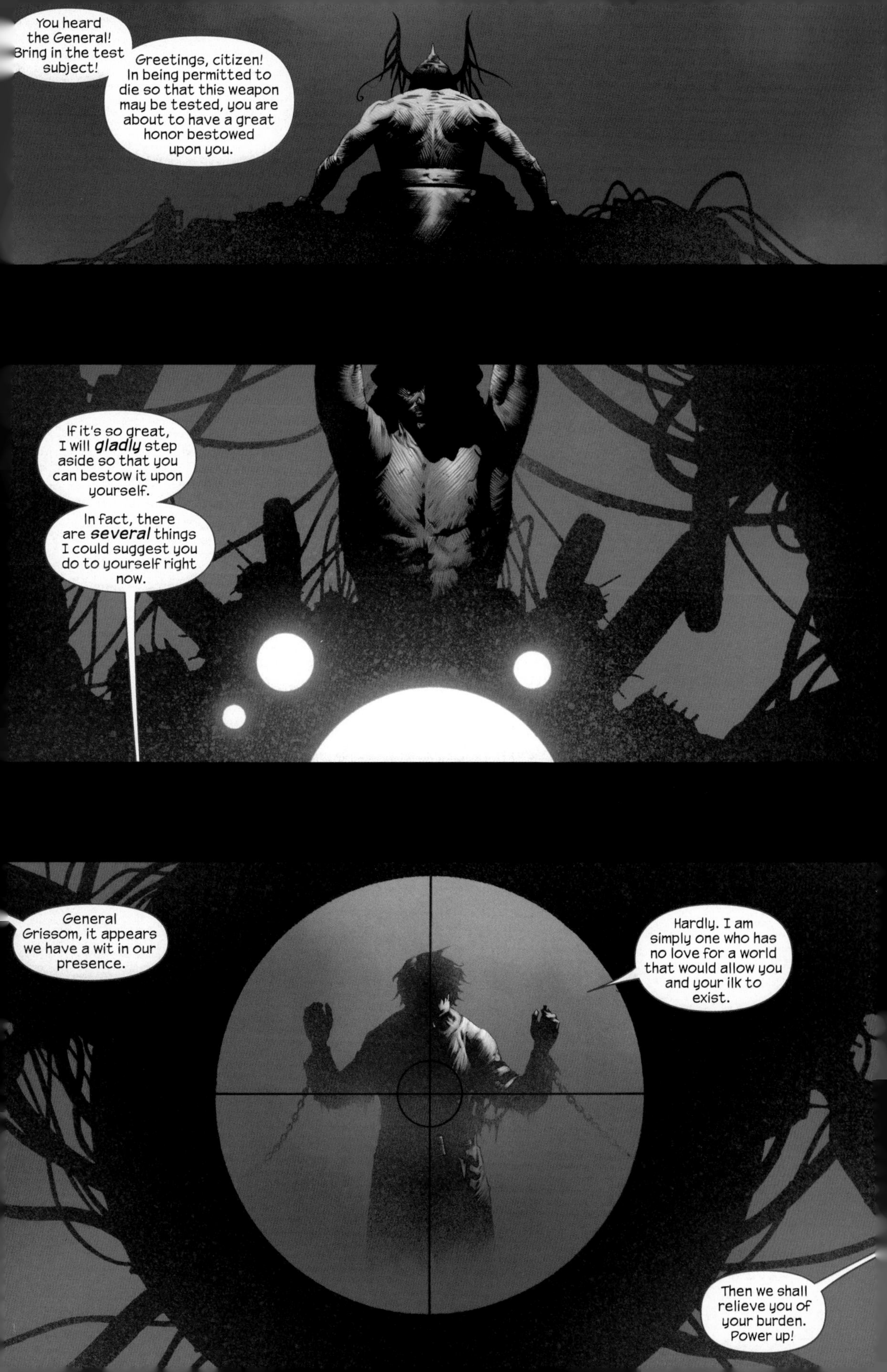

You heard the General! Bring in the test subject!
Greetings, citizen! In being permitted to die so that this weapon may be tested, you are about to have a great honor bestowed upon you.
If it's so great, I will *gladly* step aside so that you can bestow it upon yourself.
In fact, there are *several* things I could suggest you do to yourself right now.
General Grissom, it appears we have a wit in our presence.
Hardly. I am simply one who has no love for a world that would allow you and your ilk to exist.
Then we shall relieve you of your burden. Power up!

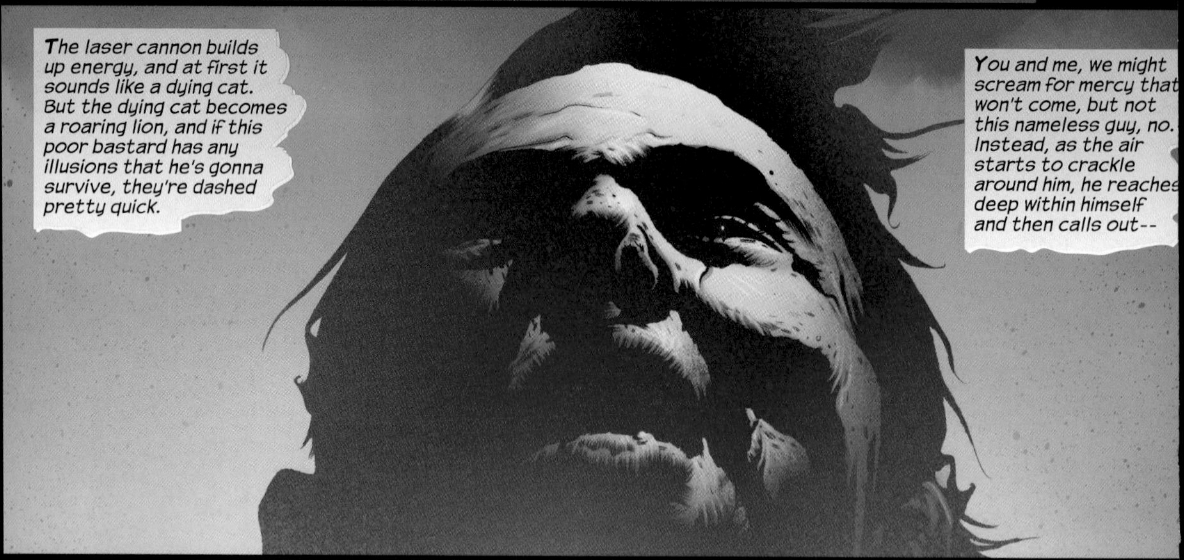
The laser cannon builds up energy, and at first it sounds like a dying cat. But the dying cat becomes a roaring lion, and if this poor bastard has any illusions that he's gonna survive, they're dashed pretty quick.
You and me, we might scream for mercy that won't come, but not this nameless guy, no. Instead, as the air starts to crackle around him, he reaches deep within himself and then calls out--

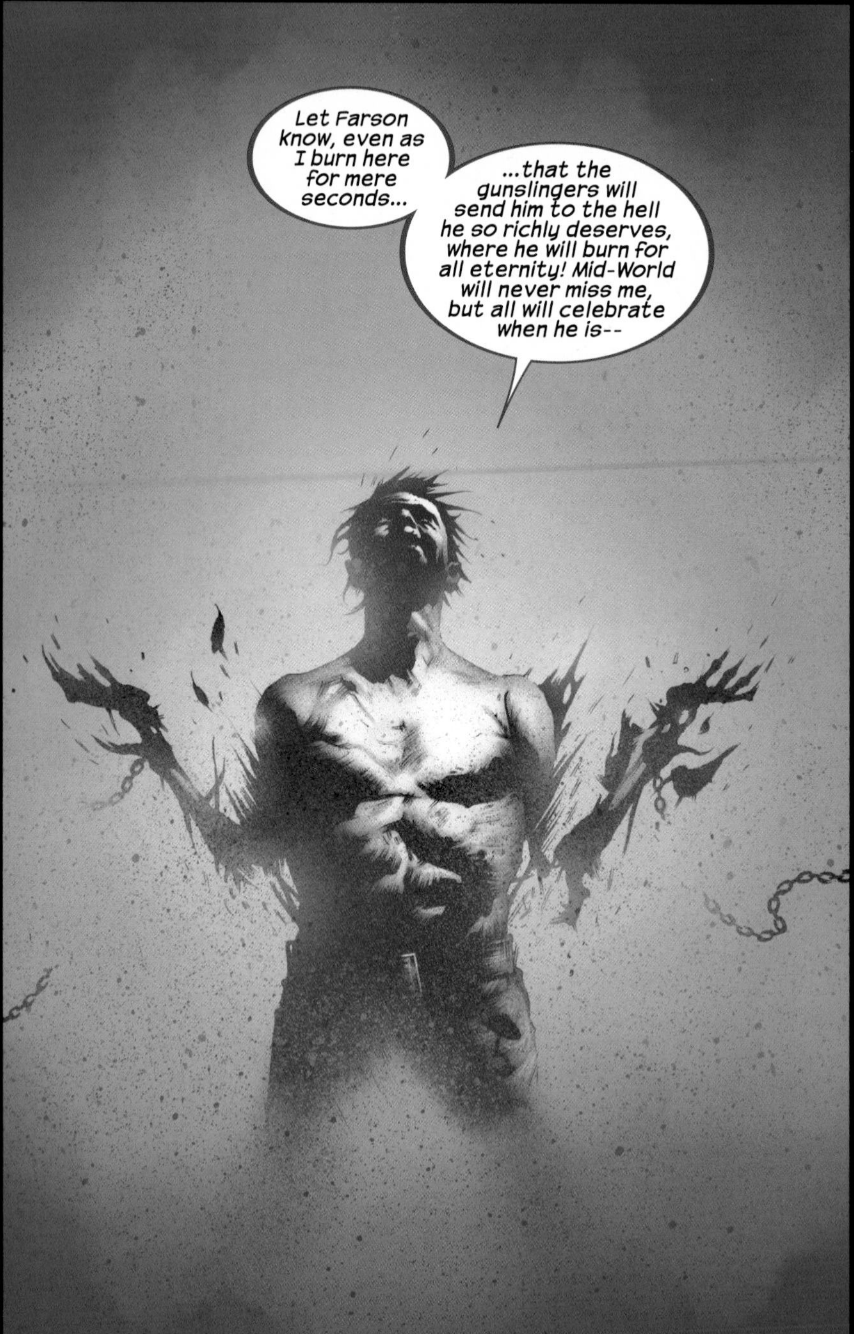
Let Farson know, even as I burn here for mere seconds...
...that the gunslingers will send him to the hell he so richly deserves, where he will burn for all eternity! Mid-World will never miss me, but all will celebrate when he is--

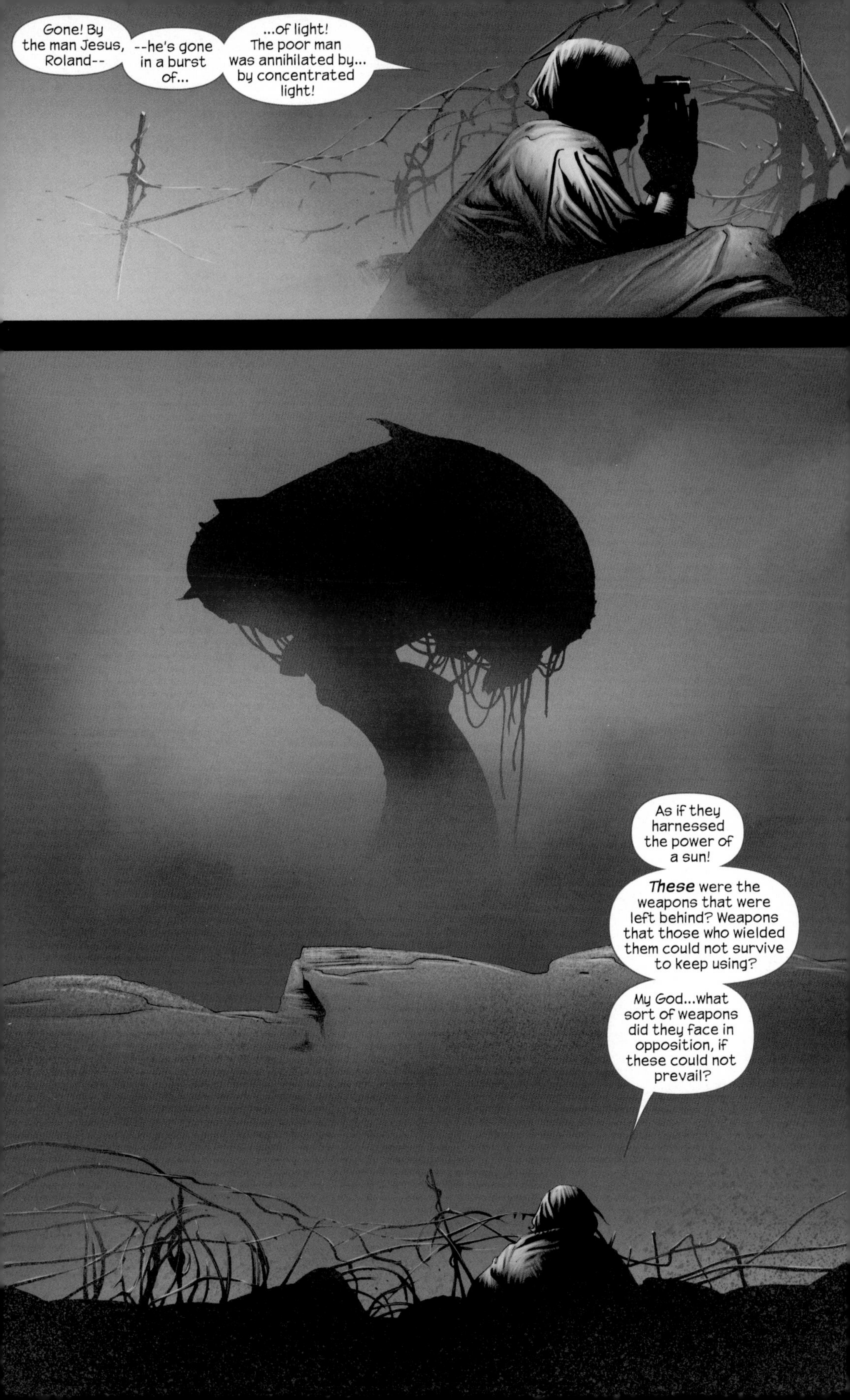
Gone! By the man Jesus, Roland--
--he's gone in a burst of...
...of light! The poor man was annihilated by... by concentrated light!
As if they harnessed the power of a sun!
These were the weapons that were left behind? Weapons that those who wielded them could not survive to keep using?
My God...what sort of weapons did they face in opposition, if these could not prevail?

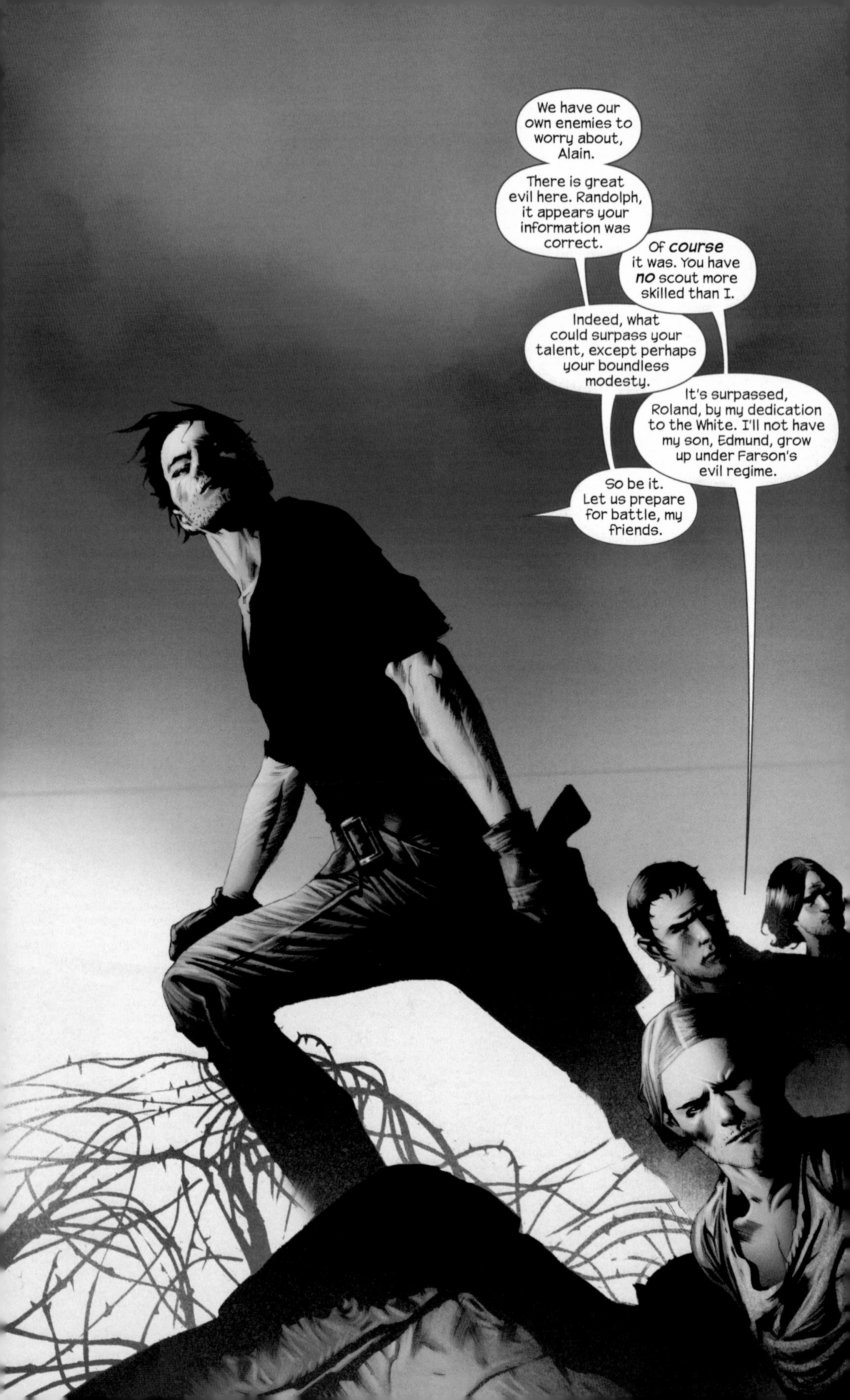

We have our own enemies to worry about, Alain.
There is great evil here. Randolph, it appears your information was correct.
Of *course* it was. You have ***no*** scout more skilled than I.
Indeed, what could surpass your talent, except perhaps your boundless modesty.
It's surpassed, Roland, by my dedication to the White. I'll not have my son, Edmund, grow up under Farson's evil regime.
So be it. Let us prepare for battle, my friends.

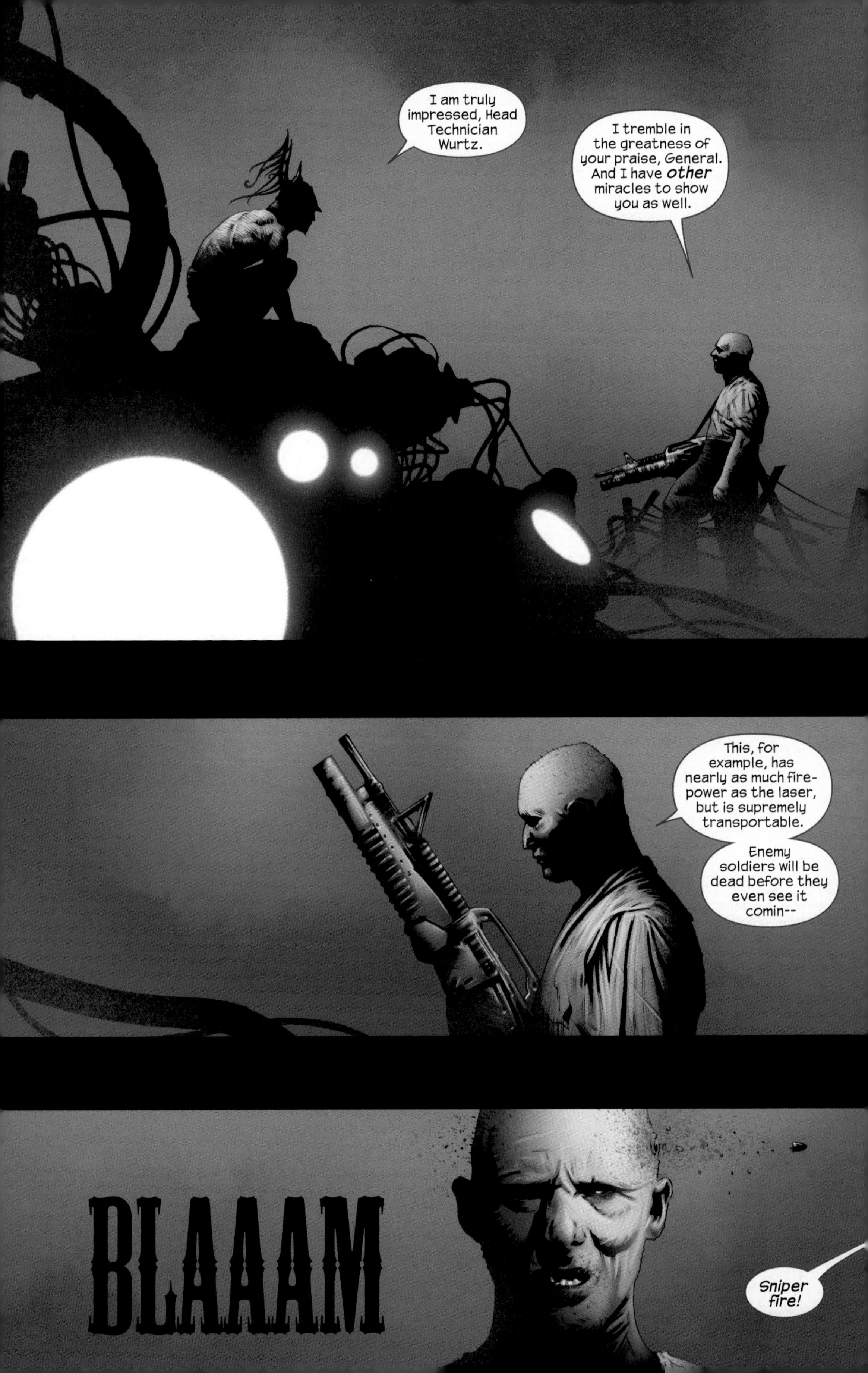

I am truly impressed, Head Technician Wurtz.
I tremble in the greatness of your praise, General. And I have *other* miracles to show you as well.
This, for example, has nearly as much fire-power as the laser, but is supremely transportable.
Enemy soldiers will be dead before they even see it comin--
BLAAAM
Sniper fire!

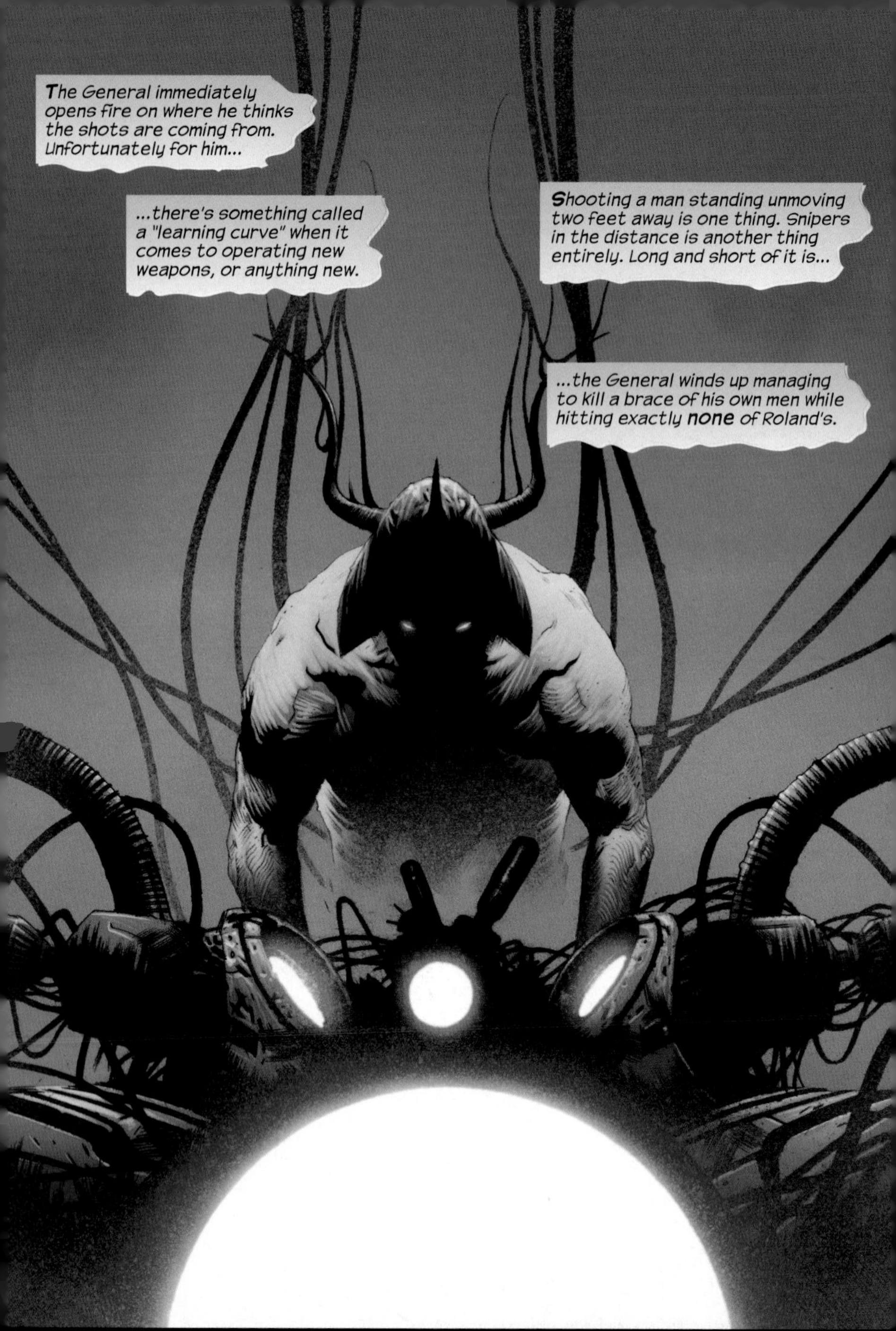
The General immediately opens fire on where he thinks the shots are coming from. Unfortunately for him...
...there's something called a "learning curve" when it comes to operating new weapons, or anything new.
Shooting a man standing unmoving two feet away is one thing. Snipers in the distance is another thing entirely. Long and short of it is...
...the General winds up managing to kill a brace of his own men while hitting exactly **none** of Roland's.

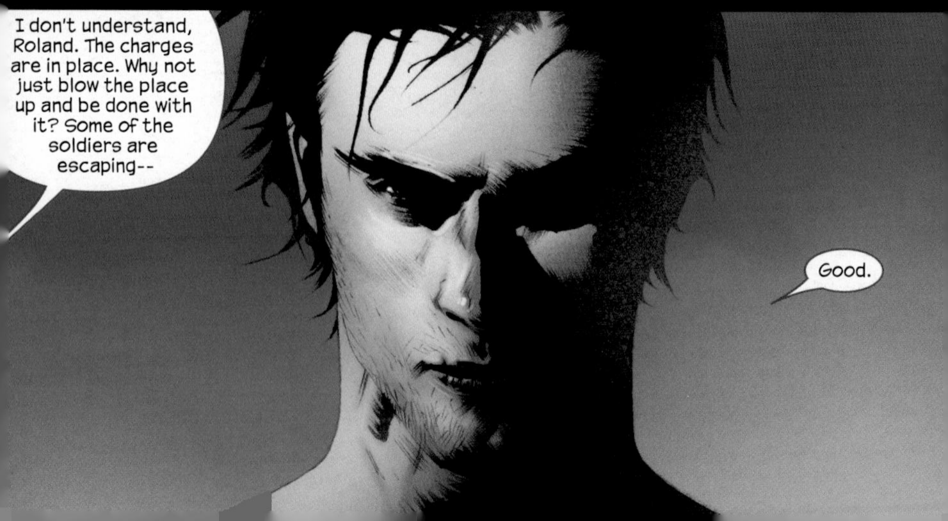
I don't understand, Roland. The charges are in place. Why not just blow the place up and be done with it? Some of the soldiers are escaping--
Good.

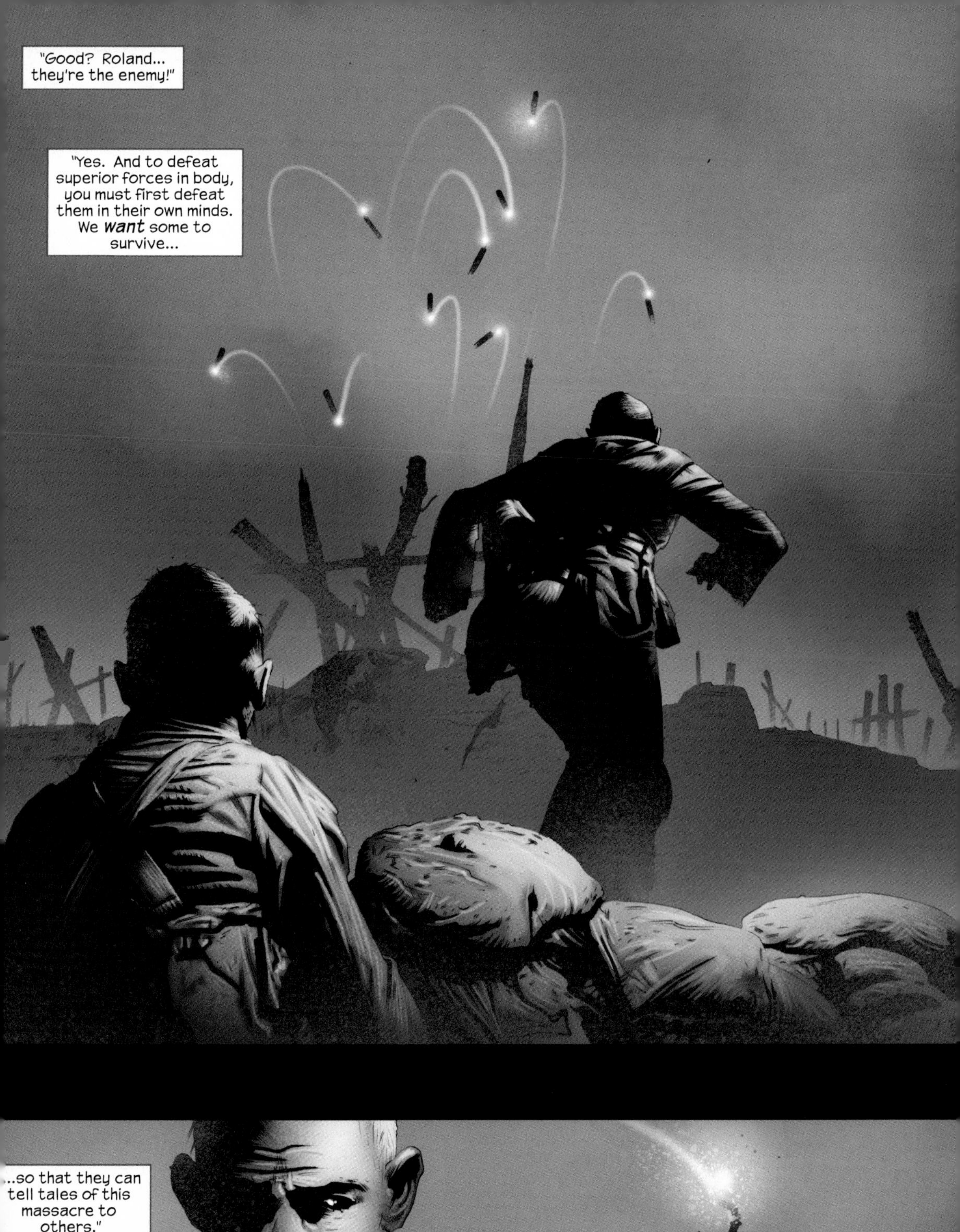
"Good? Roland... they're the enemy!"
"Yes. And to defeat superior forces in body, you must first defeat them in their own minds. We *want* some to survive...
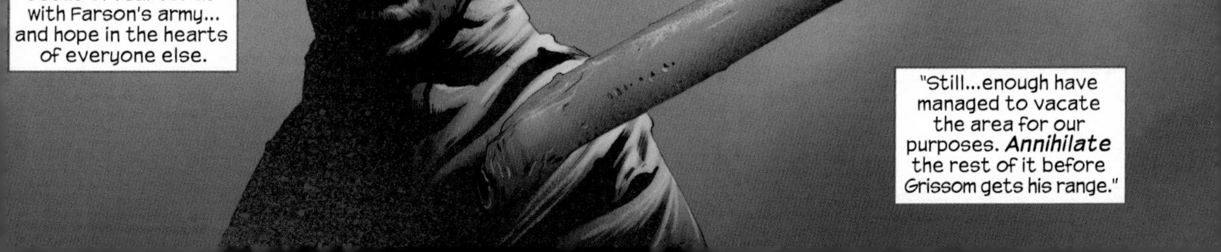
...so that they can tell tales of this massacre to others."
"They will plant the seeds of fear for us with Farson's army... and hope in the hearts of everyone else.
"Still...enough have managed to vacate the area for our purposes. *Annihilate* the rest of it before Grissom gets his range."

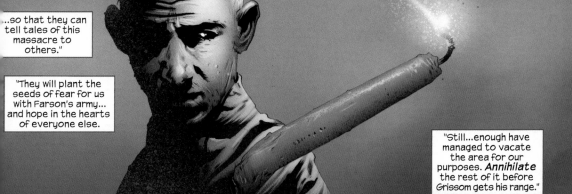

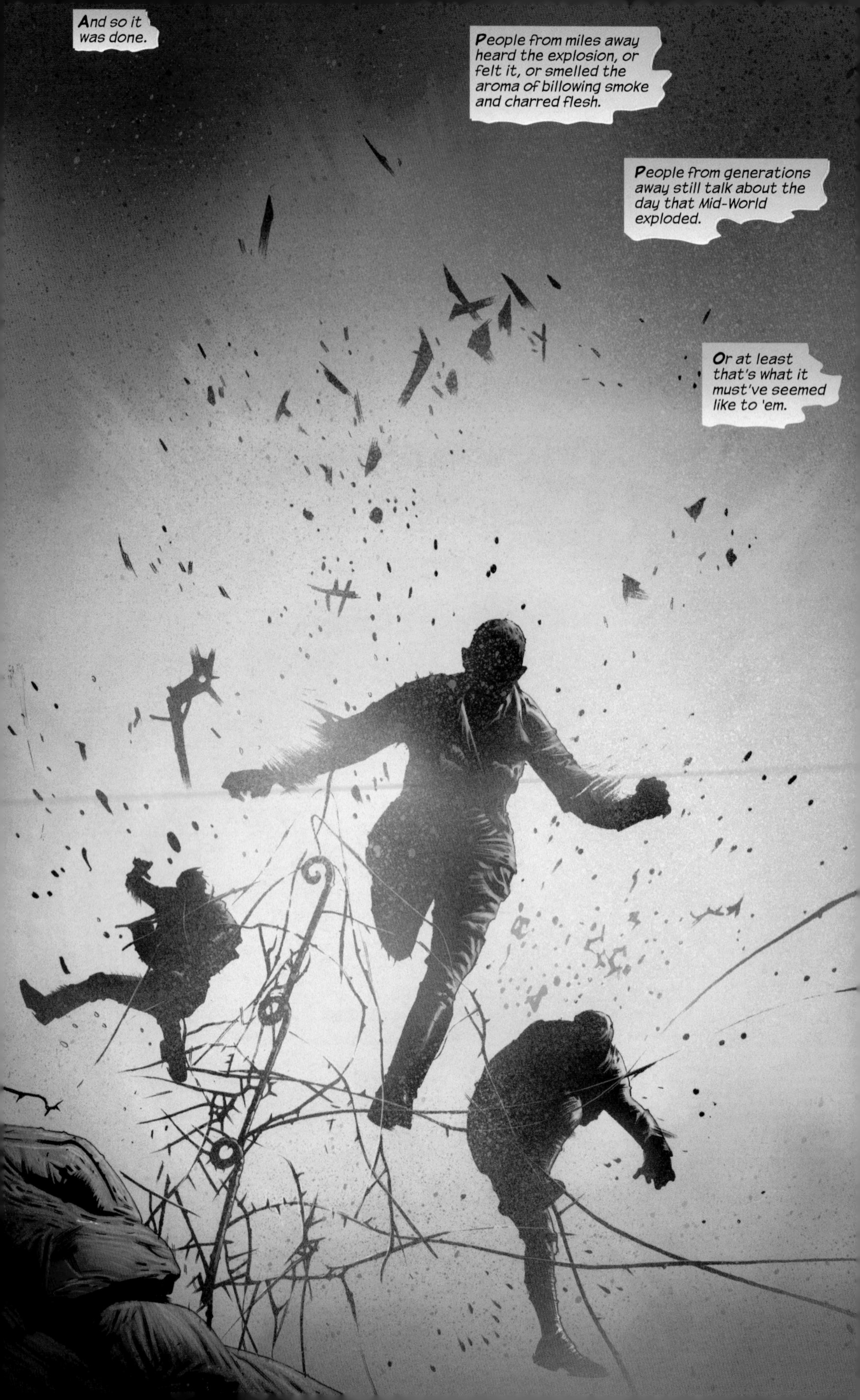
And so it was done.
People from miles away heard the explosion, or felt it, or smelled the aroma of billowing smoke and charred flesh.
People from generations away still talk about the day that Mid-World exploded.
Or at least that's what it must've seemed like to 'em.

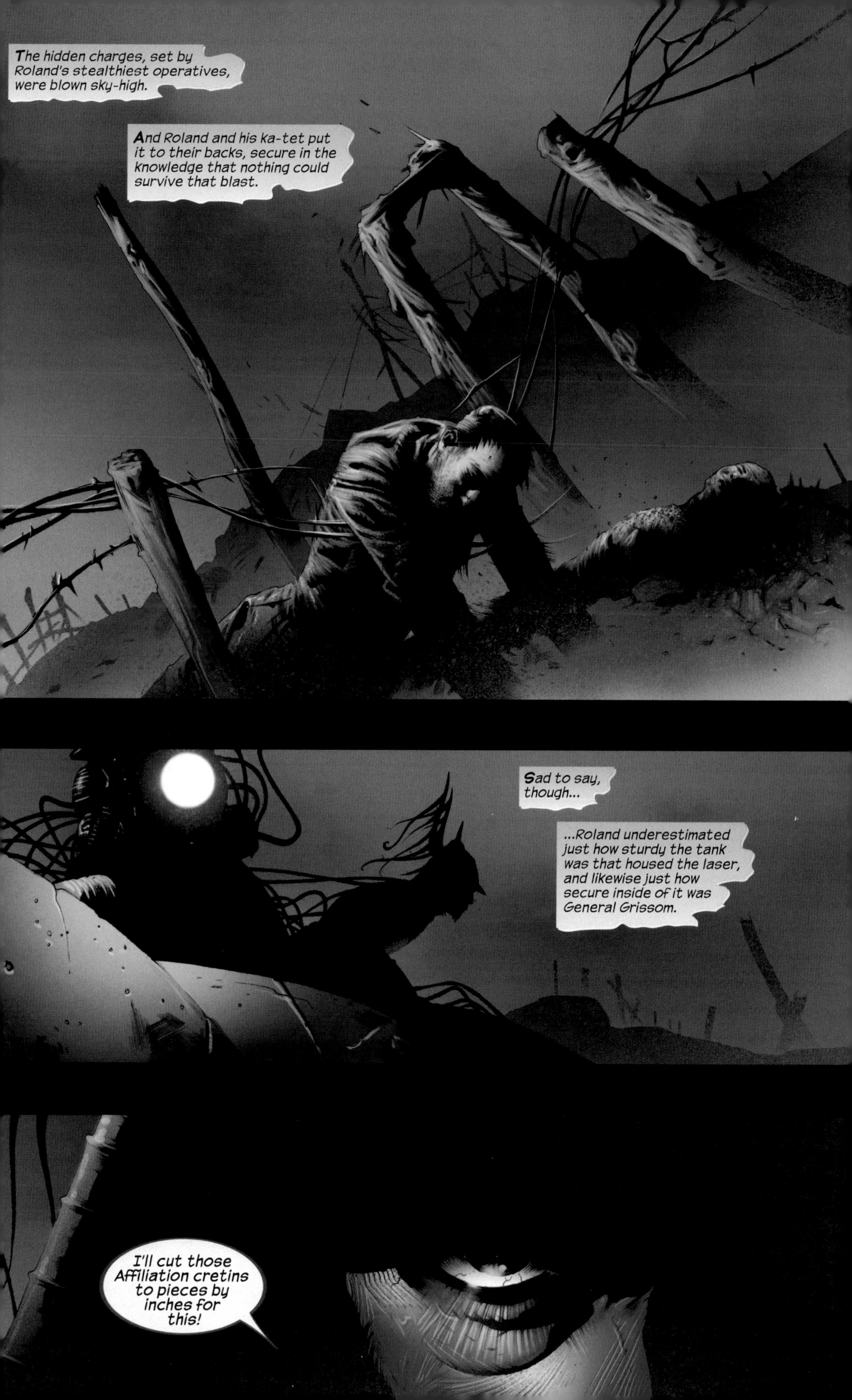
The hidden charges, set by Roland's stealthiest operatives, were blown sky-high.
And Roland and his ka-tet put it to their backs, secure in the knowledge that nothing could survive that blast.
Sad to say, though...
...Roland underestimated just how sturdy the tank was that housed the laser, and likewise just how secure inside of it was General Grissom.
I'll cut those Affiliation cretins to pieces by inches for this!

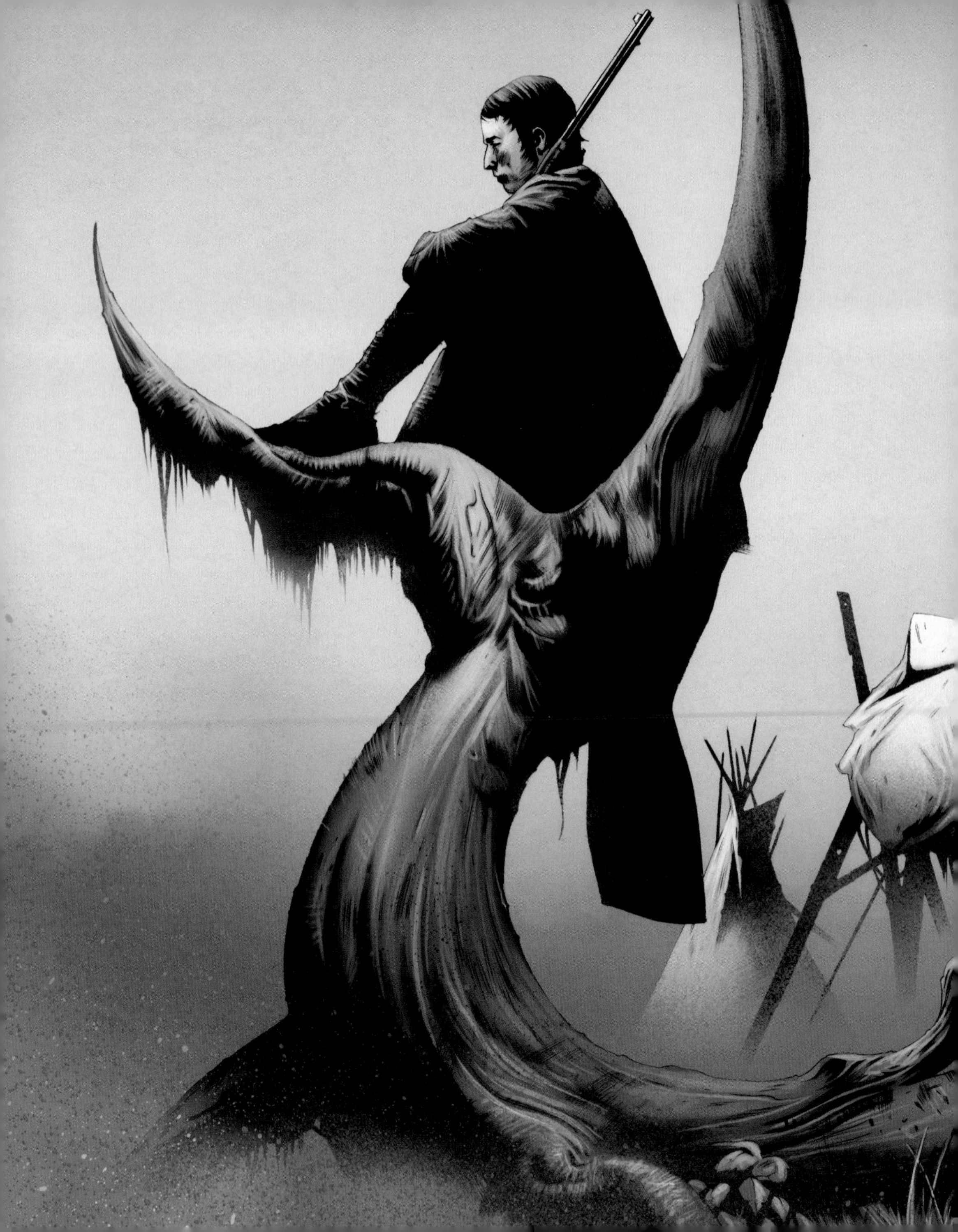

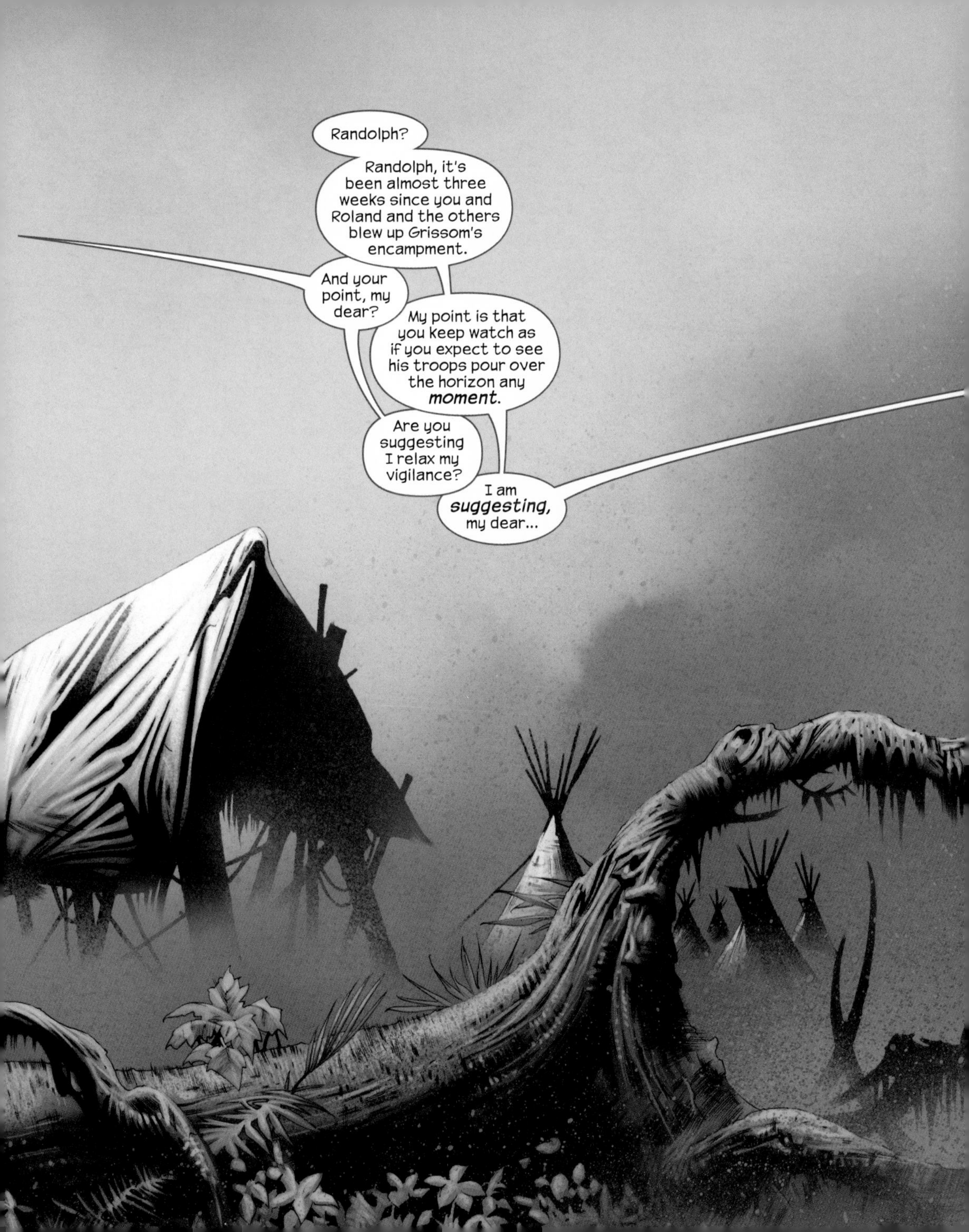
Randolph?
Randolph, it's been almost three weeks since you and Roland and the others blew up Grissom's encampment.
And your point, my dear?
My point is that you keep watch as if you expect to see his troops pour over the horizon any *moment*.
Are you suggesting I relax my vigilance?
I am *suggesting,* my dear...

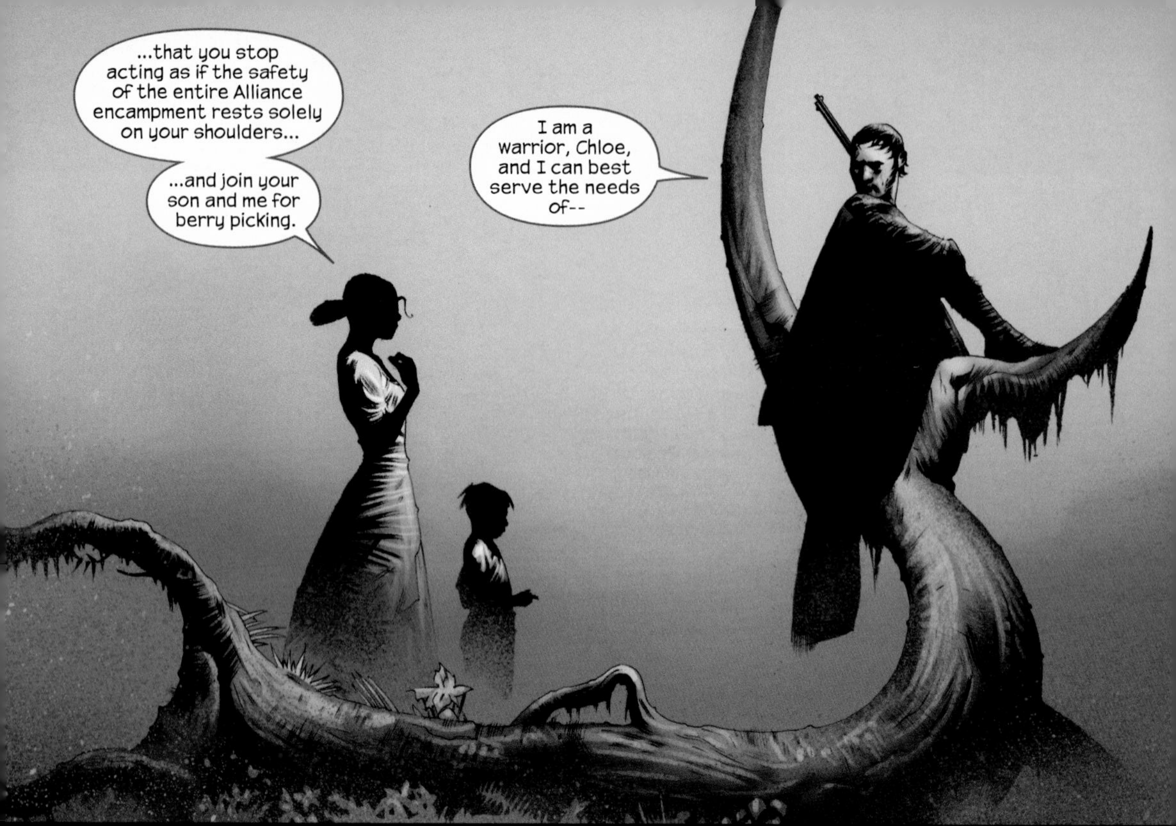
...that you stop acting as if the safety of the entire Alliance encampment rests solely on your shoulders...
...and join your son and me for berry picking.
I am a warrior, Chloe, and I can best serve the needs of--

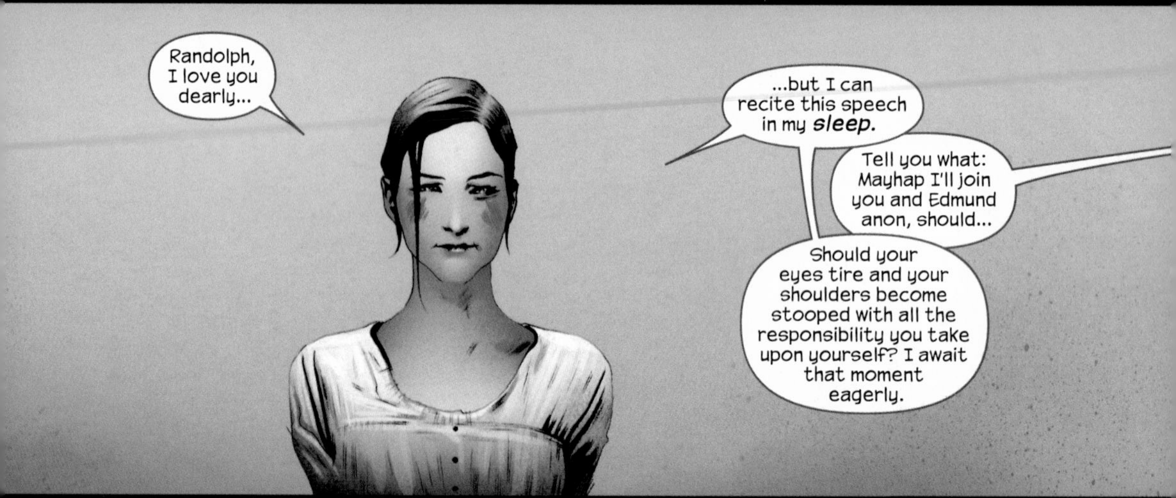
Randolph, I love you dearly...
...but I can recite this speech in my *sleep.*
Tell you what: Mayhap I'll join you and Edmund anon, should...
Should your eyes tire and your shoulders become stooped with all the responsibility you take upon yourself? I await that moment eagerly.

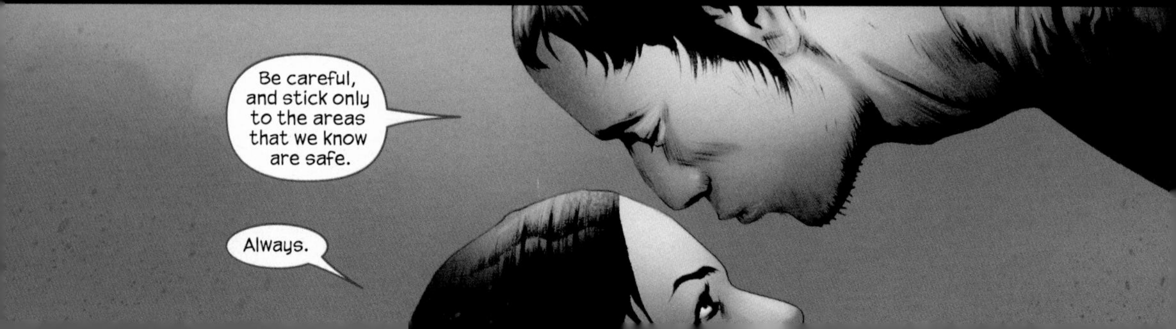
Be careful, and stick only to the areas that we know are safe.
Always.

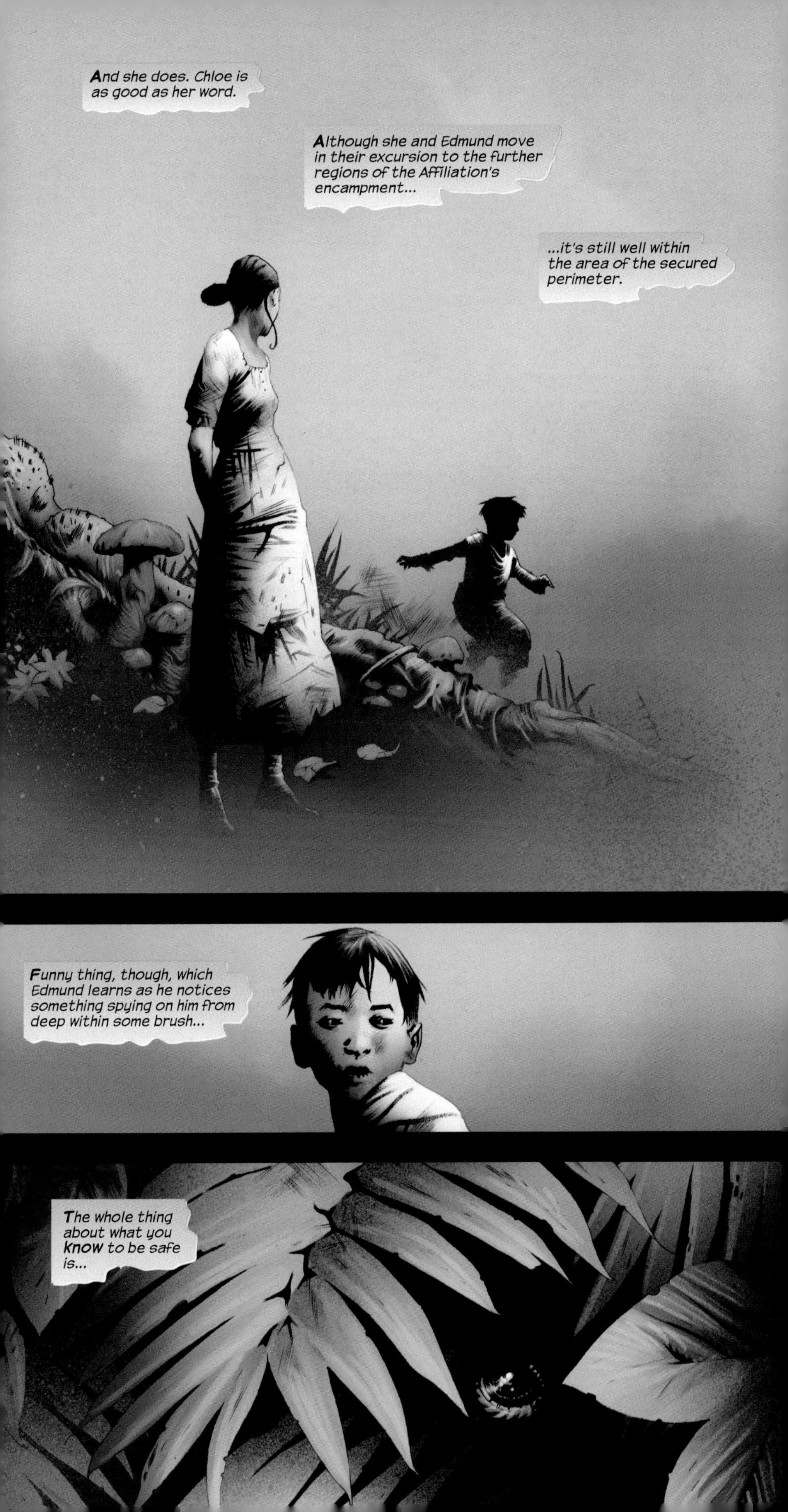
And she does. Chloe is as good as her word.
Although she and Edmund move in their excursion to the further regions of the Affiliation's encampment...
...it's still well within the area of the secured perimeter.
Funny thing, though, which Edmund learns as he notices something spying on him from deep within some brush...
The whole thing about what you KNOW to be safe is...

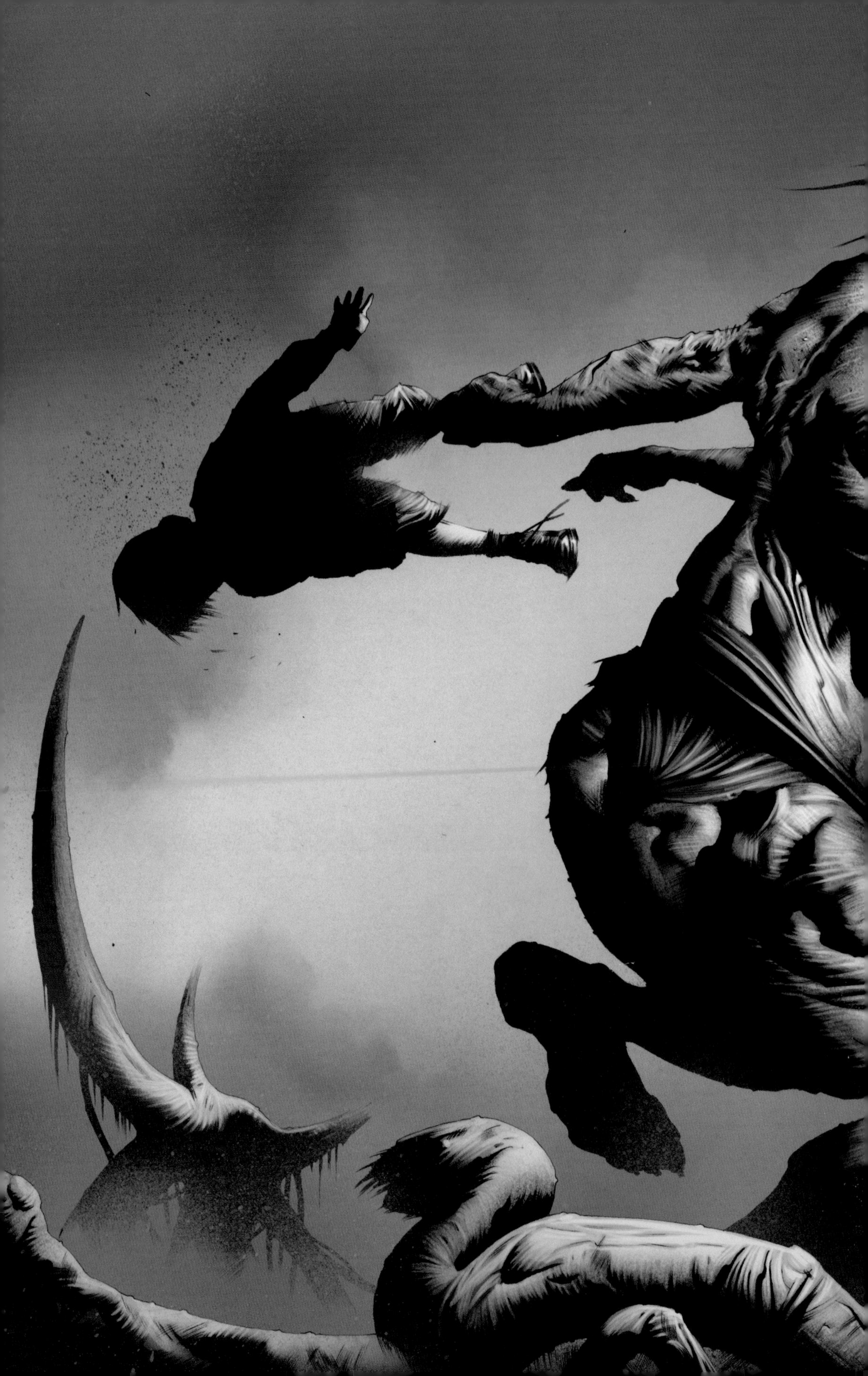

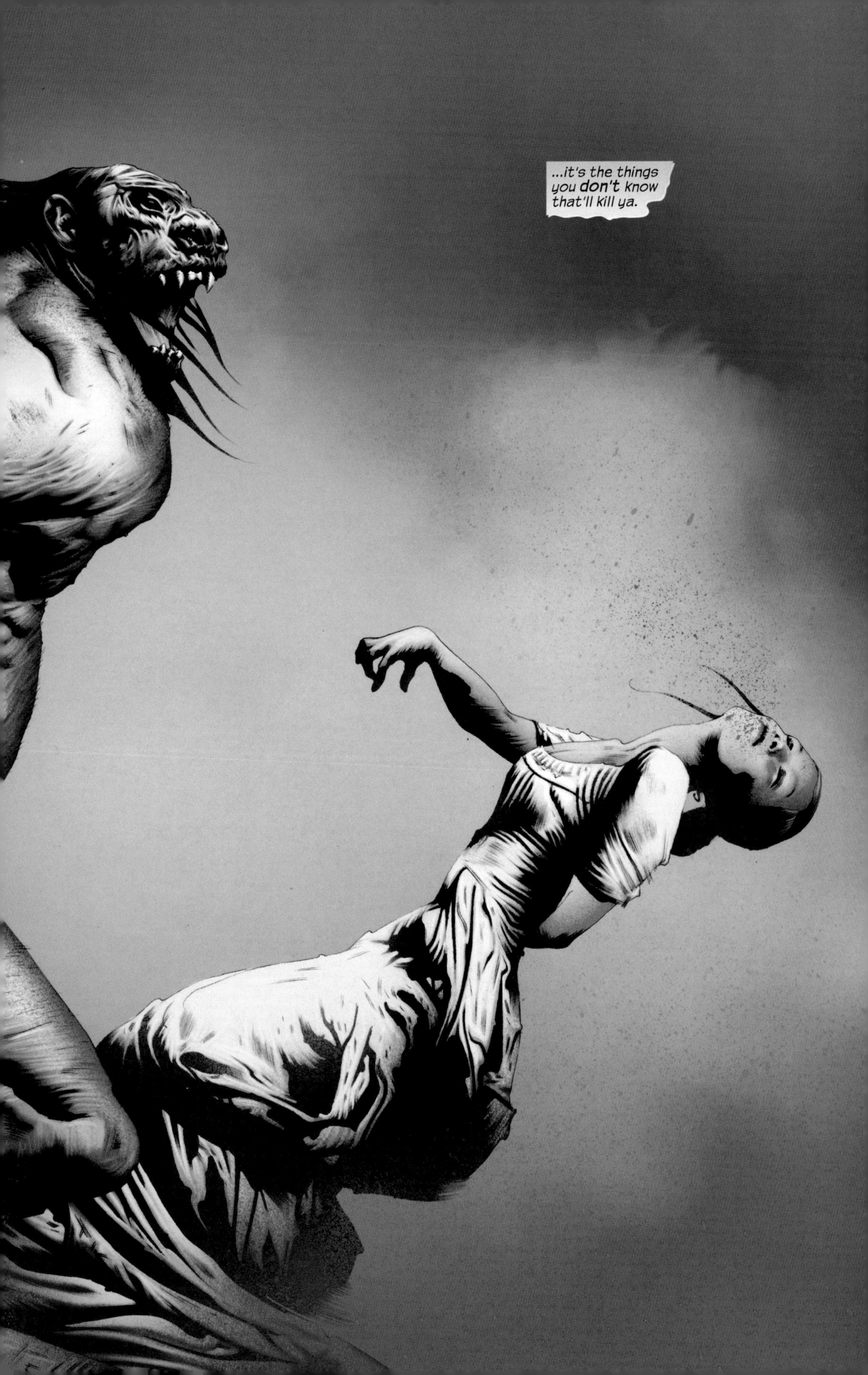
...it's the things you don't know that'll kill ya.

STEPHEN KING

THE DARK TOWER

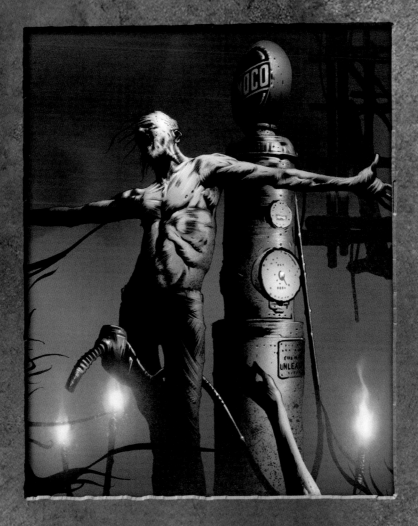

BATTLE OF JERICHO HILL

CHAPTER THREE

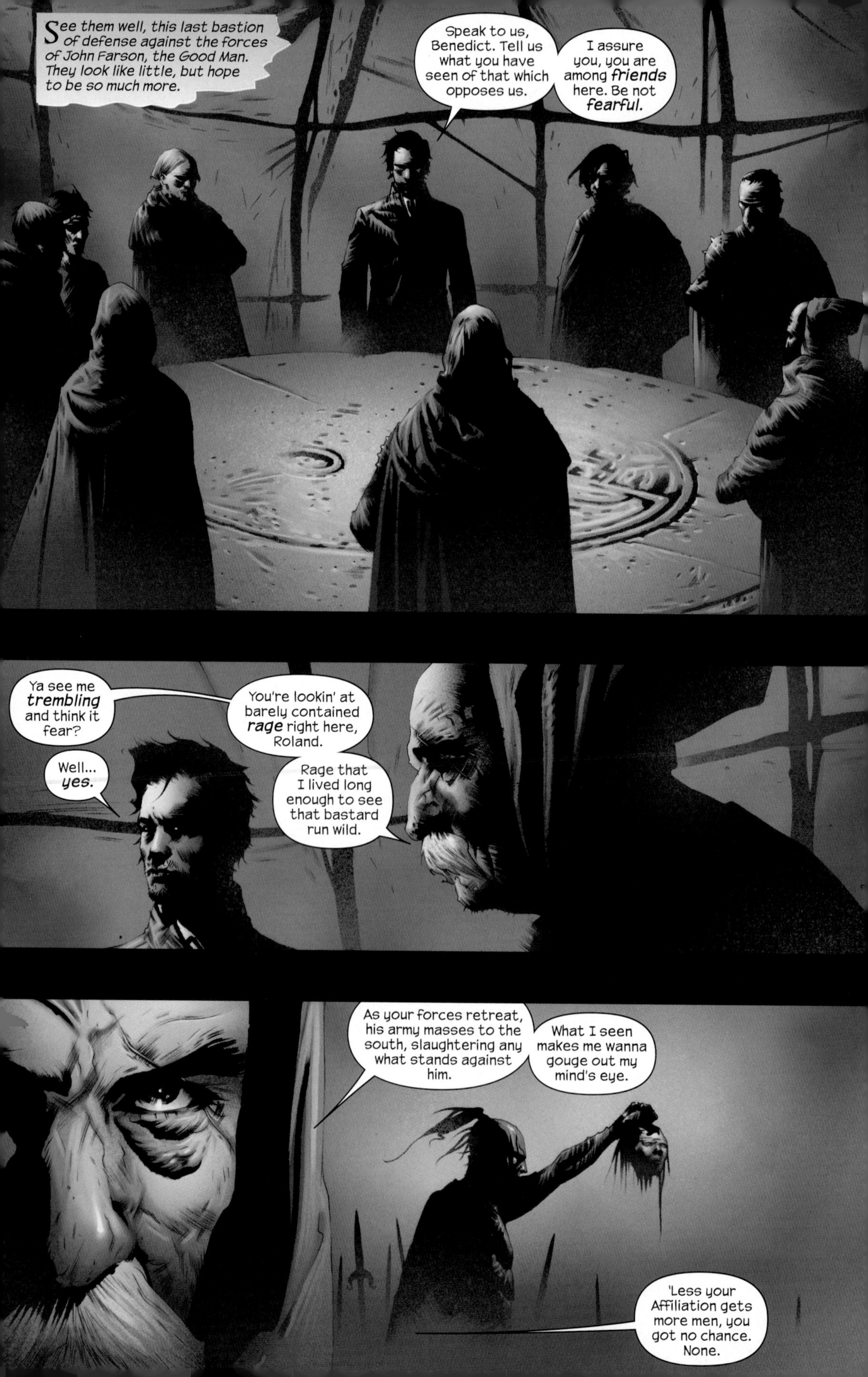
See them well, this last bastion of defense against the forces of John Farson, the Good Man. They look like little, but hope to be so much more.
Speak to us, Benedict. Tell us what you have seen of that which opposes us.
I assure you, you are among *friends* here. Be not *fearful.*
Ya see me *trembling* and think it fear?
Well... *yes.*
You're lookin' at barely contained *rage* right here, Roland.
Rage that I lived long enough to see that bastard run wild.
As your forces retreat, his army masses to the south, slaughtering any what stands against him.
What I seen makes me wanna gouge out my mind's eye.
'Less your Affiliation gets more men, you got no chance. None.

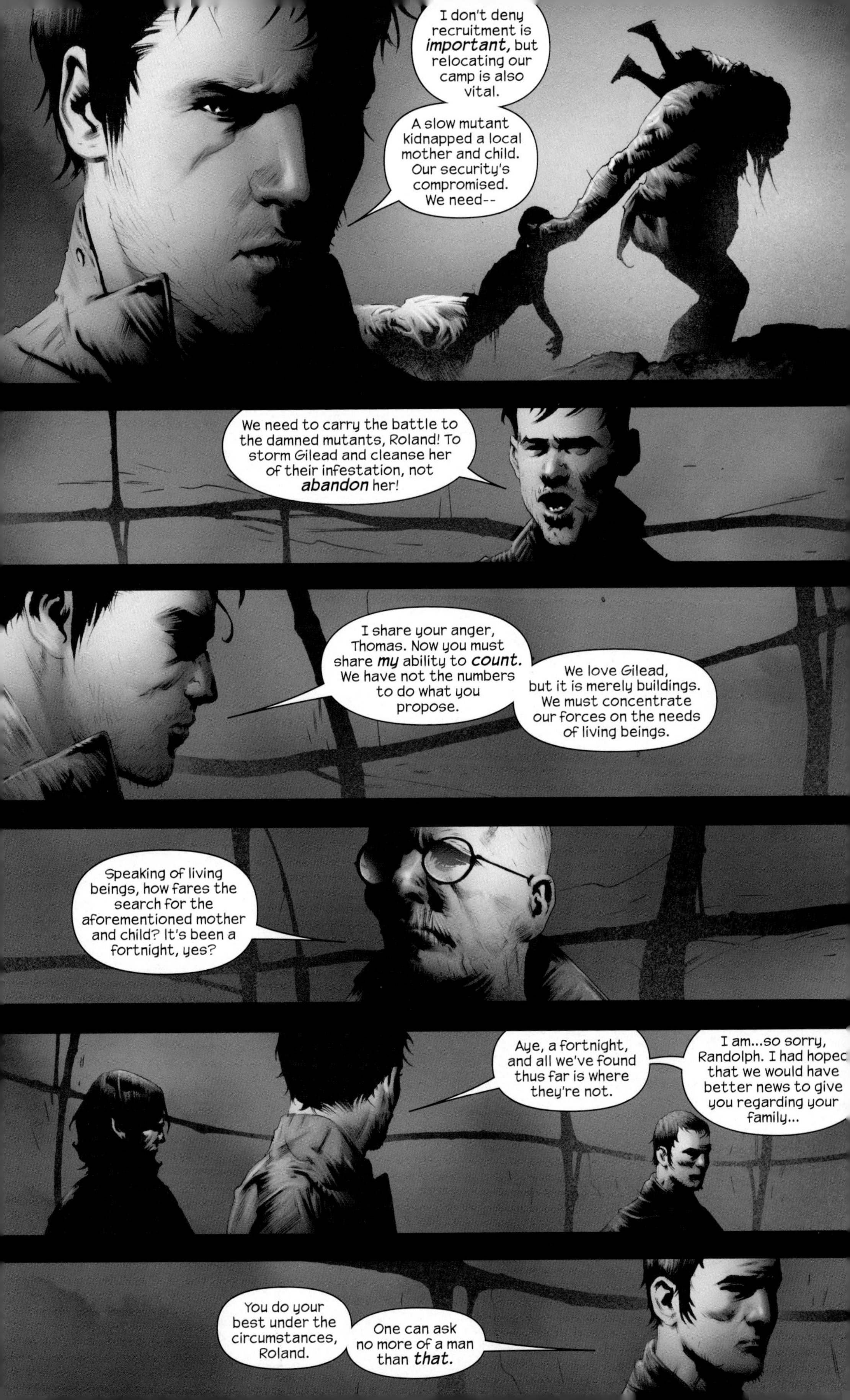
I don't deny recruitment is *important,* but relocating our camp is also vital.
A slow mutant kidnapped a local mother and child. Our security's compromised. We need--
We need to carry the battle to the damned mutants, Roland! To storm Gilead and cleanse her of their infestation, not *abandon* her!
I share your anger, Thomas. Now you must share *my* ability to *count.* We have not the numbers to do what you propose.
We love Gilead, but it is merely buildings. We must concentrate our forces on the needs of living beings.
Speaking of living beings, how fares the search for the aforementioned mother and child? It's been a fortnight, yes?
Aye, a fortnight, and all we've found thus far is where they're not.
I am...so sorry, Randolph. I had hoped that we would have better news to give you regarding your family...
You do your best under the circumstances, Roland.
One can ask no more of a man than *that.*

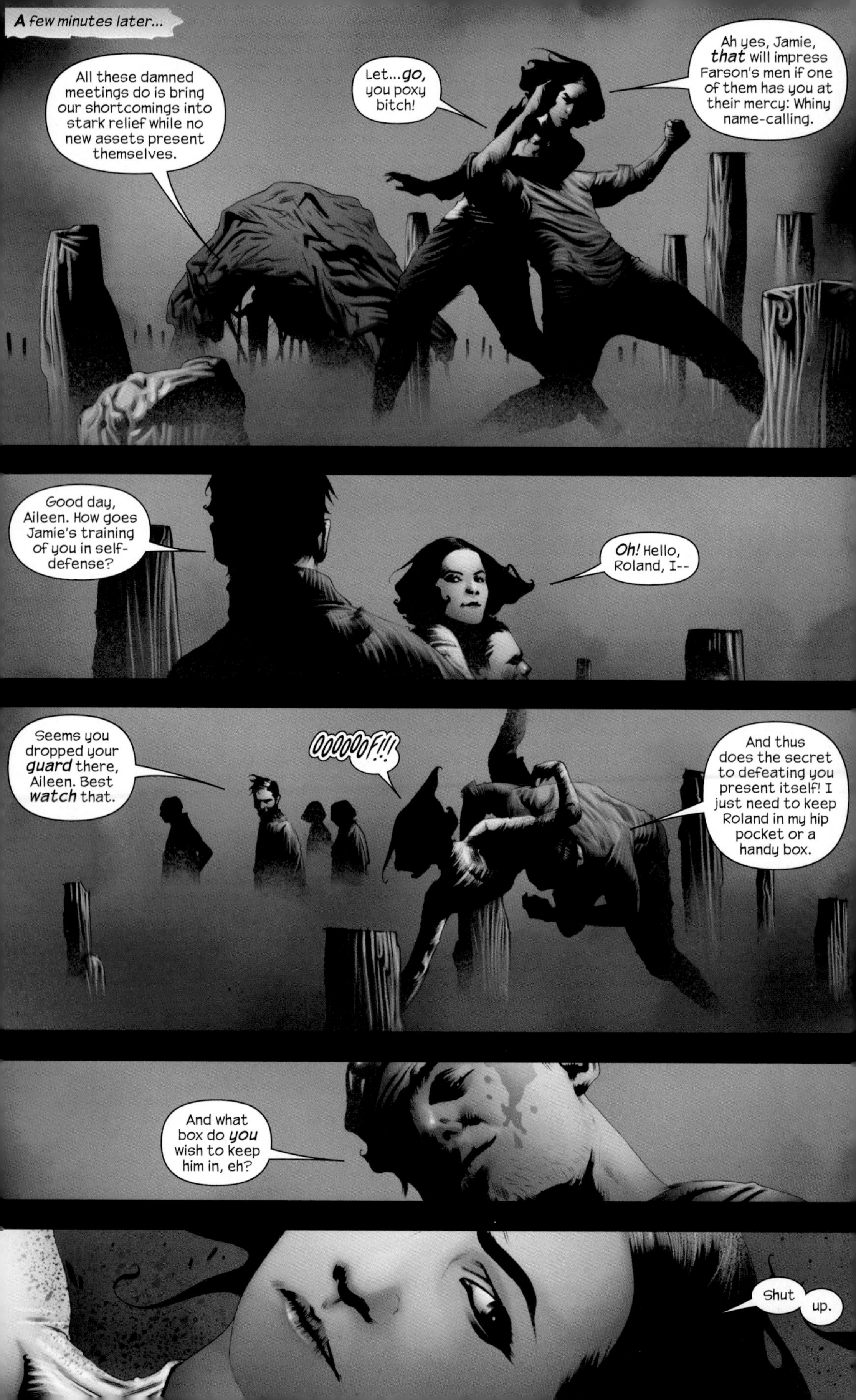
A few minutes later...
All these damned meetings do is bring our shortcomings into stark relief while no new assets present themselves.
Let...go, you poxy bitch!
Ah yes, Jamie, that will impress Farson's men if one of them has you at their mercy: Whiny name-calling.
Good day, Aileen. How goes Jamie's training of you in self-defense?
Oh! Hello, Roland, I--
Seems you dropped your guard there, Aileen. Best watch that.
OOOOOOF!!!
And thus does the secret to defeating you present itself! I just need to keep Roland in my hip pocket or a handy box.
And what box do you wish to keep him in, eh?
Shut
up.

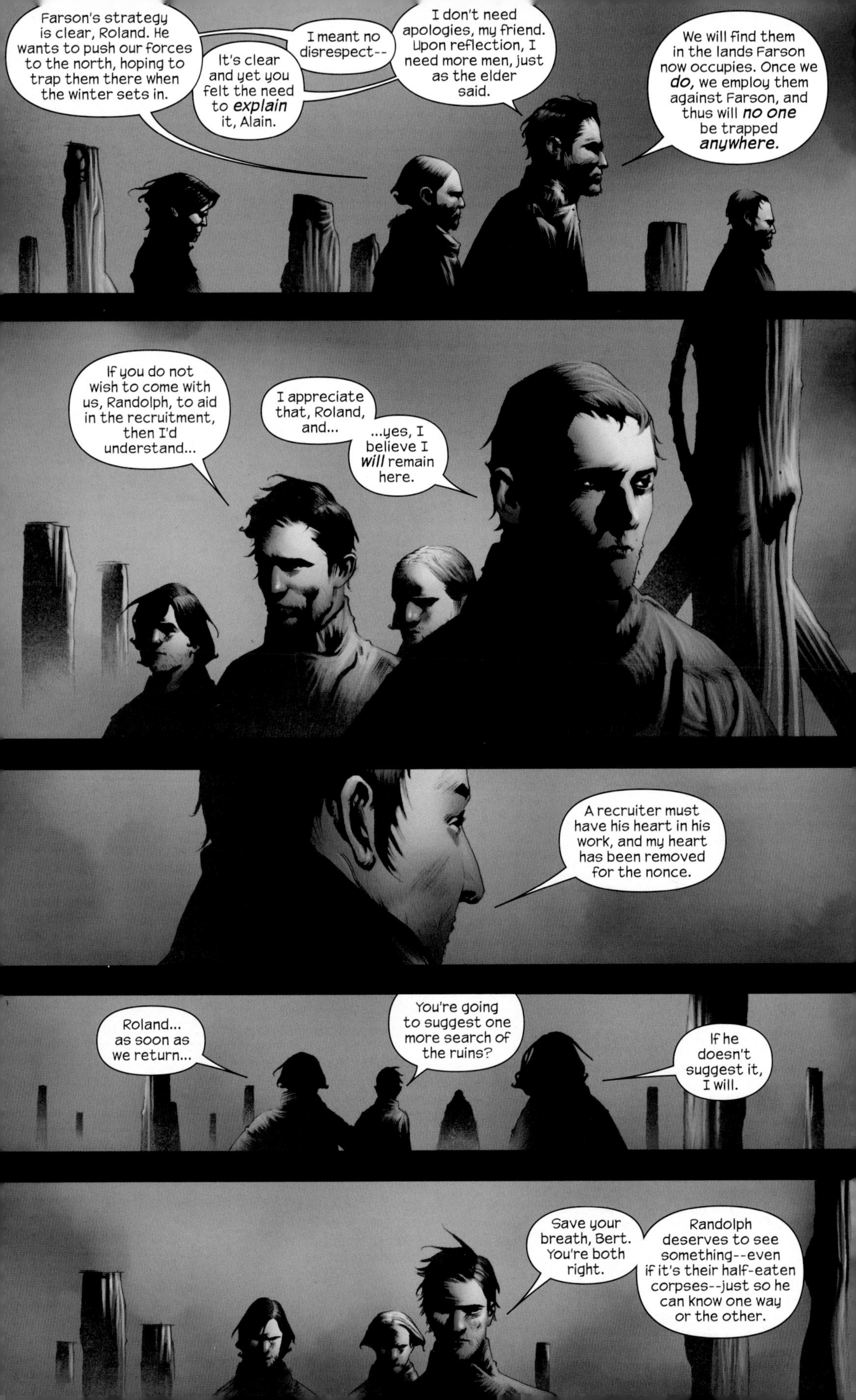
Farson's strategy is clear, Roland. He wants to push our forces to the north, hoping to trap them there when the winter sets in.
I meant no disrespect--
It's clear and yet you felt the need to *explain* it, Alain.
I don't need apologies, my friend. Upon reflection, I need more men, just as the elder said.
We will find them in the lands Farson now occupies. Once we *do,* we employ them against Farson, and thus will *no one* be trapped *anywhere.*
If you do not wish to come with us, Randolph, to aid in the recruitment, then I'd understand...
I appreciate that, Roland, and...
...yes, I believe I *will* remain here.
A recruiter must have his heart in his work, and my heart has been removed for the nonce.
Roland... as soon as we return...
You're going to suggest one more search of the ruins?
If he doesn't suggest it, I will.
Save your breath, Bert. You're both right.
Randolph deserves to see something--even if it's their half-eaten corpses--just so he can know one way or the other.

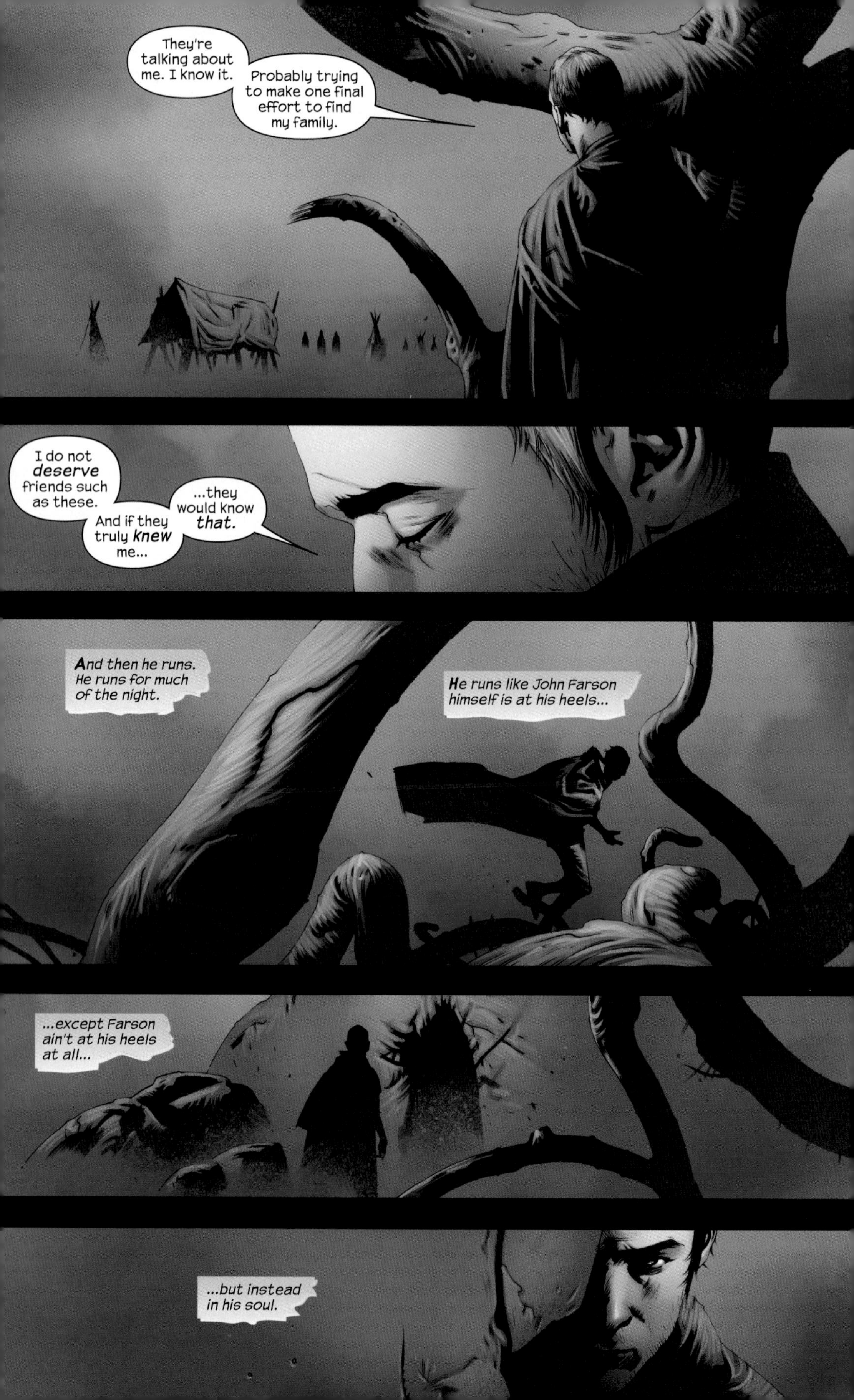

They're talking about me. I know it.
Probably trying to make one final effort to find my family.
I do not *deserve* friends such as these.
And if they truly *knew* me...
...they would know *that.*
And then he runs. He runs for much of the night.
He runs like John Farson himself is at his heels...
...except Farson ain't at his heels at all...
...but instead in his soul.

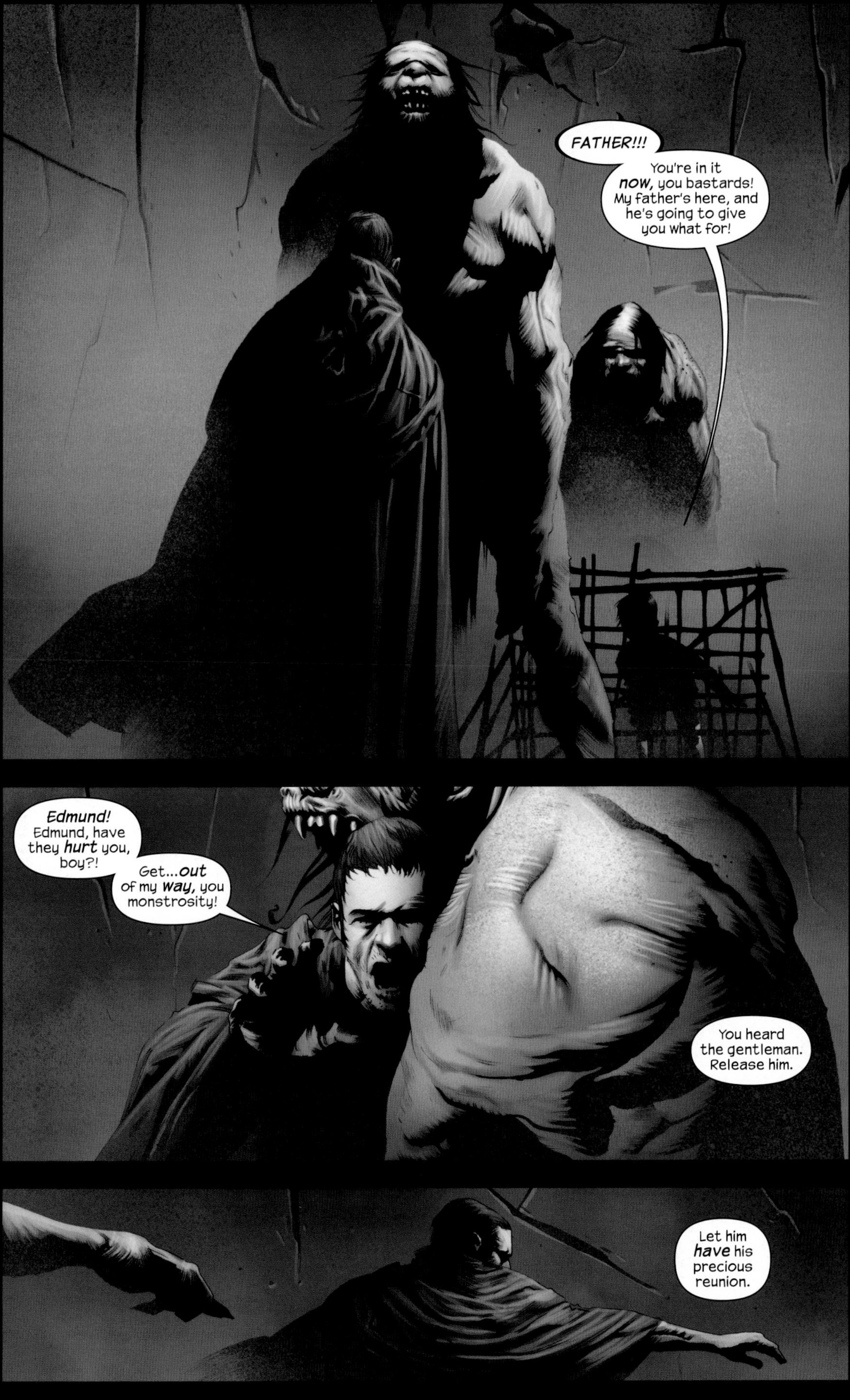
FATHER!!!
You're in it *now,* you bastards! My father's here, and he's going to give you what for!
Edmund! Edmund, have they *hurt* you, boy?!
Get...*out* of my *way,* you monstrosity!
You heard the gentleman. Release him.
Let him *have* his precious reunion.

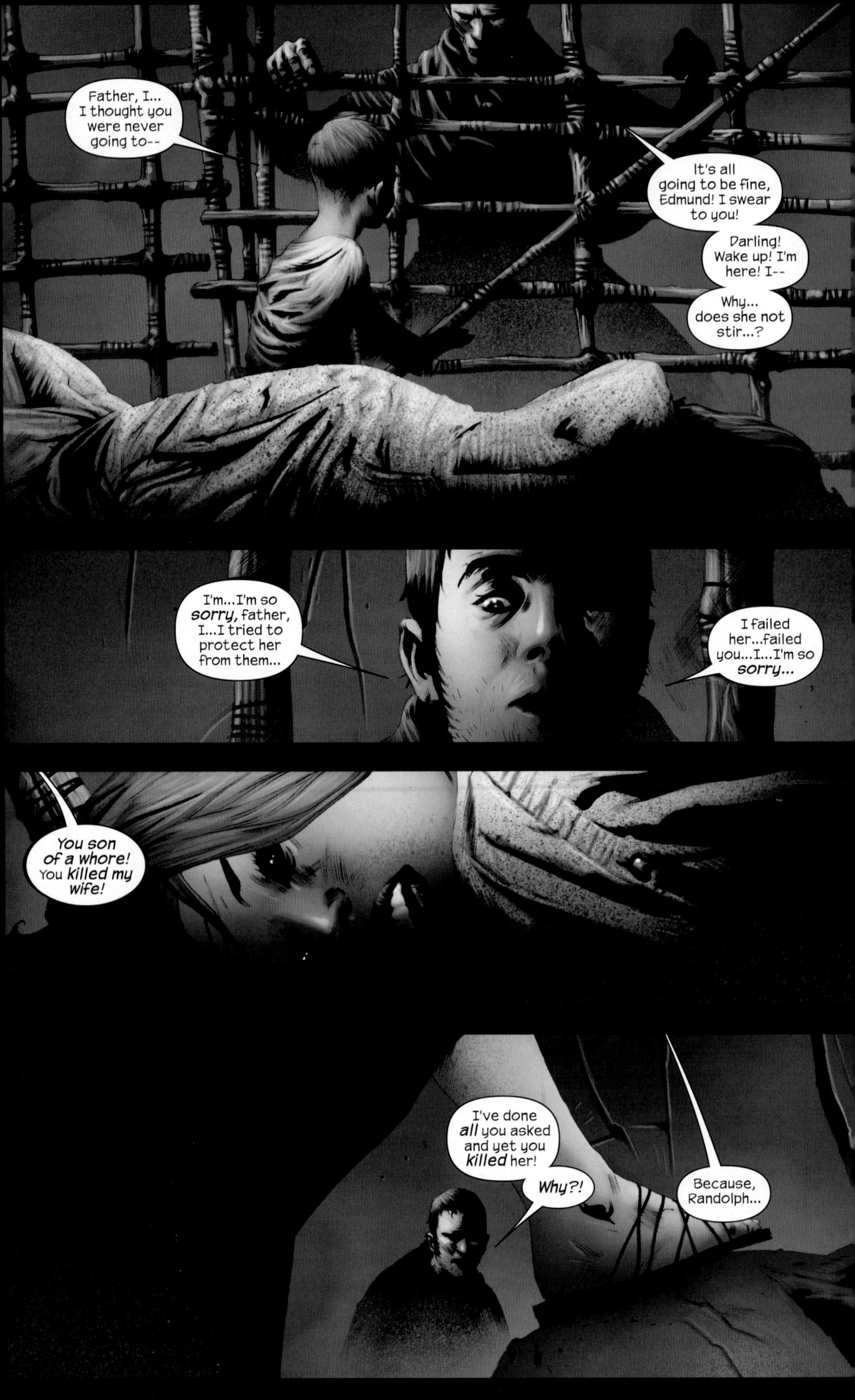
Father, I... I thought you were never going to--
It's all going to be fine, Edmund! I swear to you!
Darling! Wake up! I'm here! I--
Why... does she not stir...?
I'm...I'm so *sorry,* father, I...I tried to protect her from them...
I failed her...failed you...I...I'm so *sorry...*
You son of a whore! You *killed my wife!*
I've done *all* you asked and yet you *killed* her!
Why?!
Because, Randolph...

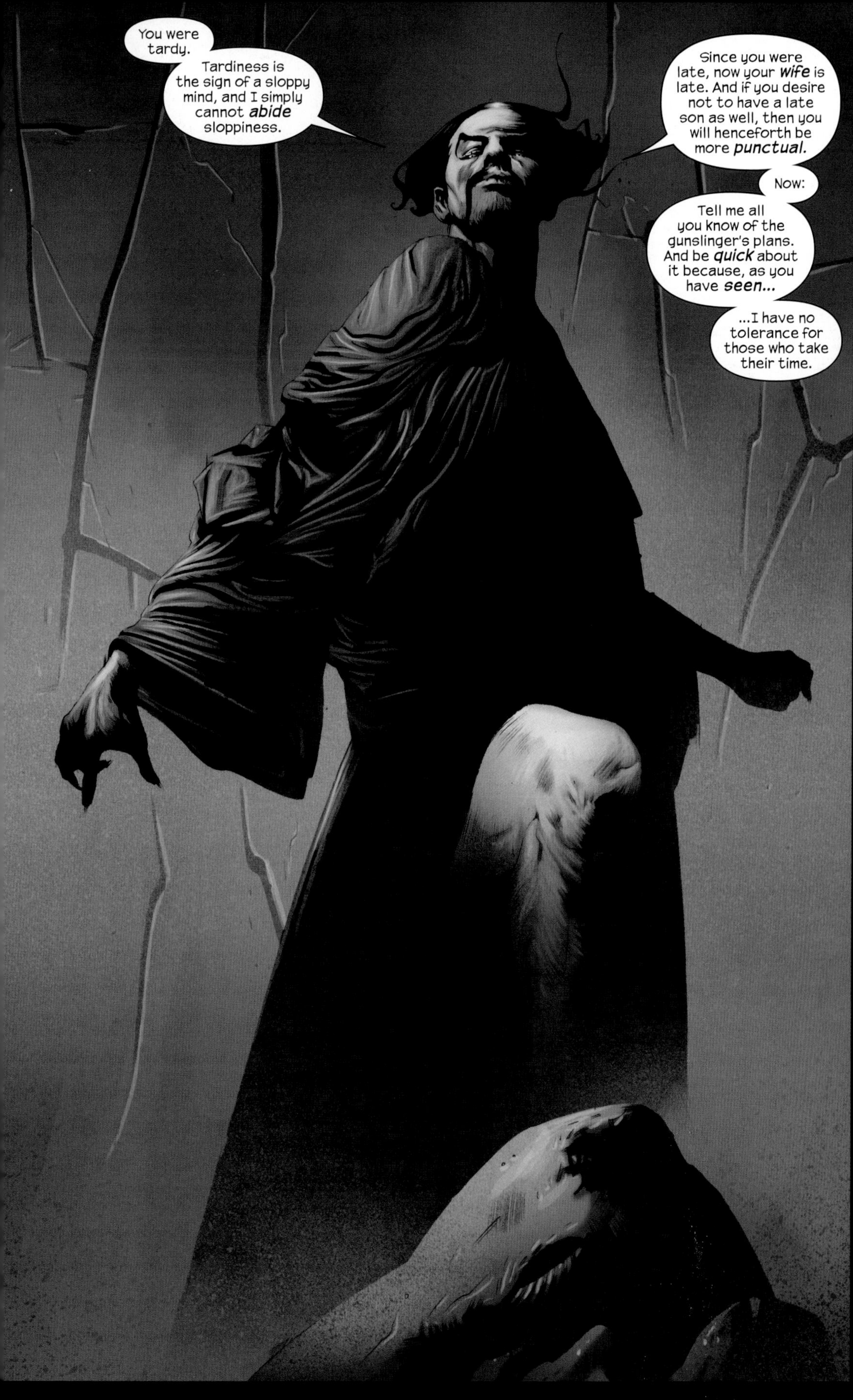
You were tardy.
Tardiness is the sign of a sloppy mind, and I simply cannot *abide* sloppiness.
Since you were late, now your *wife* is late. And if you desire not to have a late son as well, then you will henceforth be more *punctual.*
Now:
Tell me all you know of the gunslinger's plans. And be *quick* about it because, as you have *seen...*
...I have no tolerance for those who take their time.

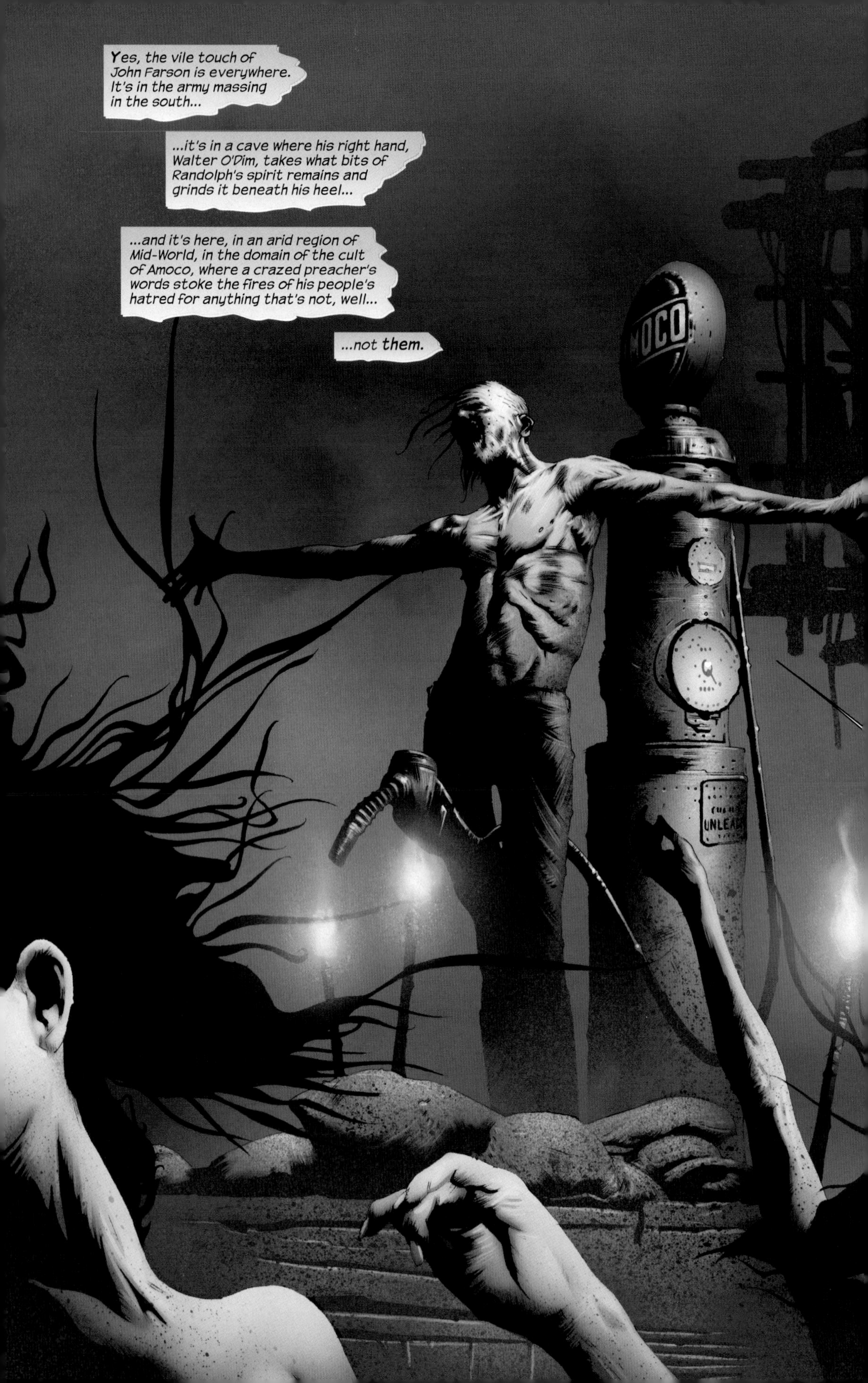
Yes, the vile touch of John Farson is everywhere. It's in the army massing in the south...
...it's in a cave where his right hand, Walter O'Dim, takes what bits of Randolph's spirit remains and grinds it beneath his heel...
...and it's here, in an arid region of Mid-World, in the domain of the cult of Amoco, where a crazed preacher's words stoke the fires of his people's hatred for anything that's not, well...
...not them.
MOCO
UNLEAD

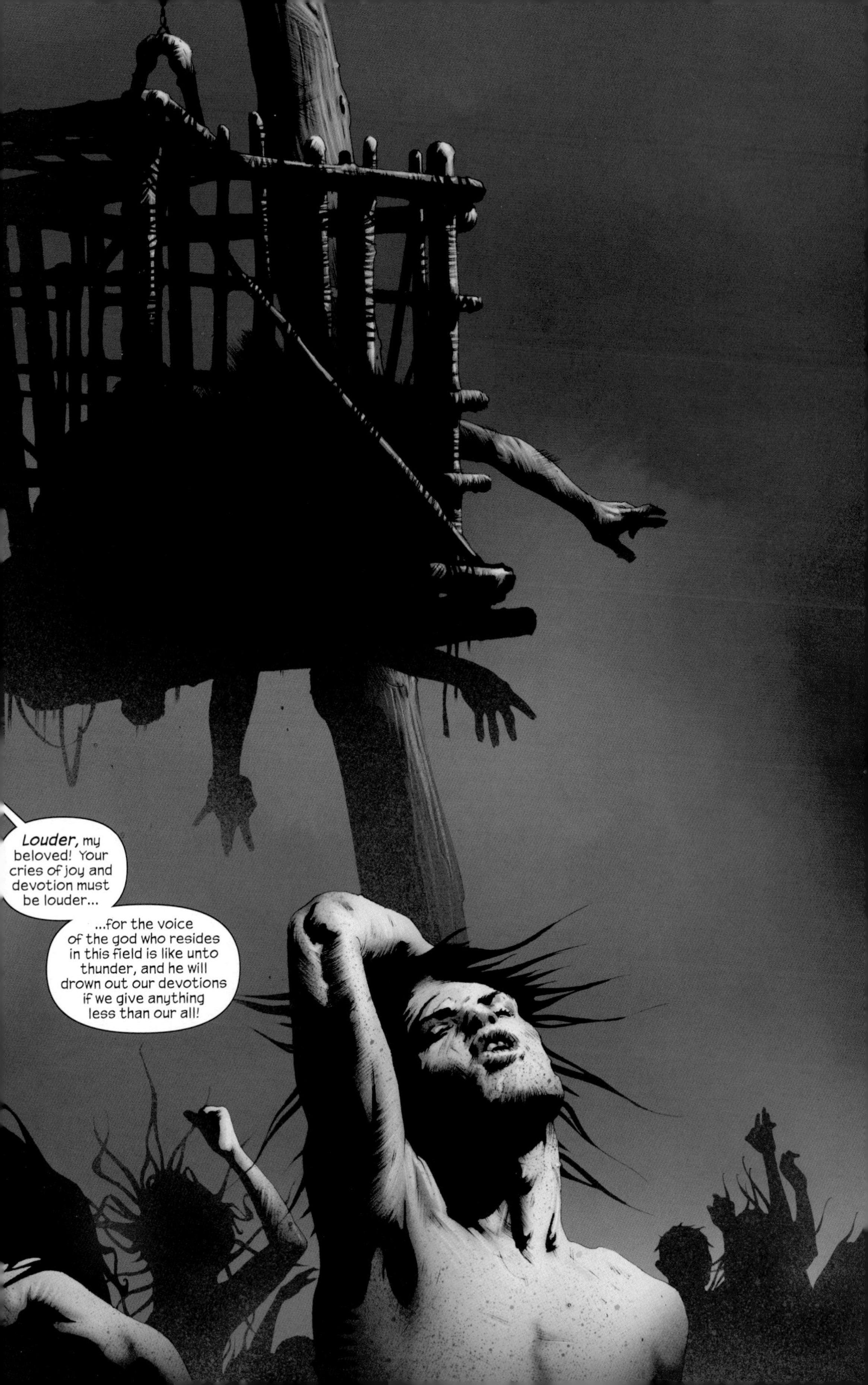
Louder, my beloved! Your cries of joy and devotion must be louder...
...for the voice of the god who resides in this field is like unto thunder, and he will drown out our devotions if we give anything less than our all!

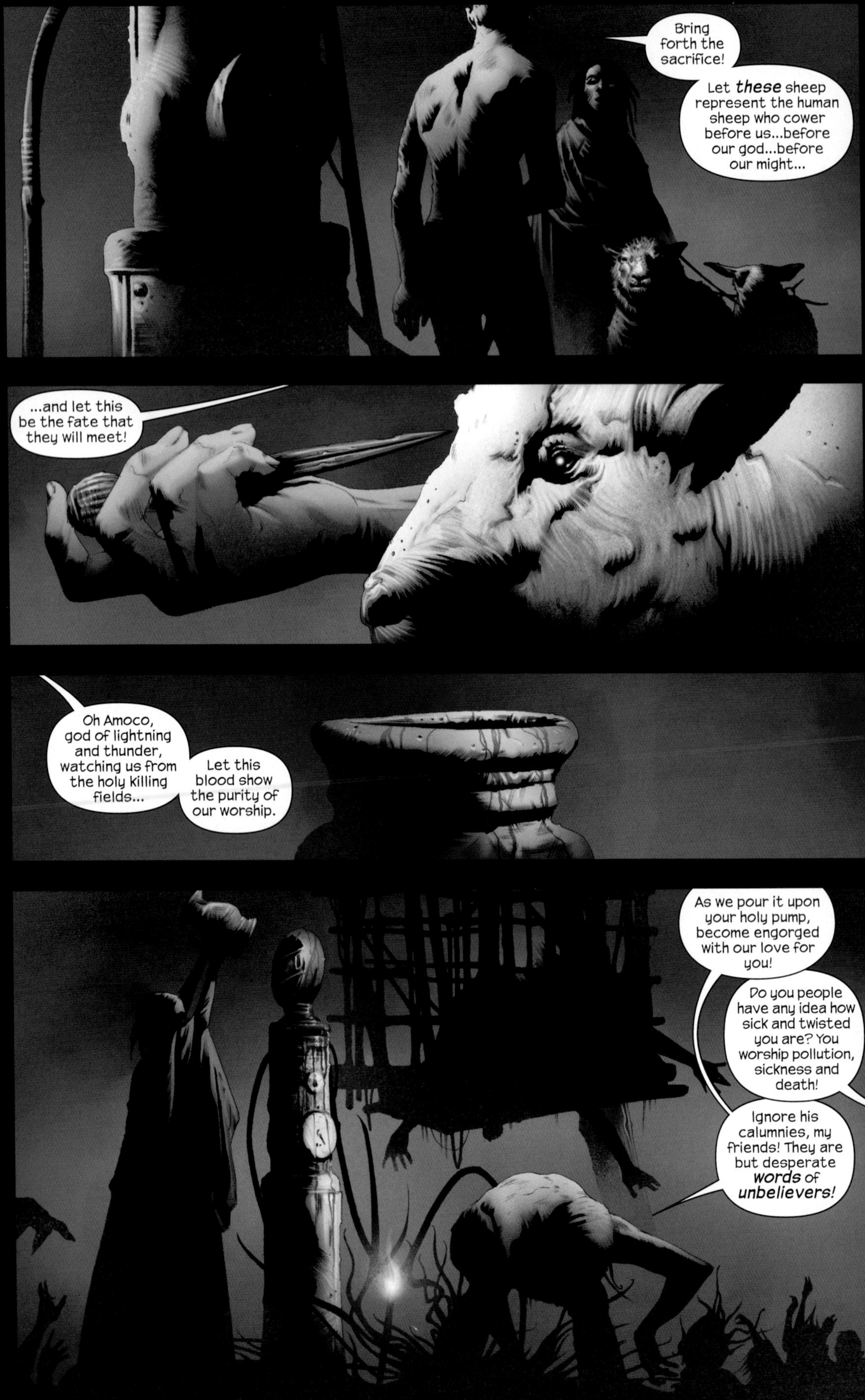
Bring forth the sacrifice!
Let *these* sheep represent the human sheep who cower before us...before our god...before our might...
...and let this be the fate that they will meet!
Oh Amoco, god of lightning and thunder, watching us from the holy killing fields...
Let this blood show the purity of our worship.
As we pour it upon your holy pump, become engorged with our love for you!
Do you people have any idea how sick and twisted you are? You worship pollution, sickness and death!
Ignore his calumnies, my friends! They are but desperate *words* of *unbelievers!*

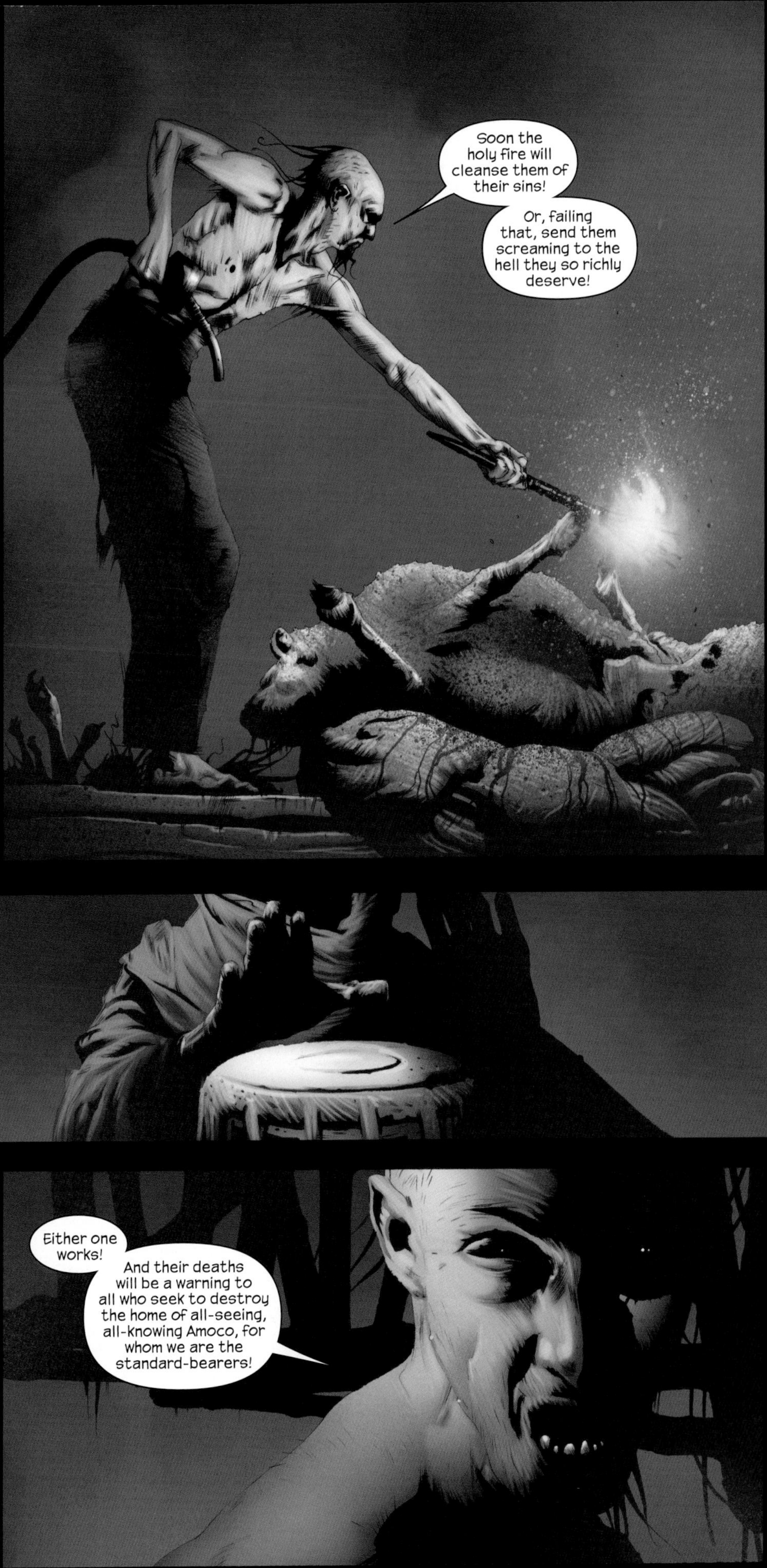
Soon the holy fire will cleanse them of their sins!
Or, failing that, send them screaming to the hell they so richly deserve!
Either one works!
And their deaths will be a warning to all who seek to destroy the home of all-seeing, all-knowing Amoco, for whom we are the standard-bearers!

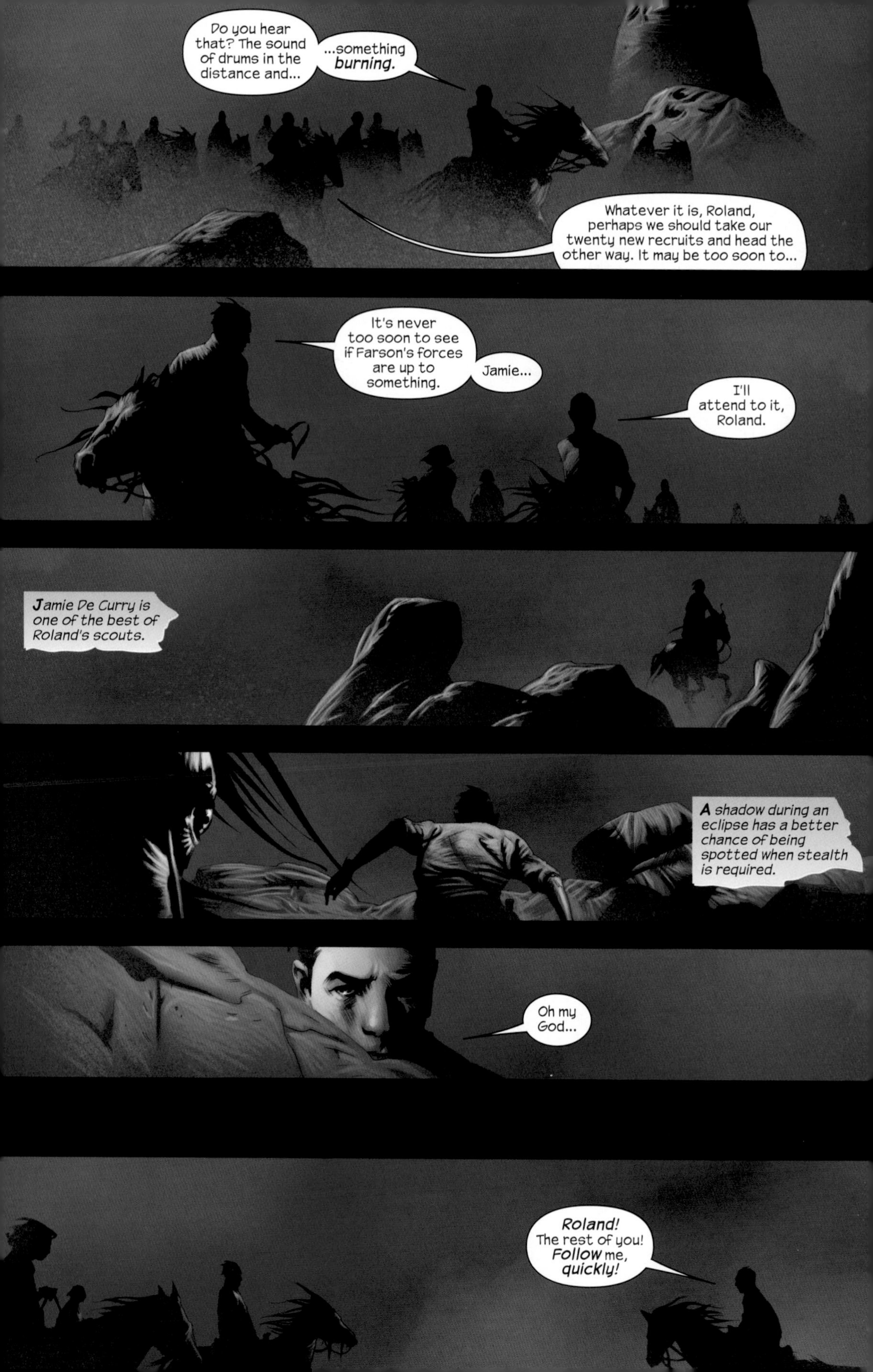
Do you hear that? The sound of drums in the distance and...
...something *burning.*
Whatever it is, Roland, perhaps we should take our twenty new recruits and head the other way. It may be too soon to...
It's never too soon to see if Farson's forces are up to something.
Jamie...
I'll attend to it, Roland.
Jamie De Curry is one of the best of Roland's scouts.
A shadow during an eclipse has a better chance of being spotted when stealth is required.
Oh my God...
Roland! *The rest of you!* ***Follow*** *me,* ***quickly!***

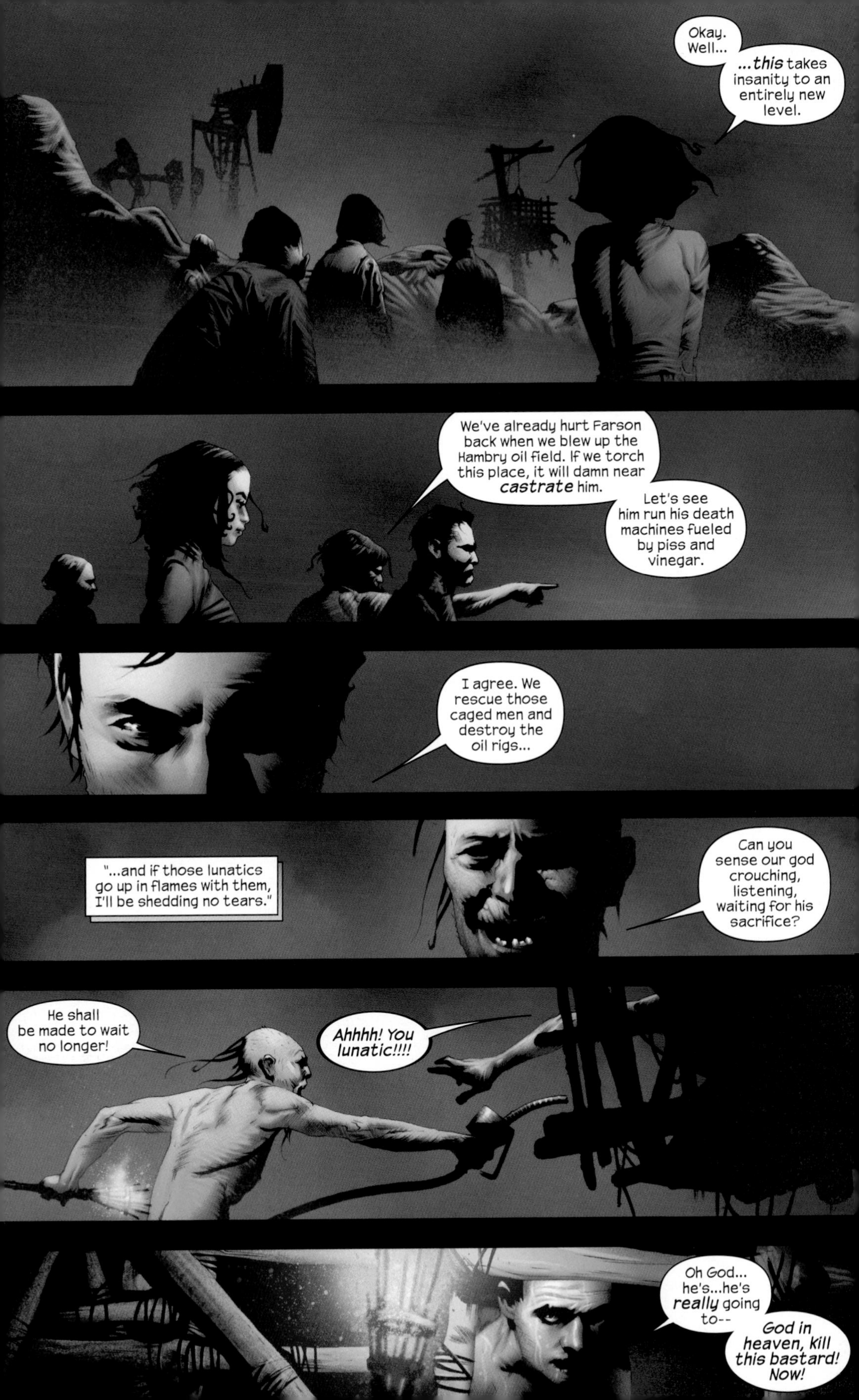
Okay. Well...
...*this* takes insanity to an entirely new level.
We've already hurt Farson back when we blew up the Hambry oil field. If we torch this place, it will damn near *castrate* him.
Let's see him run his death machines fueled by piss and vinegar.
I agree. We rescue those caged men and destroy the oil rigs...
"...and if those lunatics go up in flames with them, I'll be shedding no tears."
Can you sense our god crouching, listening, waiting for his sacrifice?
He shall be made to wait no longer!
Ahhhh! You lunatic!!!!
Oh God... he's...he's *really* going to--
God in heaven, kill this bastard! Now!

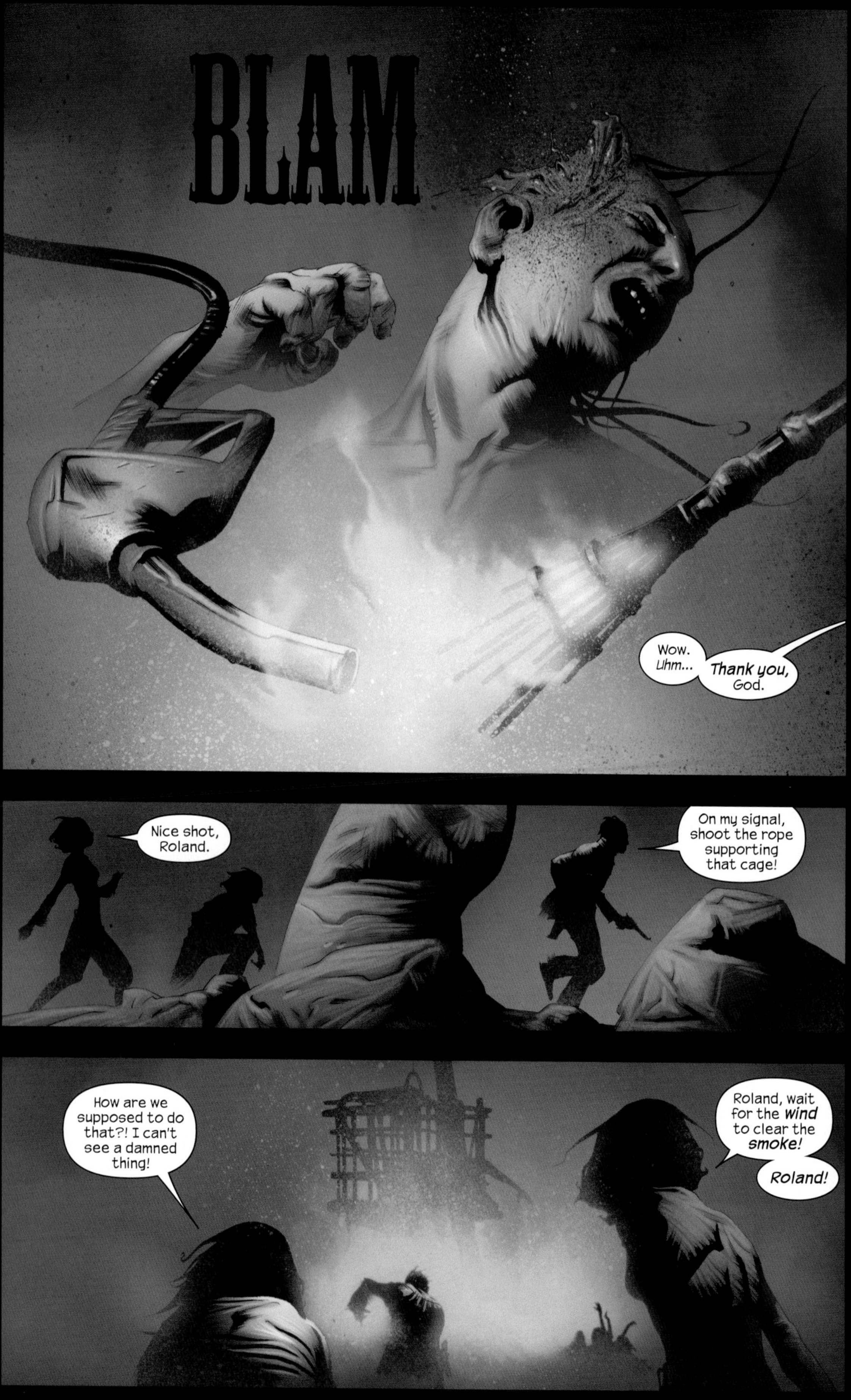
BLAM
Wow. Uhm...
Thank you, God.
Nice shot, Roland.
On my signal, shoot the rope supporting that cage!
How are we supposed to do that?! I can't see a damned thing!
Roland, wait for the wind to clear the smoke!
Roland!

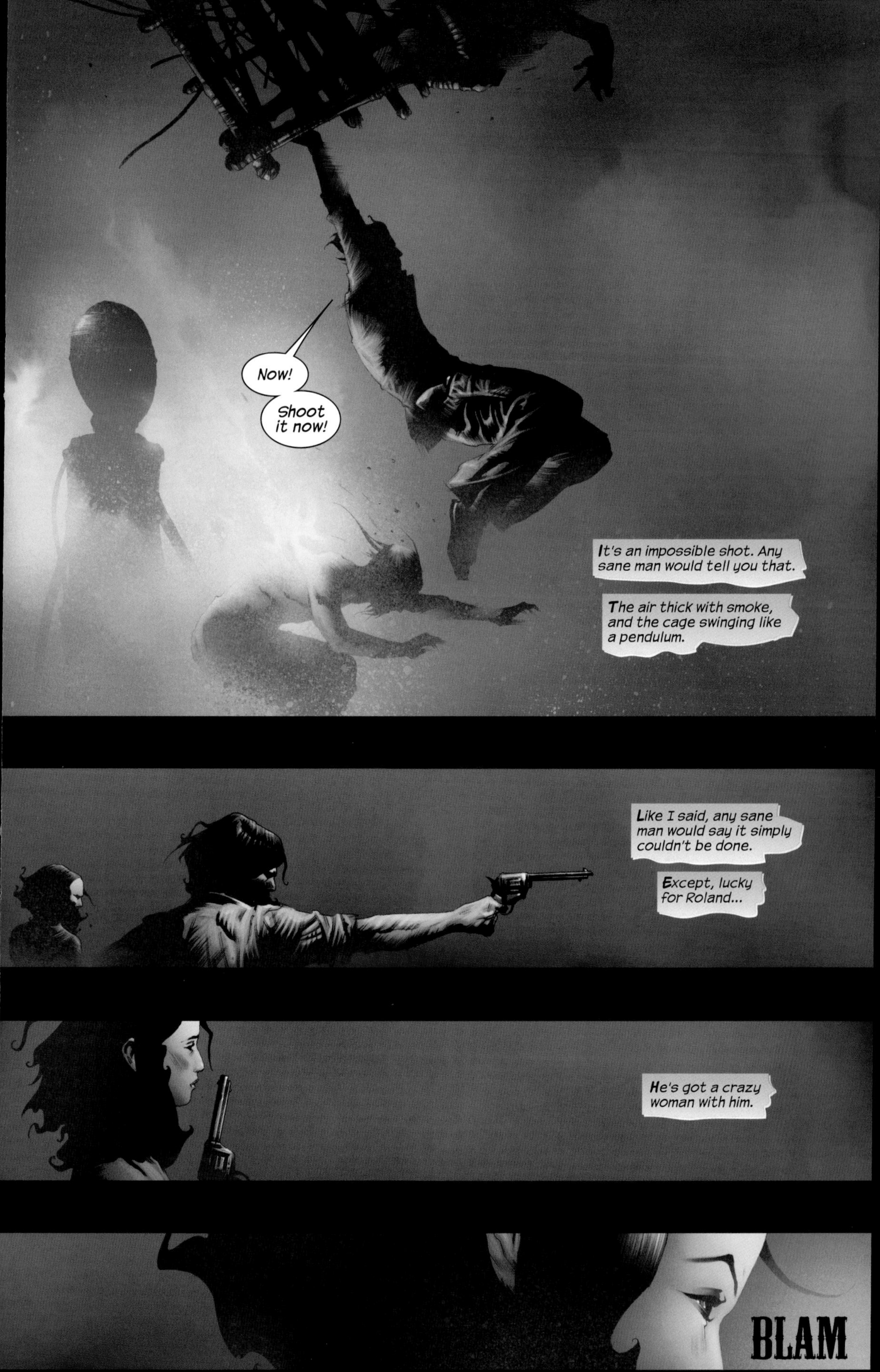
Now!
Shoot it now!
It's an impossible shot. Any sane man would tell you that.
The air thick with smoke, and the cage swinging like a pendulum.
Like I said, any sane man would say it simply couldn't be done.
Except, lucky for Roland...
He's got a crazy woman with him.
BLAM

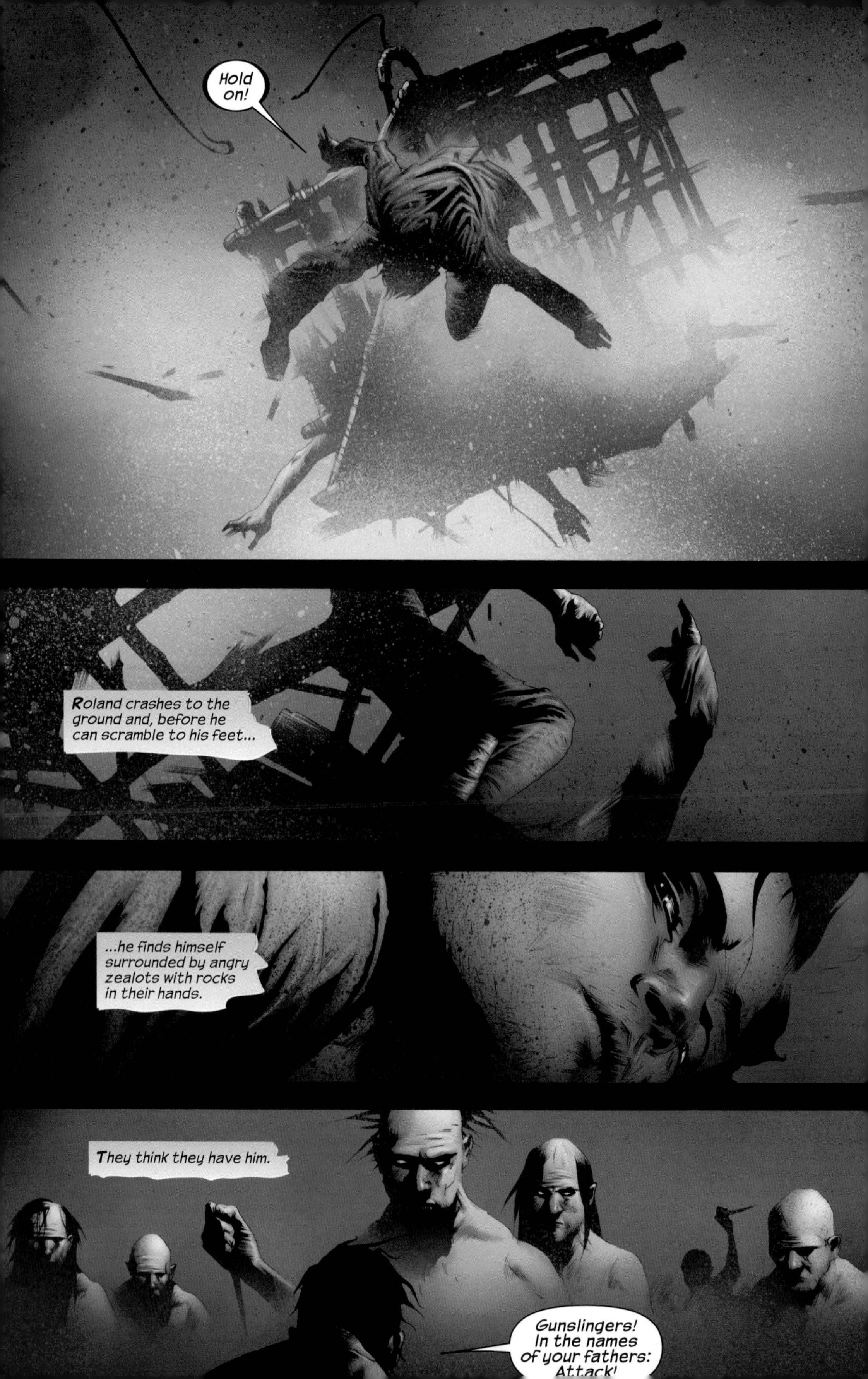
Hold on!
Roland crashes to the ground and, before he can scramble to his feet...
...he finds himself surrounded by angry zealots with rocks in their hands.
They think they have him.
Gunslingers! In the names of your fathers: Attack!

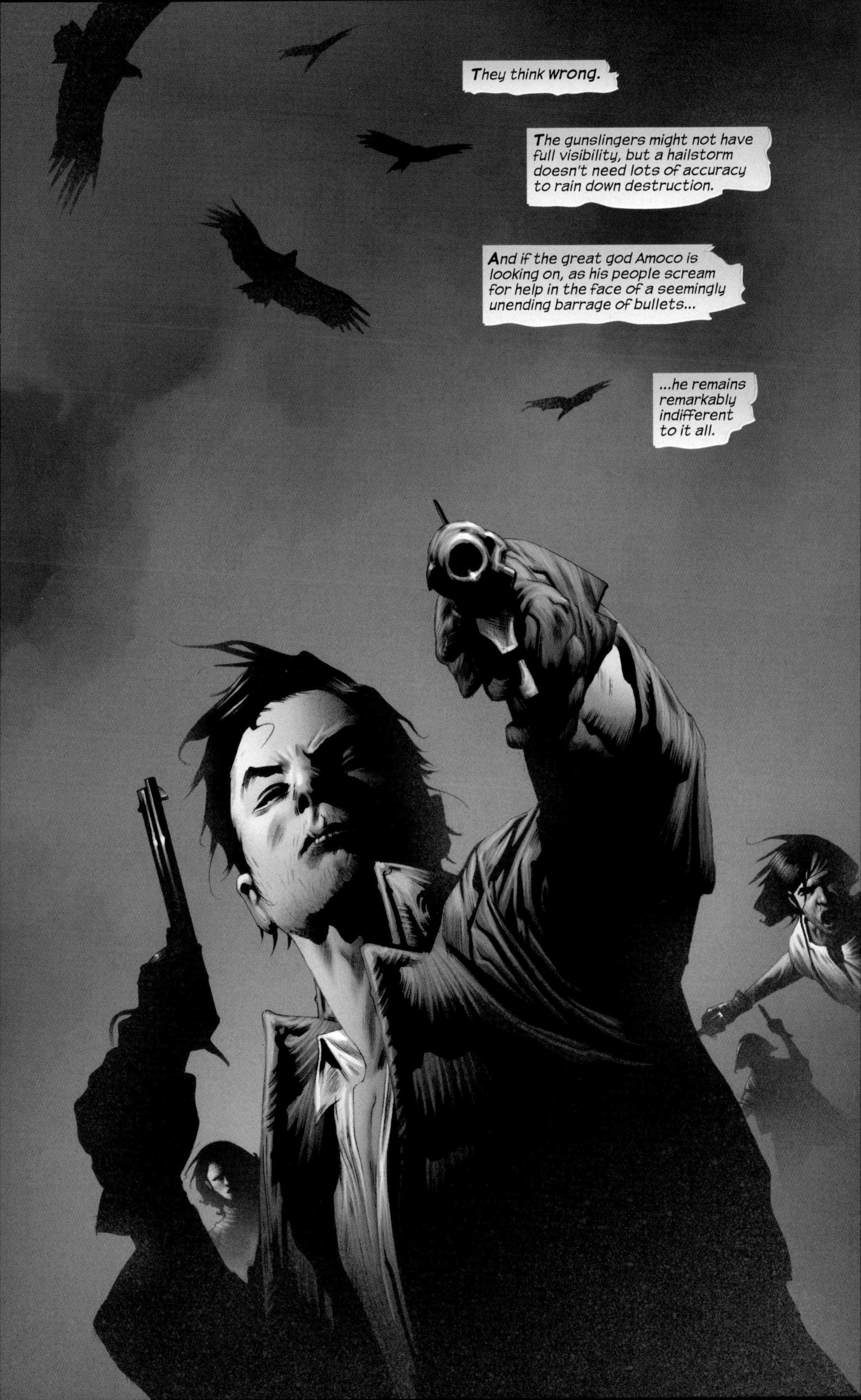

They think wrong.
The gunslingers might not have full visibility, but a hailstorm doesn't need lots of accuracy to rain down destruction.
And if the great god Amoco is looking on, as his people scream for help in the face of a seemingly unending barrage of bullets...
...he remains remarkably indifferent to it all.

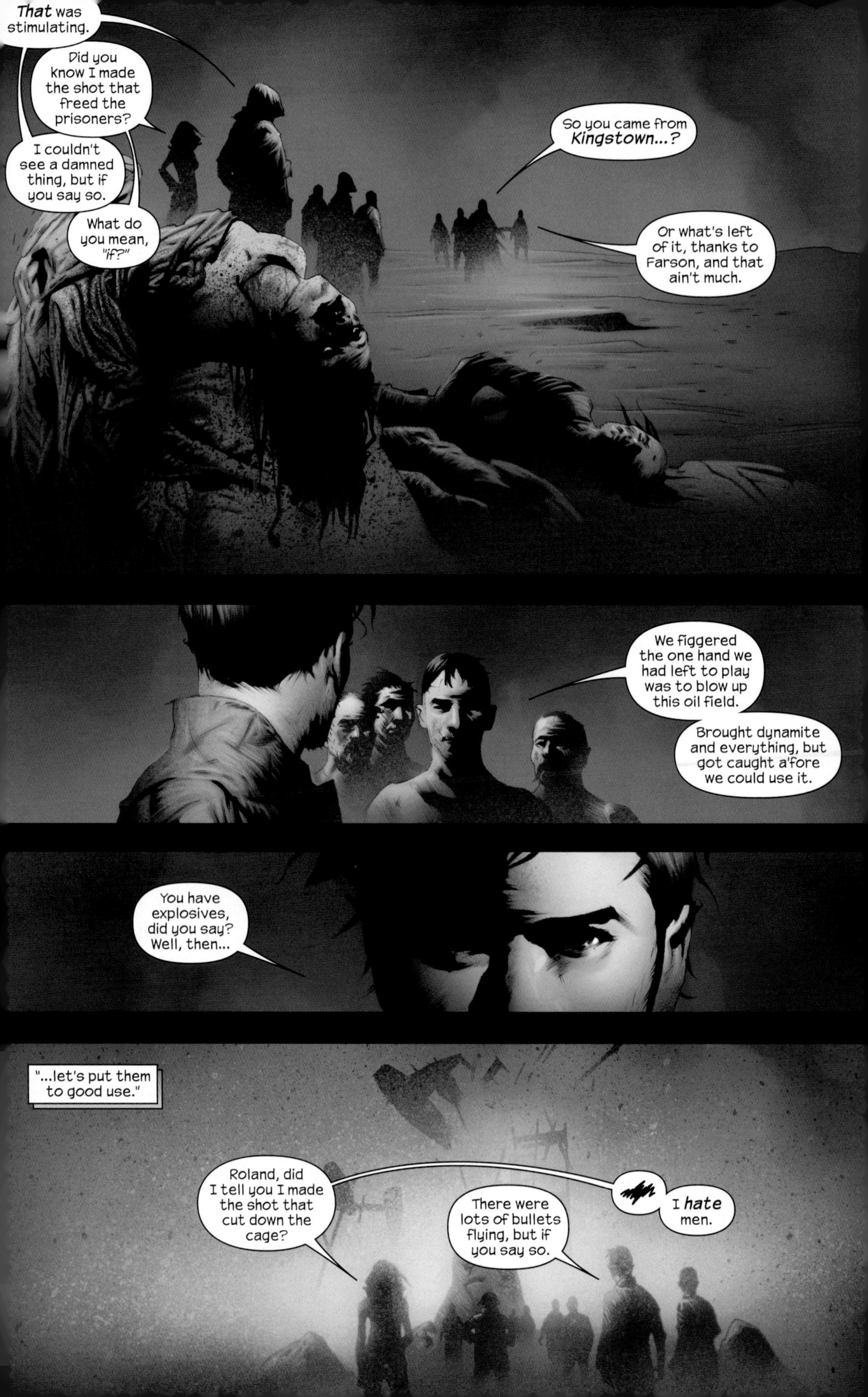
That was stimulating.
Did you know I made the shot that freed the prisoners?
I couldn't see a damned thing, but if you say so.
What do you mean, "*if?*"
So you came from *Kingstown...?*
Or what's left of it, thanks to Farson, and that ain't much.
We figgered the one hand we had left to play was to blow up this oil field.
Brought dynamite and everything, but got caught a'fore we could use it.
You have explosives, did you say? Well, then...
"...let's put them to good use."
Roland, did I tell you I made the shot that cut down the cage?
There were lots of bullets flying, but if you say so.
I *hate* men.

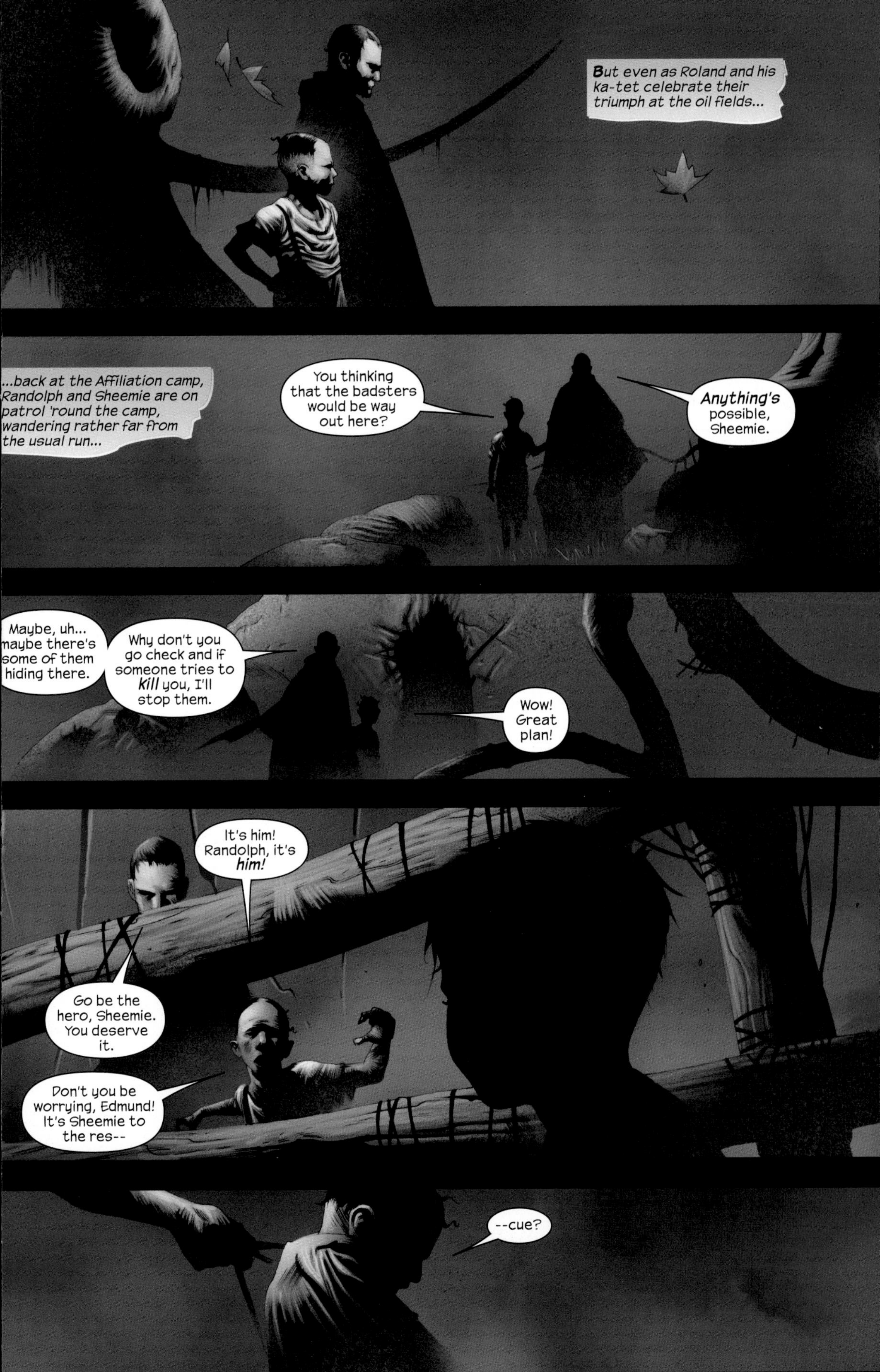
But even as Roland and his ka-tet celebrate their triumph at the oil fields...
...back at the Affiliation camp, Randolph and Sheemie are on patrol 'round the camp, wandering rather far from the usual run...
You thinking that the badsters would be way out here?
Anything's possible, Sheemie.
Maybe, uh... maybe there's some of them hiding there.
Why don't you go check and if someone tries to kill you, I'll stop them.
Wow! Great plan!
It's him! Randolph, it's him!
Go be the hero, Sheemie. You deserve it.
Don't you be worrying, Edmund! It's Sheemie to the res--
--cue?

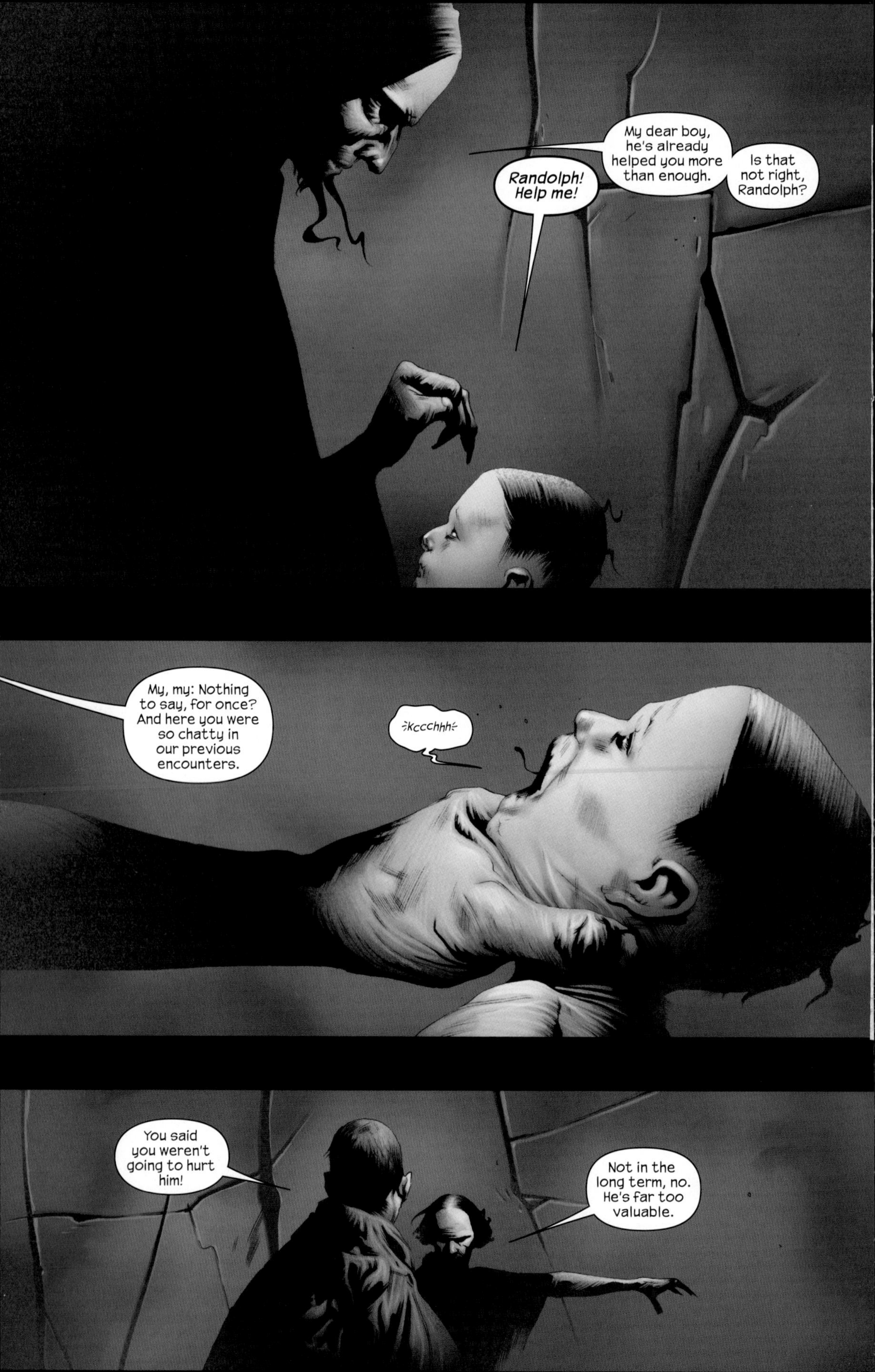
Randolph! Help me!
My dear boy, he's already helped you more than enough.
Is that not right, Randolph?
My, my: Nothing to say, for once? And here you were so chatty in our previous encounters.
kccchhh
You said you weren't going to hurt him!
Not in the long term, no. He's far too valuable.

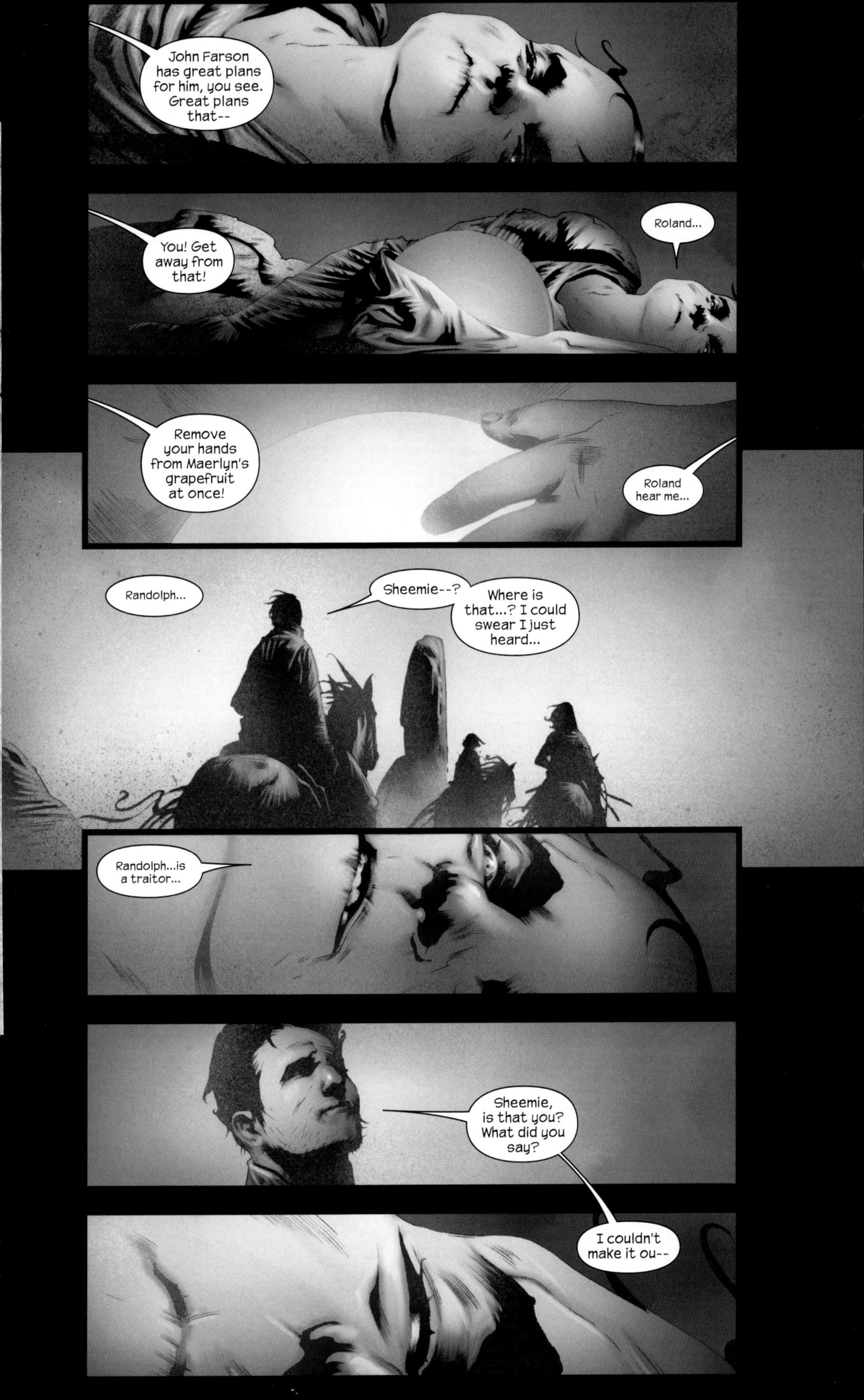
John Farson has great plans for him, you see. Great plans that--
You! Get away from that!
Roland...
Remove your hands from Maerlyn's grapefruit at once!
Roland hear me...
Randolph...
Sheemie--?
Where is that...? I could swear I just heard...
Randolph...is a traitor...
Sheemie, is that you? What did you say?
I couldn't make it ou--

STEPHEN KING

THE DARK TOWER

BATTLE OF JERICHO HILL

CHAPTER FOUR

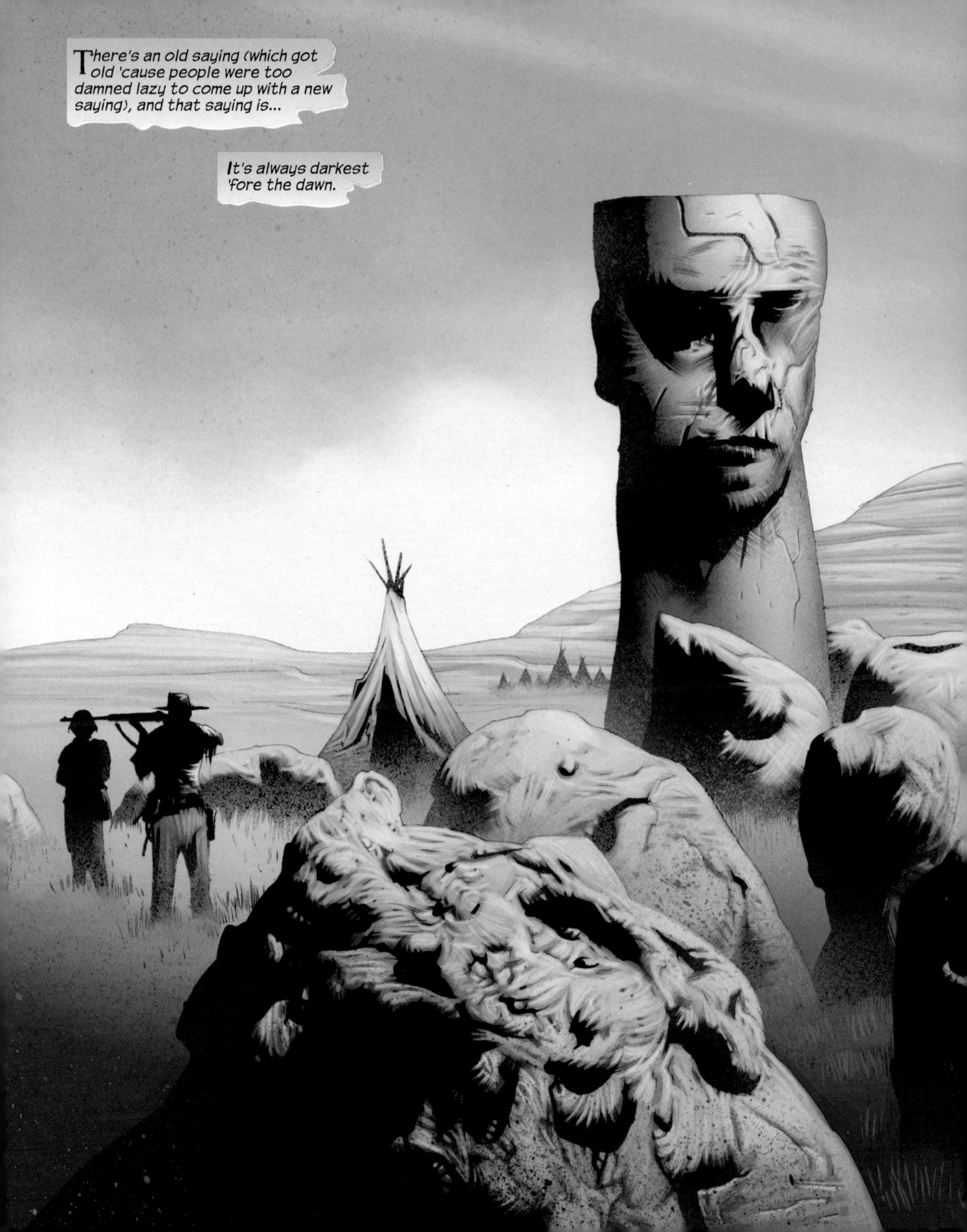
There's an old saying (which got old 'cause people were too damned lazy to come up with a new saying), and that saying is...
It's always darkest 'fore the dawn.

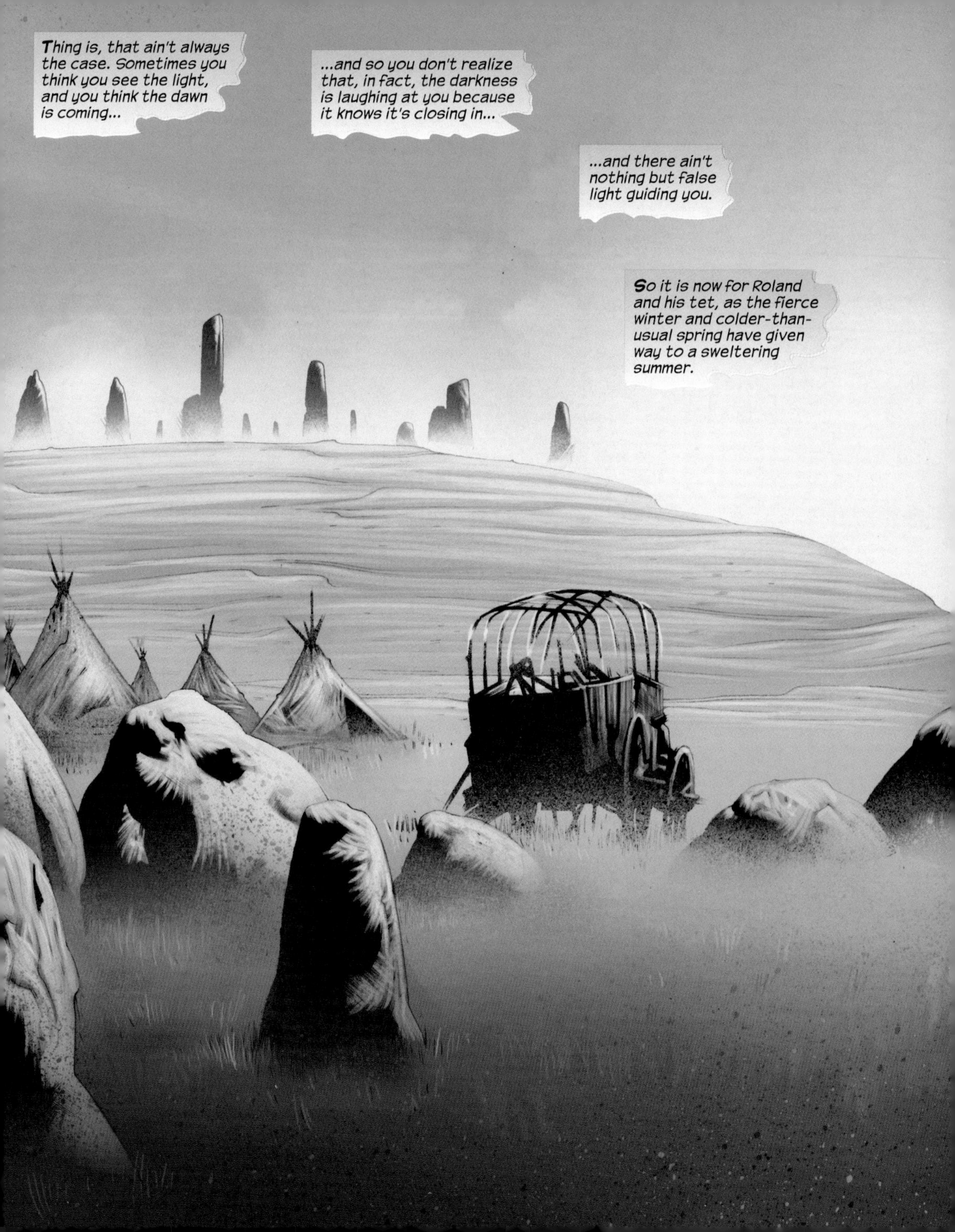
Thing is, that ain't always the case. Sometimes you think you see the light, and you think the dawn is coming...
...and so you don't realize that, in fact, the darkness is laughing at you because it knows it's closing in...
...and there ain't nothing but false light guiding you.
So it is now for Roland and his tet, as the fierce winter and colder-than-usual spring have given way to a sweltering summer.

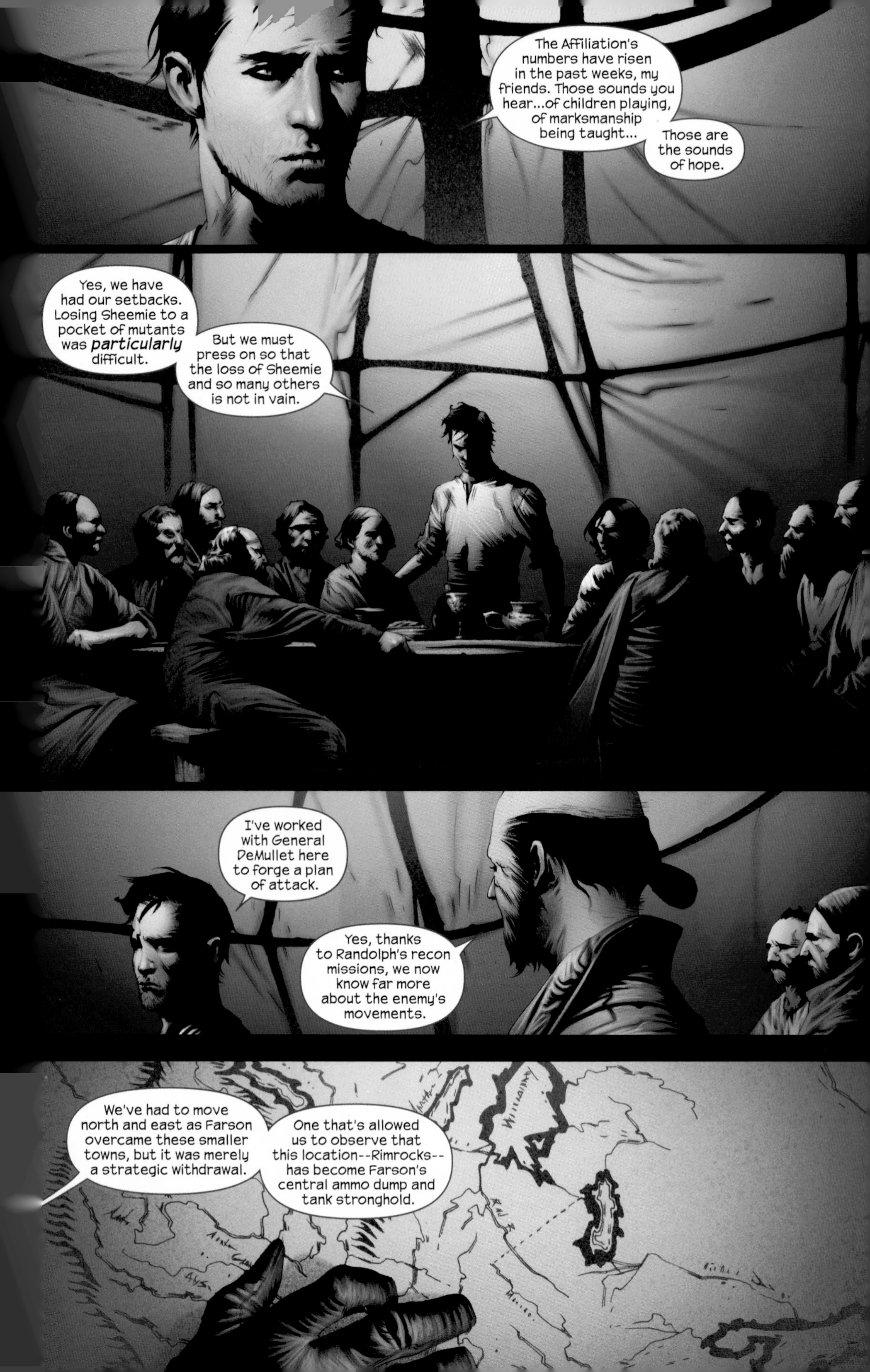
The Affiliation's numbers have risen in the past weeks, my friends. Those sounds you hear...of children playing, of marksmanship being taught...
Those are the sounds of hope.
Yes, we have had our setbacks. Losing Sheemie to a pocket of mutants was *particularly* difficult.
But we must press on so that the loss of Sheemie and so many others is not in vain.
I've worked with General DeMullet here to forge a plan of attack.
Yes, thanks to Randolph's recon missions, we now know far more about the enemy's movements.
We've had to move north and east as Farson overcame these smaller towns, but it was merely a strategic withdrawal.
One that's allowed us to observe that this location--Rimrocks--has become Farson's central ammo dump and tank stronghold.

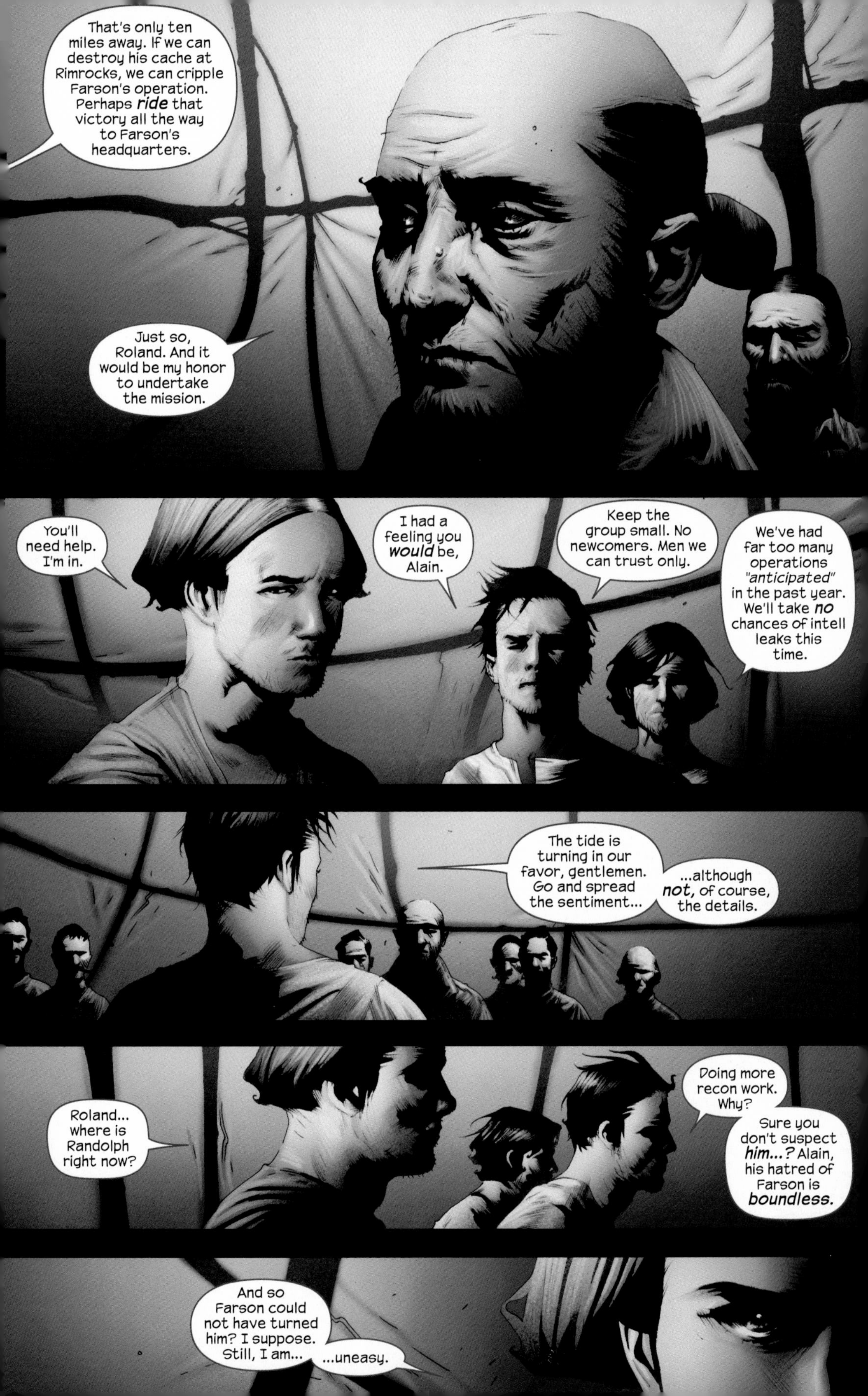

That's only ten miles away. If we can destroy his cache at Rimrocks, we can cripple Farson's operation. Perhaps *ride* that victory all the way to Farson's headquarters.
Just so, Roland. And it would be my honor to undertake the mission.
You'll need help. I'm in.
I had a feeling you *would* be, Alain.
Keep the group small. No newcomers. Men we can trust only.
We've had far too many operations *"anticipated"* in the past year. We'll take *no* chances of intell leaks this time.
The tide is turning in our favor, gentlemen. Go and spread the sentiment...
...although *not,* of course, the details.
Roland... where is Randolph right now?
Doing more recon work. Why?
Sure you don't suspect *him...?* Alain, his hatred of Farson is *boundless.*
And so Farson could not have turned him? I suppose. Still, I am...
...uneasy.

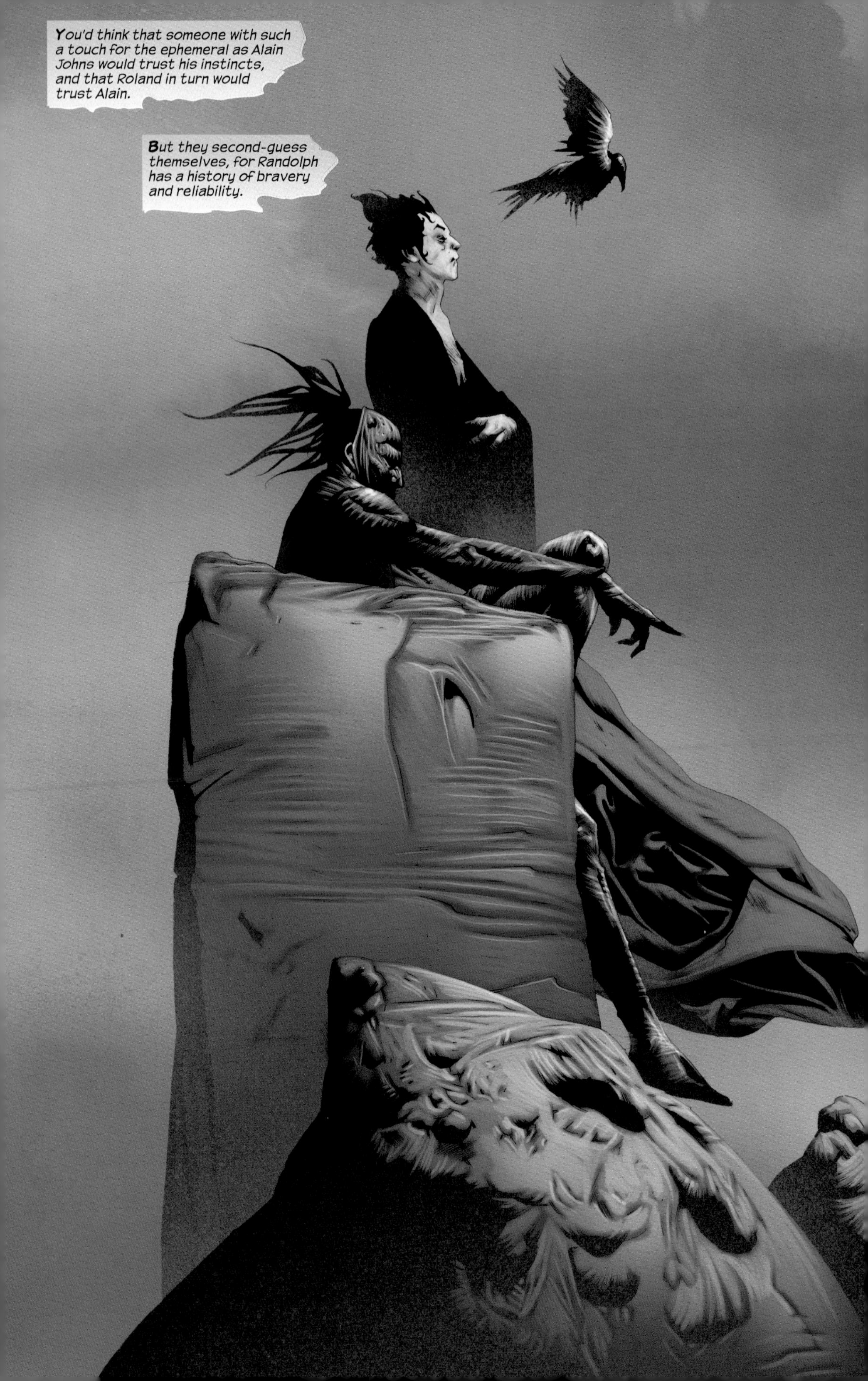
You'd think that someone with such a touch for the ephemeral as Alain Johns would trust his instincts, and that Roland in turn would trust Alain.
But they second-guess themselves, for Randolph has a history of bravery and reliability.

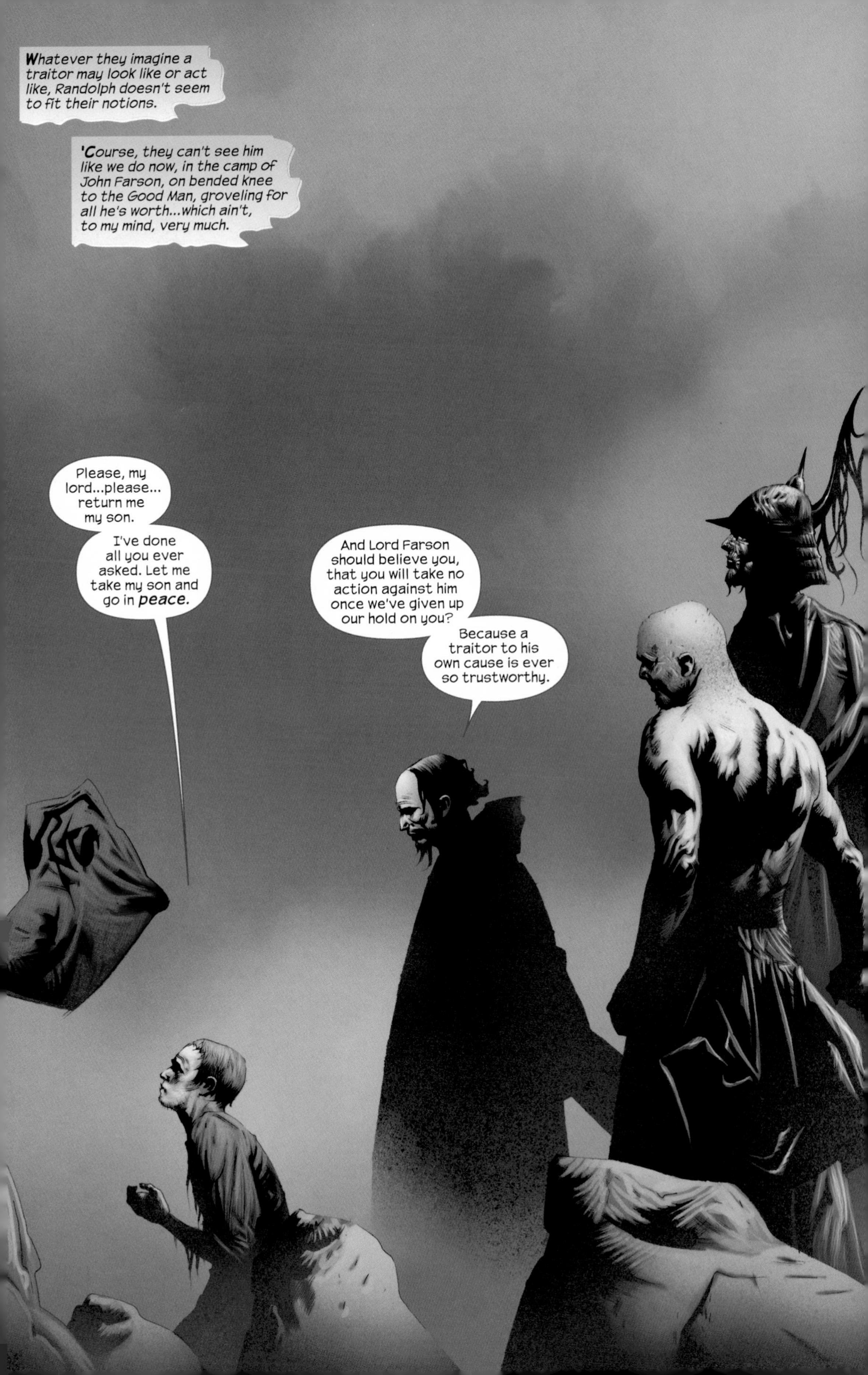
Whatever they imagine a traitor may look like or act like, Randolph doesn't seem to fit their notions.
'Course, they can't see him like we do now, in the camp of John Farson, on bended knee to the Good Man, groveling for all he's worth...which ain't, to my mind, very much.
Please, my lord...please... return me my son.
I've done all you ever asked. Let me take my son and go in *peace.*
And Lord Farson should believe you, that you will take no action against him once we've given up our hold on you?
Because a traitor to his own cause is ever so trustworthy.

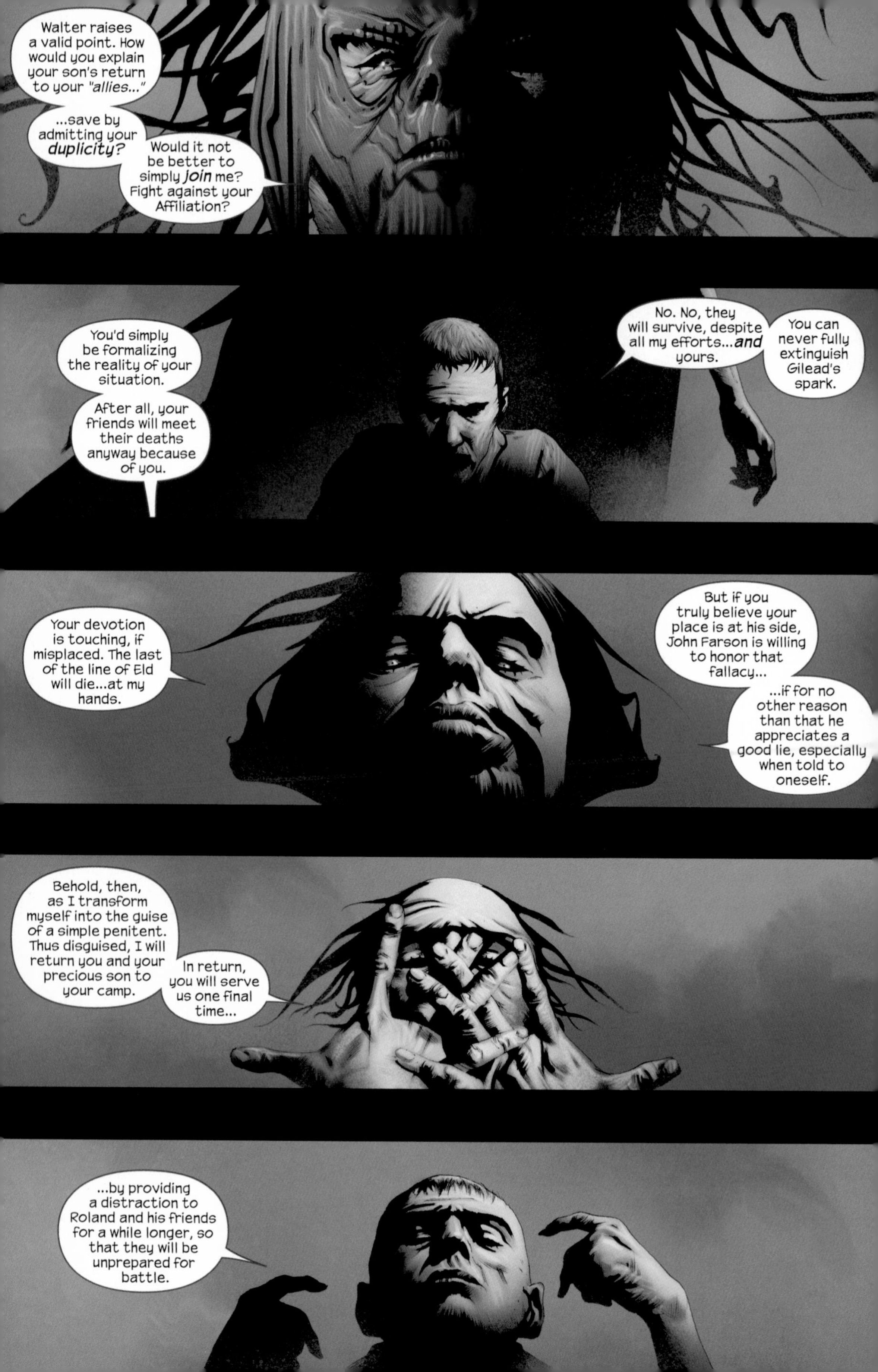
Walter raises a valid point. How would you explain your son's return to your "allies..."
...save by admitting your *duplicity*?
Would it not be better to simply *join* me? Fight against your Affiliation?
You'd simply be formalizing the reality of your situation.
After all, your friends will meet their deaths anyway because of you.
No. No, they will survive, despite all my efforts...*and* yours.
You can never fully extinguish Gilead's spark.
Your devotion is touching, if misplaced. The last of the line of Eld will die...at my hands.
But if you truly believe your place is at his side, John Farson is willing to honor that fallacy...
...if for no other reason than that he appreciates a good lie, especially when told to oneself.
Behold, then, as I transform myself into the guise of a simple penitent. Thus disguised, I will return you and your precious son to your camp.
In return, you will serve us one final time...
...by providing a distraction to Roland and his friends for a while longer, so that they will be unprepared for battle.

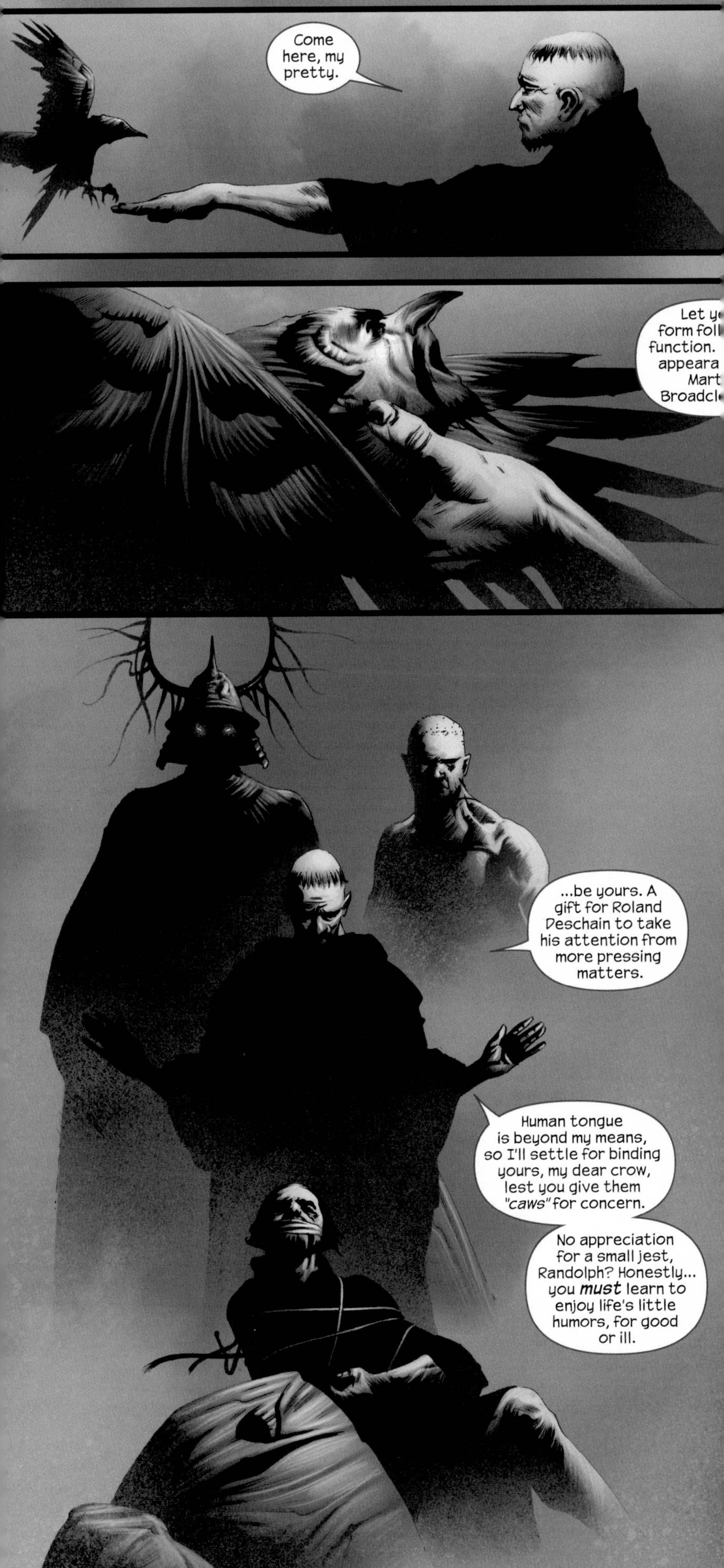
Come here, my pretty.
Let y form foll function. appeara Mart Broadcl
...be yours. A gift for Roland Deschain to take his attention from more pressing matters.
Human tongue is beyond my means, so I'll settle for binding yours, my dear crow, lest you give them *"caws"* for concern.
No appreciation for a small jest, Randolph? Honestly... you ***must*** learn to enjoy life's little humors, for good or ill.

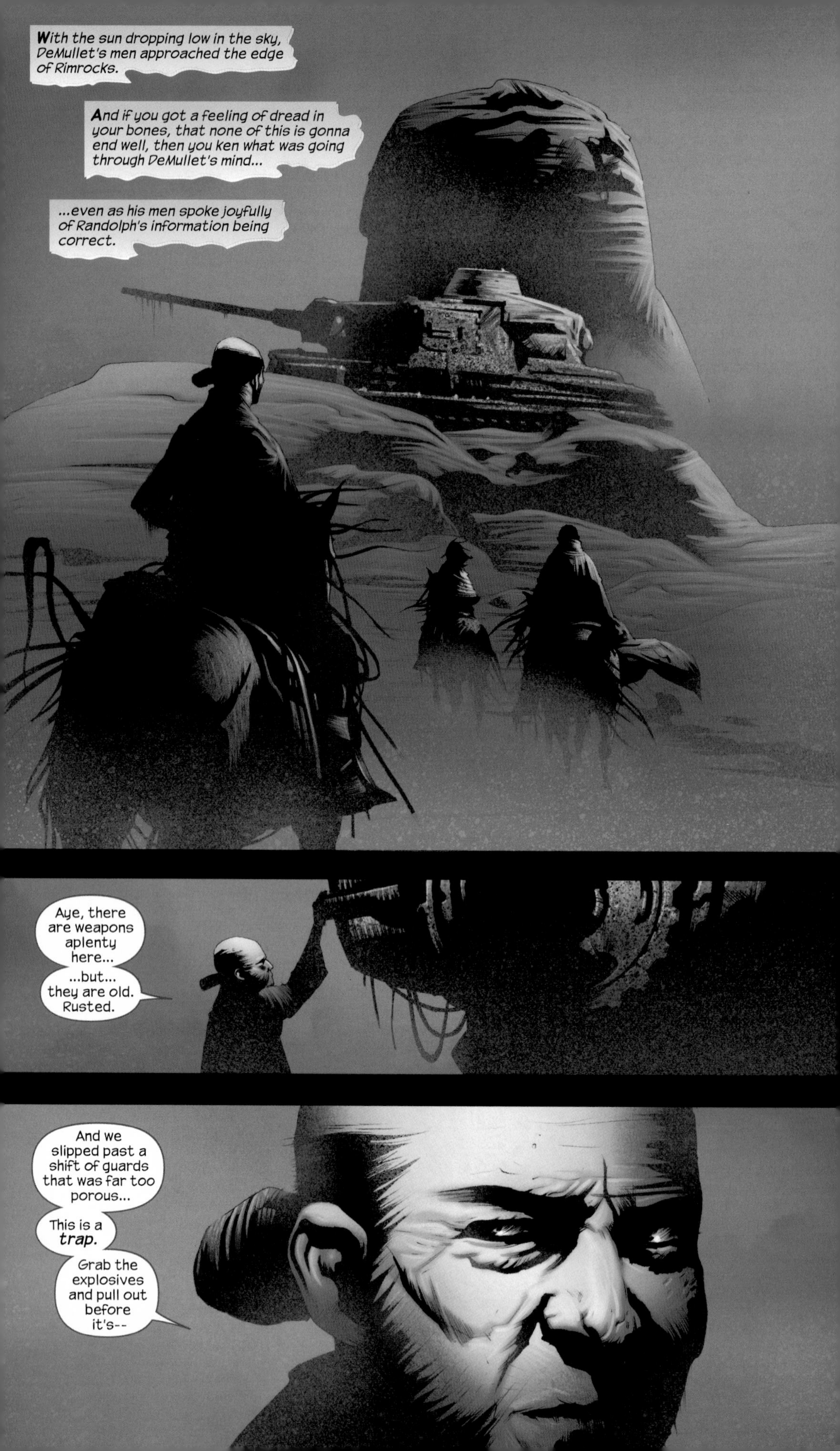
With the sun dropping low in the sky, DeMullet's men approached the edge of Rimrocks.
And if you got a feeling of dread in your bones, that none of this is gonna end well, then you ken what was going through DeMullet's mind...
...even as his men spoke joyfully of Randolph's information being correct.
Aye, there are weapons aplenty here...
...but... they are old. Rusted.
And we slipped past a shift of guards that was far too porous...
This is a *trap.*
Grab the explosives and pull out before it's--

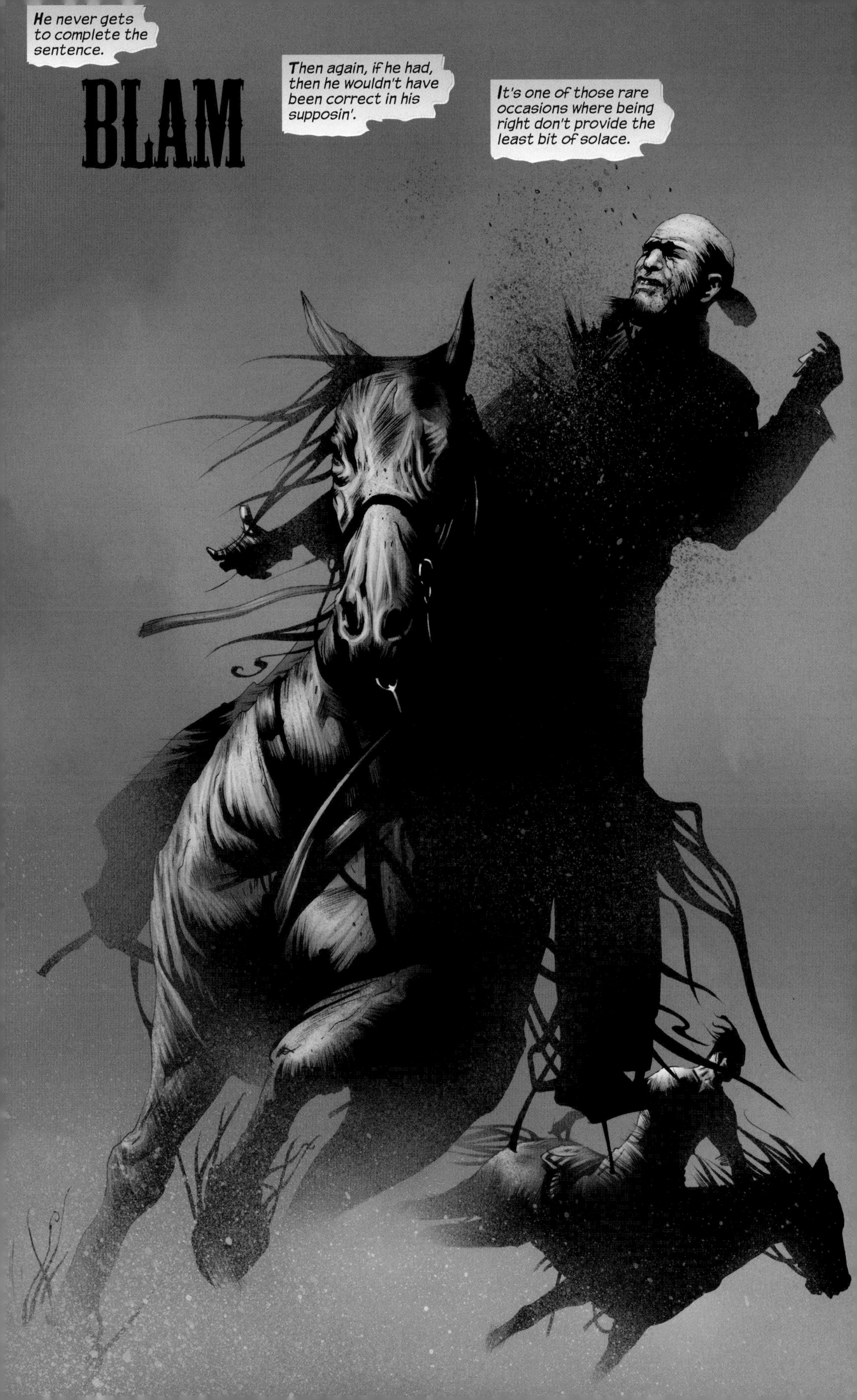
He never gets to complete the sentence.
BLAM
Then again, if he had, then he wouldn't have been correct in his supposin'.
It's one of those rare occasions where being right don't provide the least bit of solace.

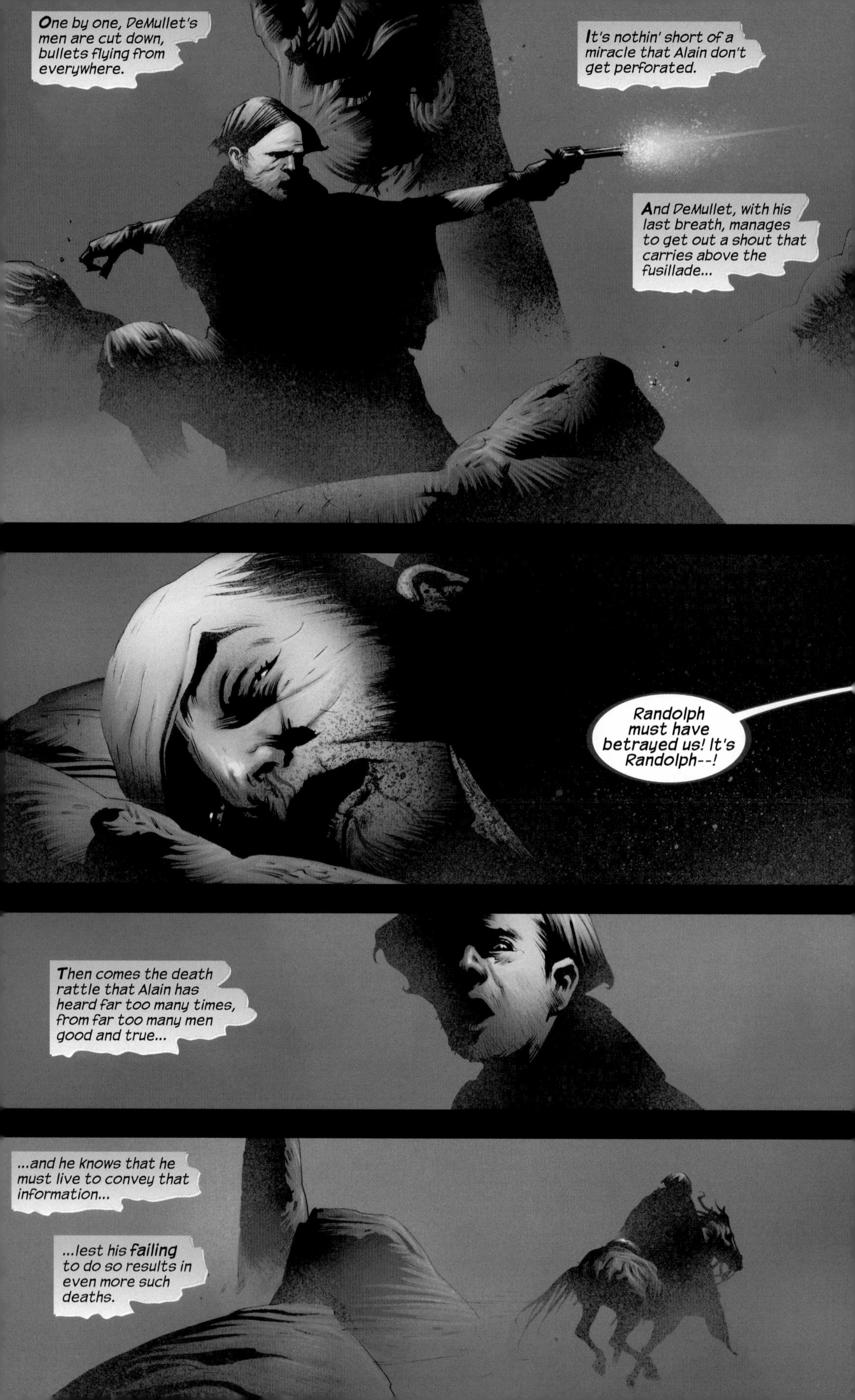
One by one, DeMullet's men are cut down, bullets flying from everywhere.
It's nothin' short of a miracle that Alain don't get perforated.
And DeMullet, with his last breath, manages to get out a shout that carries above the fusillade...
Randolph must have betrayed us! It's Randolph--!
Then comes the death rattle that Alain has heard far too many times, from far too many men good and true...
...and he knows that he must live to convey that information...
...lest his failing to do so results in even more such deaths.

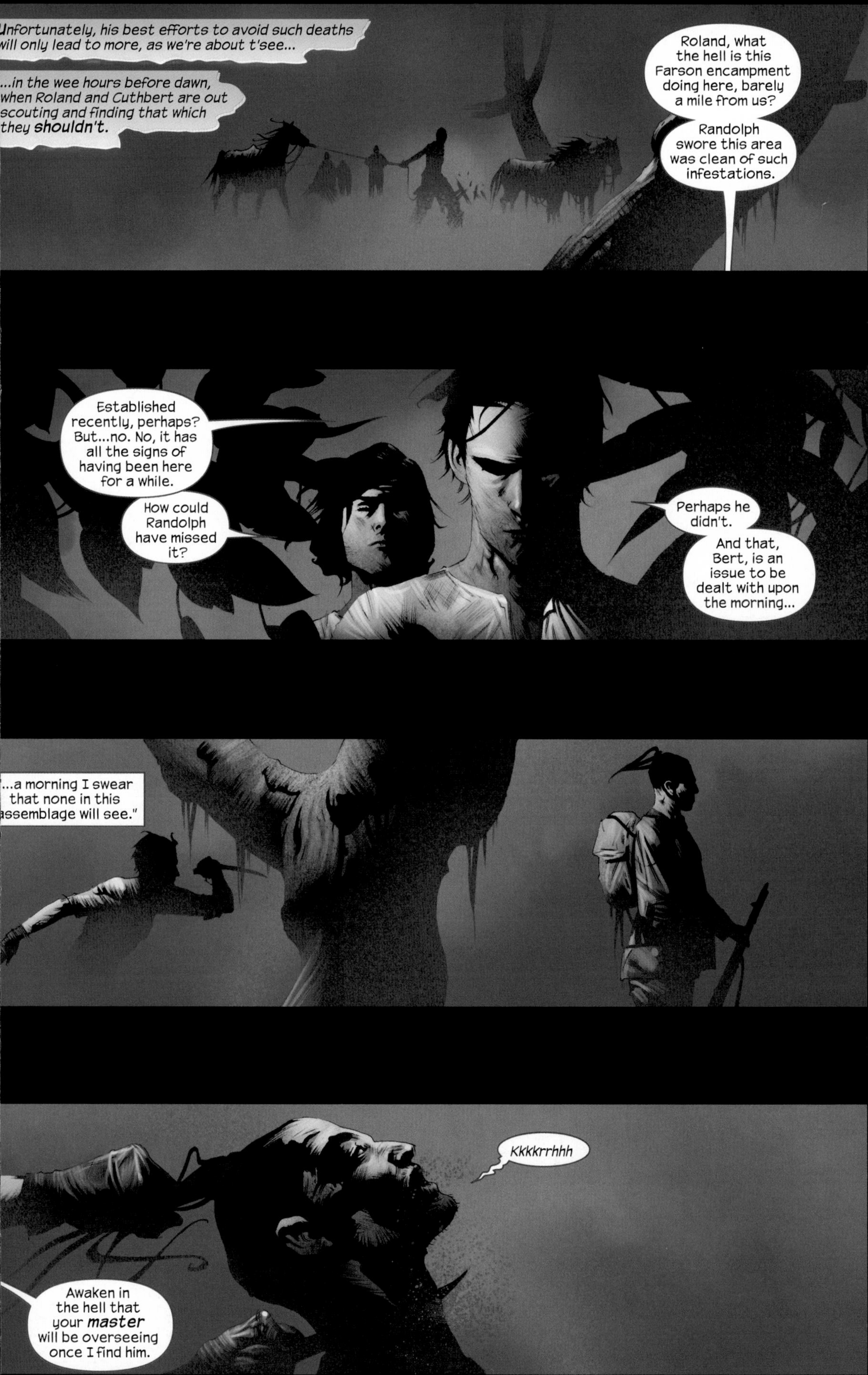
Unfortunately, his best efforts to avoid such deaths will only lead to more, as we're about t'see...
...in the wee hours before dawn, when Roland and Cuthbert are out scouting and finding that which they **shouldn't.**
Roland, what the hell is this Farson encampment doing here, barely a mile from us?
Randolph swore this area was clean of such infestations.
Established recently, perhaps? But...no. No, it has all the signs of having been here for a while.
How could Randolph have missed it?
Perhaps he didn't.
And that, Bert, is an issue to be dealt with upon the morning...
...a morning I swear that none in this assemblage will see."
Kkkkrrhhh
Awaken in the hell that your ***master*** will be overseeing once I find him.

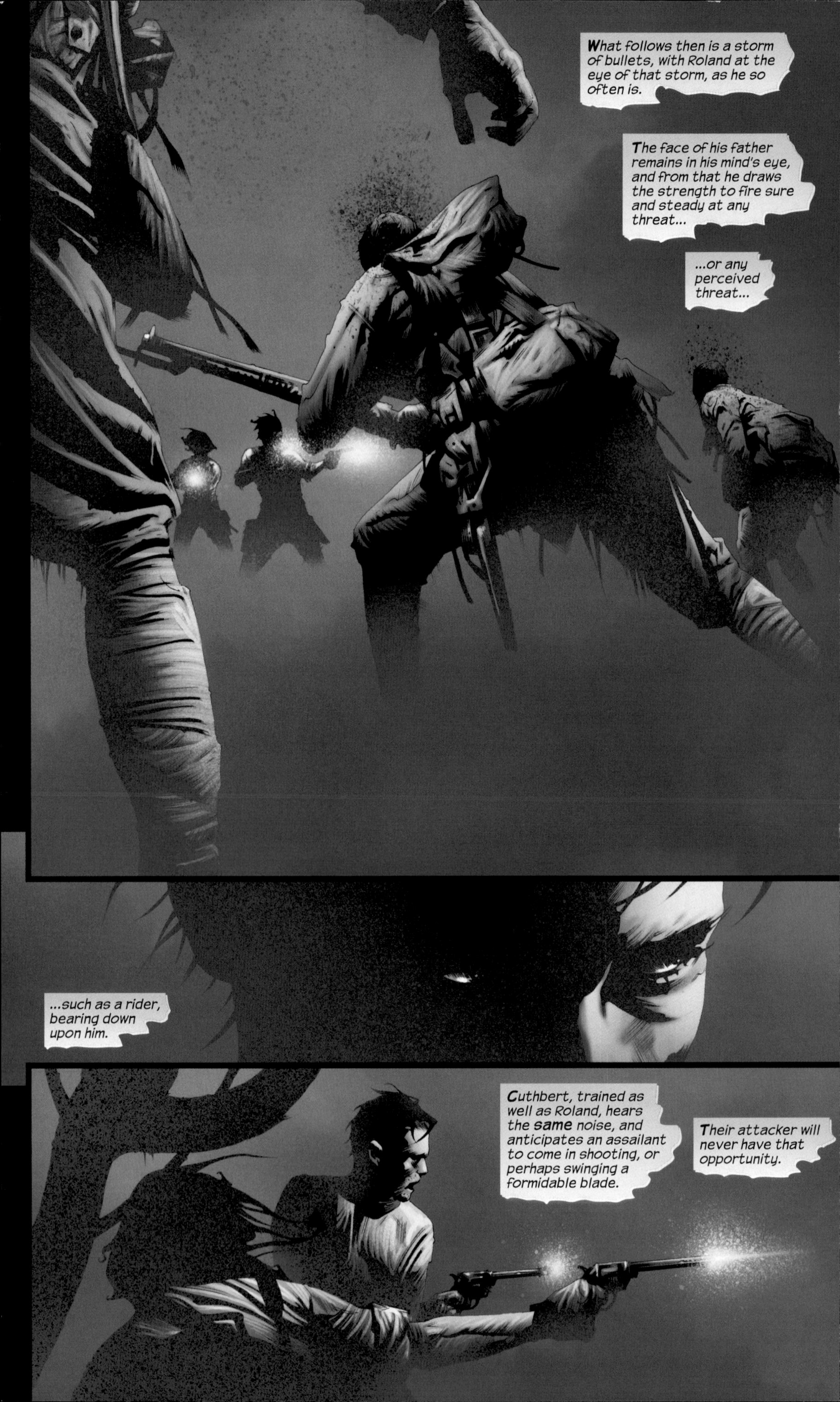
What follows then is a storm of bullets, with Roland at the eye of that storm, as he so often is.
The face of his father remains in his mind's eye, and from that he draws the strength to fire sure and steady at any threat...
...or any perceived threat...
...such as a rider, bearing down upon him.
Cuthbert, trained as well as Roland, hears the same noise, and anticipates an assailant to come in shooting, or perhaps swinging a formidable blade.
Their attacker will never have that opportunity.

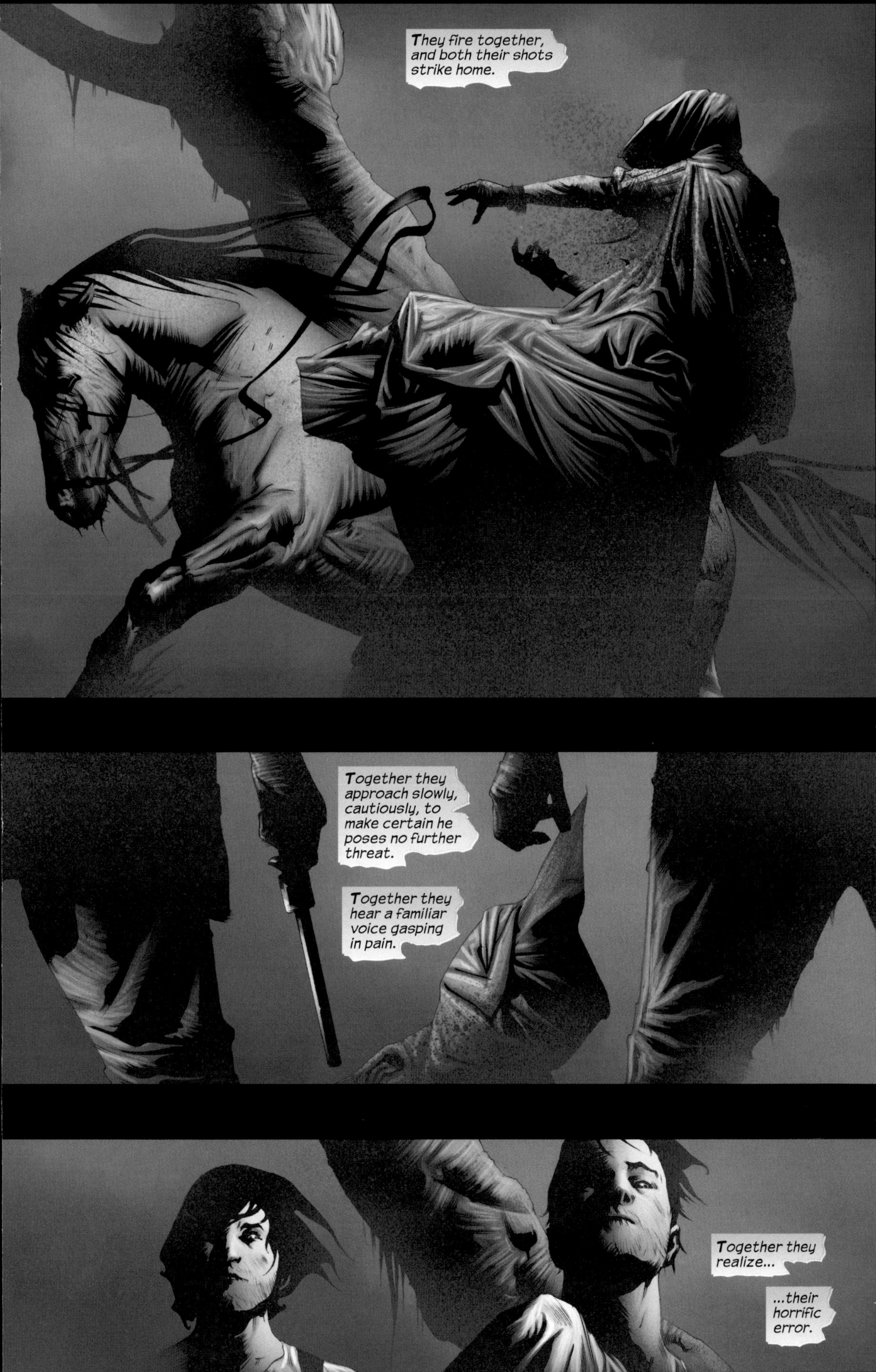
They fire together, and both their shots strike home.
Together they approach slowly, cautiously, to make certain he poses no further threat.
Together they hear a familiar voice gasping in pain.
Together they realize...
...their horrific error.

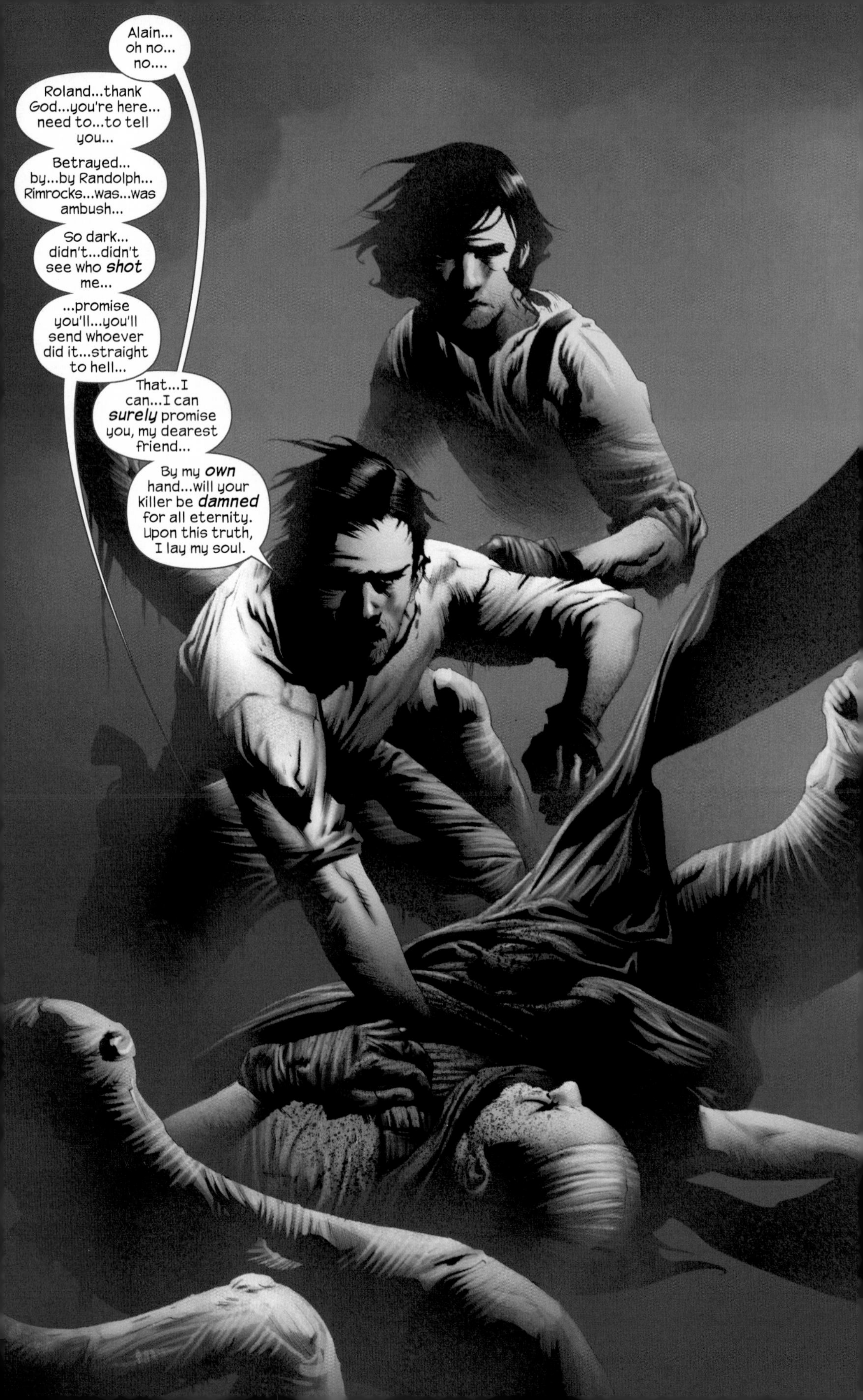
Alain... oh no... no....
Roland...thank God...you're here... need to...to tell you...
Betrayed... by...by Randolph... Rimrocks...was...was ambush...
So dark... didn't...didn't see who *shot* me...
...promise you'll...you'll send whoever did it...straight to hell...
That...I can...I can *surely* promise you, my dearest friend...
By my *own* hand...will your killer be *damned* for all eternity. Upon this truth, I lay my soul.

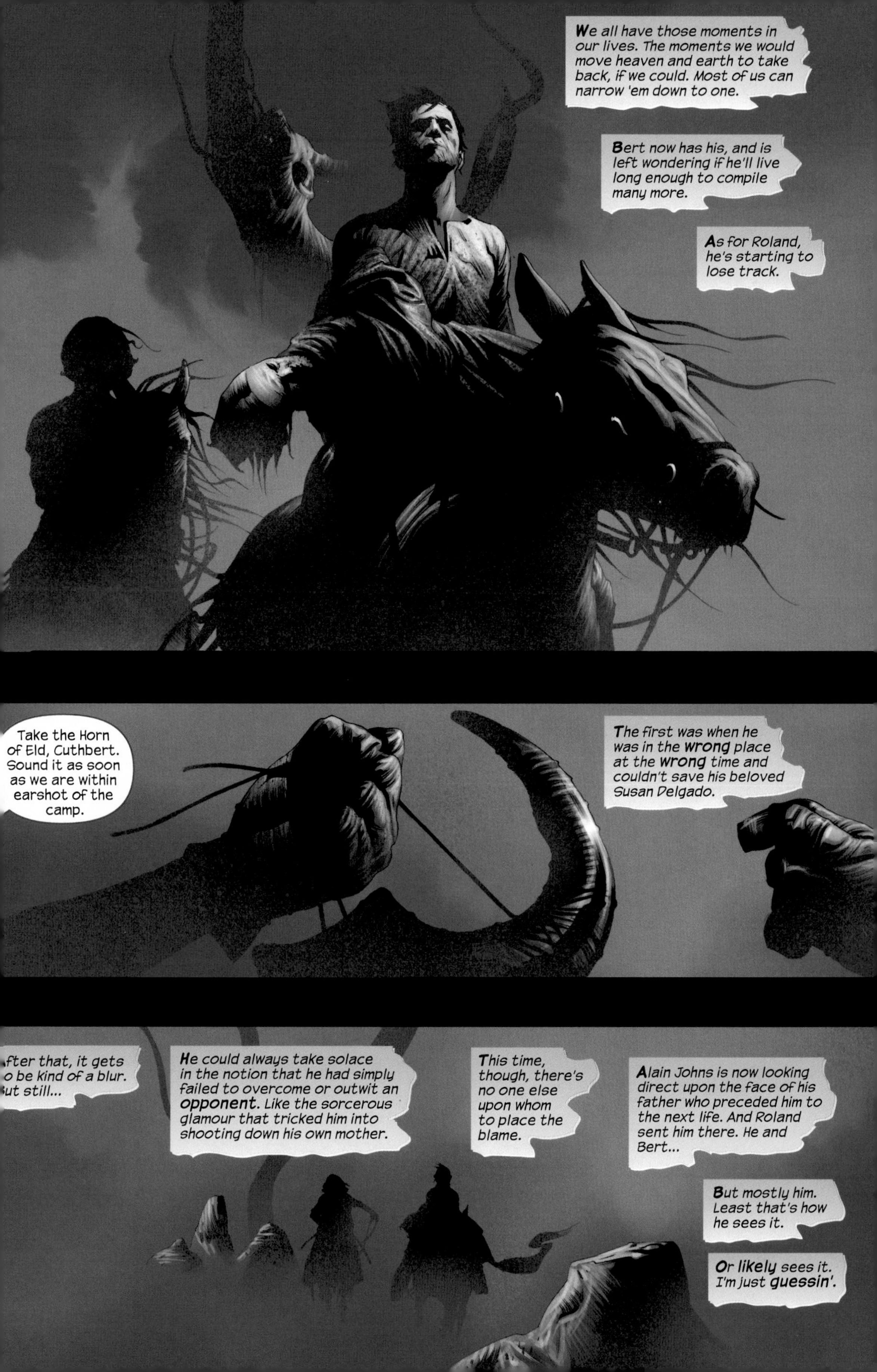
We all have those moments in our lives. The moments we would move heaven and earth to take back, if we could. Most of us can narrow 'em down to one.
Bert now has his, and is left wondering if he'll live long enough to compile many more.
As for Roland, he's starting to lose track.
Take the Horn of Eld, Cuthbert. Sound it as soon as we are within earshot of the camp.
The first was when he was in the wrong place at the wrong time and couldn't save his beloved Susan Delgado.
fter that, it gets o be kind of a blur. ut still...
He could always take solace in the notion that he had simply failed to overcome or outwit an opponent. Like the sorcerous glamour that tricked him into shooting down his own mother.
This time, though, there's no one else upon whom to place the blame.
Alain Johns is now looking direct upon the face of his father who preceded him to the next life. And Roland sent him there. He and Bert...
But mostly him. Least that's how he sees it.
Or likely sees it. I'm just guessin'.

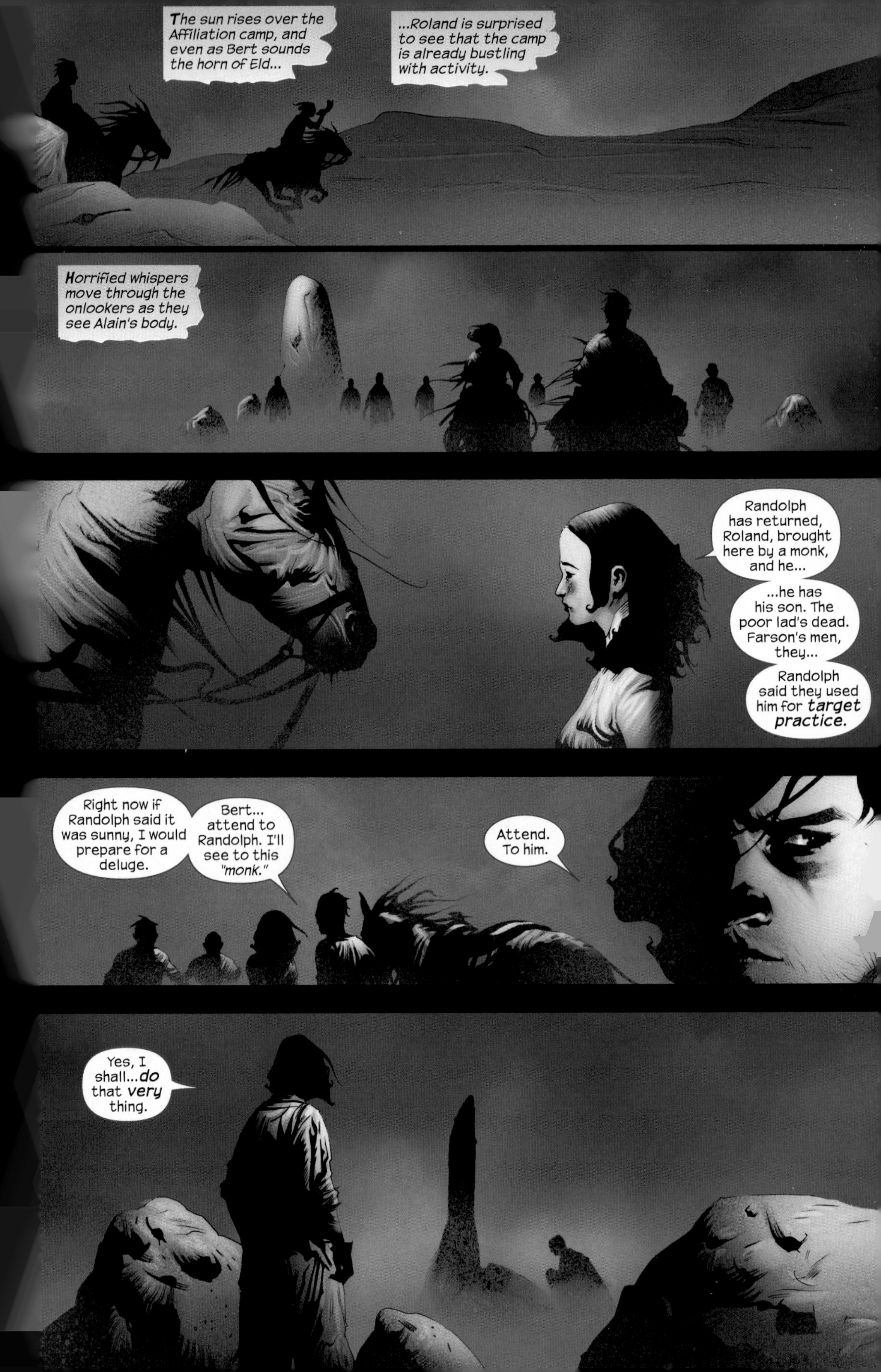
The sun rises over the Affiliation camp, and even as Bert sounds the horn of Eld...
...Roland is surprised to see that the camp is already bustling with activity.
Horrified whispers move through the onlookers as they see Alain's body.
Randolph has returned, Roland, brought here by a monk, and he...
...he has his son. The poor lad's dead. Farson's men, they...
Randolph said they used him for target practice.
Right now if Randolph said it was sunny, I would prepare for a deluge.
Bert... attend to Randolph. I'll see to this "monk."
Attend. To him.
Yes, I shall...do that very thing.

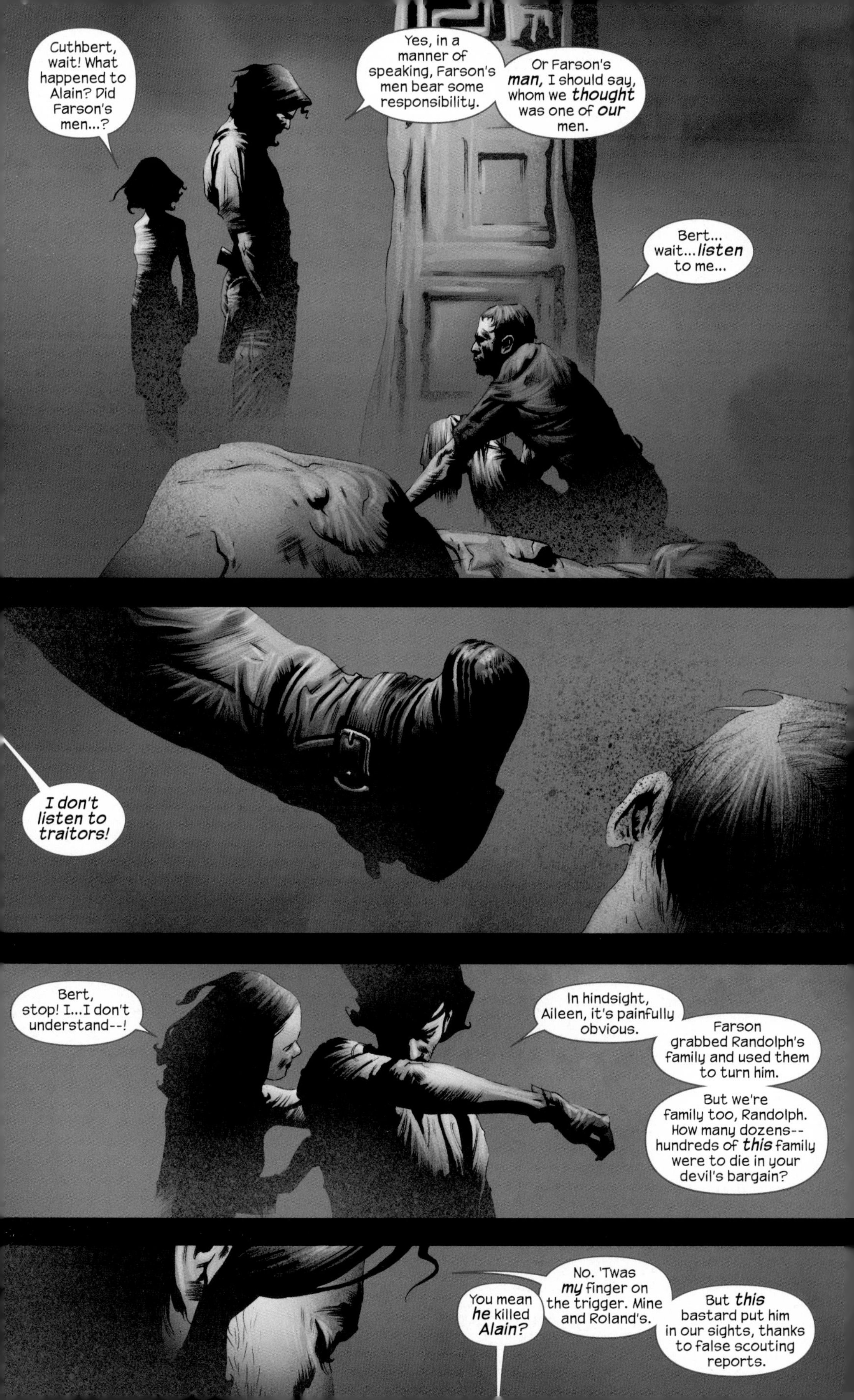
Cuthbert, wait! What happened to Alain? Did Farson's men...?
Yes, in a manner of speaking, Farson's men bear some responsibility.
Or Farson's *man*, I should say, whom we *thought* was one of *our* men.
Bert... wait... *listen* to me...
I don't listen to traitors!
Bert, stop! I...I don't understand--!
In hindsight, Aileen, it's painfully obvious.
Farson grabbed Randolph's family and used them to turn him.
But we're family too, Randolph. How many dozens--hundreds of *this* family were to die in your devil's bargain?
You mean *he* killed *Alain?*
No. 'Twas *my* finger on the trigger. Mine and Roland's.
But *this* bastard put him in our sights, thanks to false scouting reports.

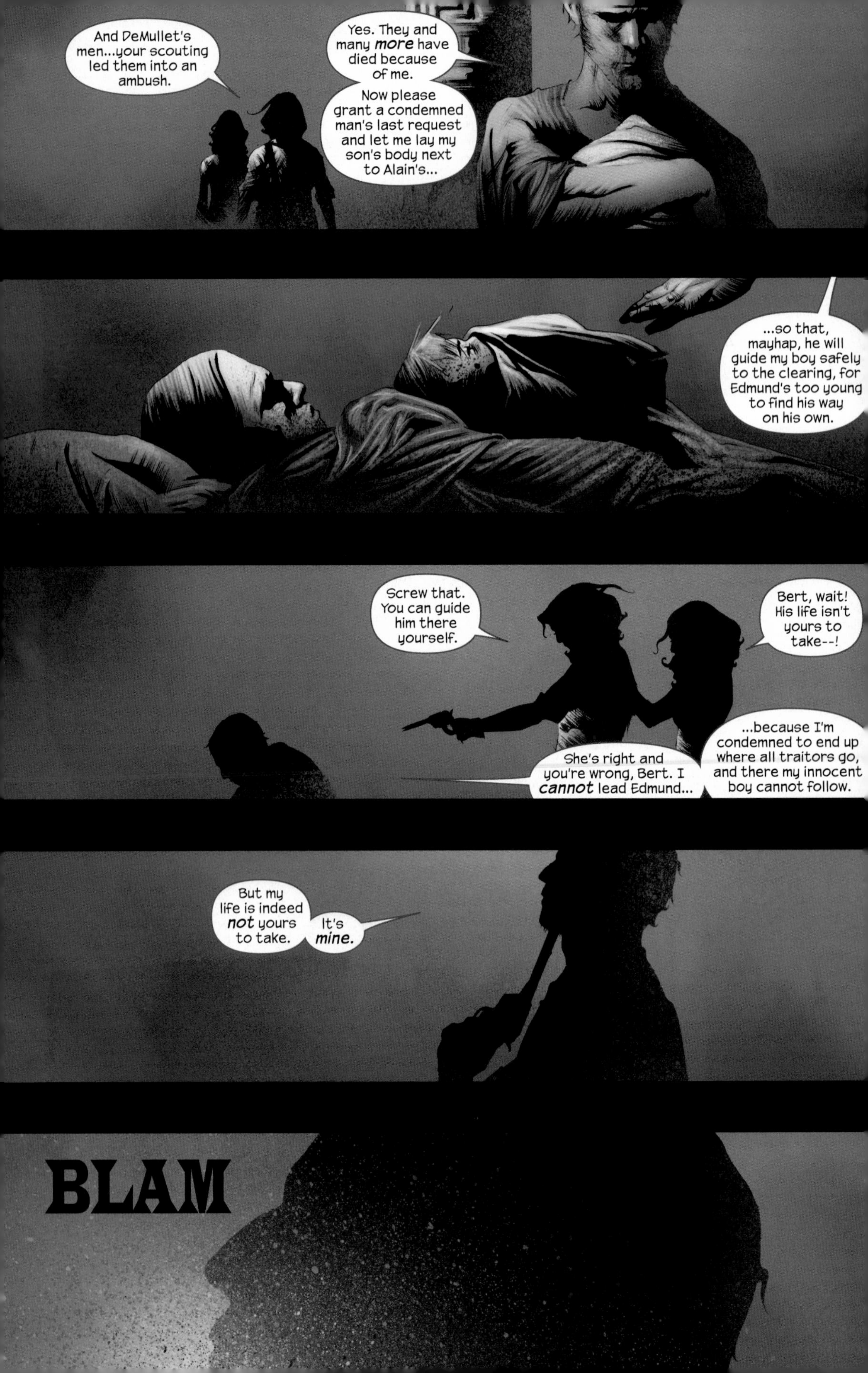
And DeMullet's men...your scouting led them into an ambush.
Yes. They and many *more* have died because of me.
Now please grant a condemned man's last request and let me lay my son's body next to Alain's...
...so that, mayhap, he will guide my boy safely to the clearing, for Edmund's too young to find his way on his own.
Screw that. You can guide him there yourself.
Bert, wait! His life isn't yours to take--!
She's right and you're wrong, Bert. I *cannot* lead Edmund...
...because I'm condemned to end up where all traitors go, and there my innocent boy cannot follow.
But my life is indeed *not* yours to take.
It's *mine.*
BLAM

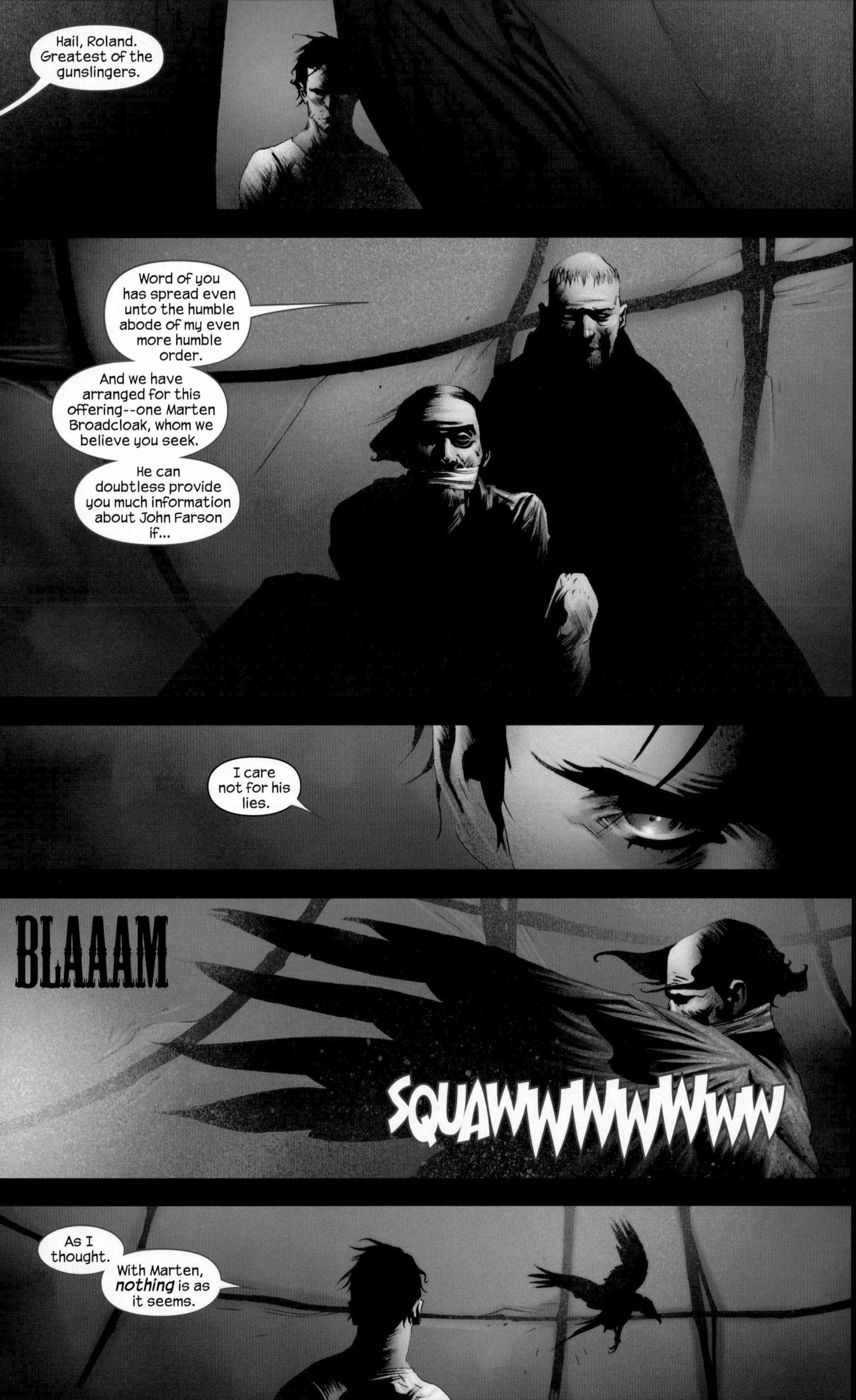
Hail, Roland. Greatest of the gunslingers.
Word of you has spread even unto the humble abode of my even more humble order.
And we have arranged for this offering--one Marten Broadcloak, whom we believe you seek.
He can doubtless provide you much information about John Farson if...
I care not for his lies.
BLAAAM
SQUAWWWWWWww
As I thought.
With Marten, *nothing* is as it seems.

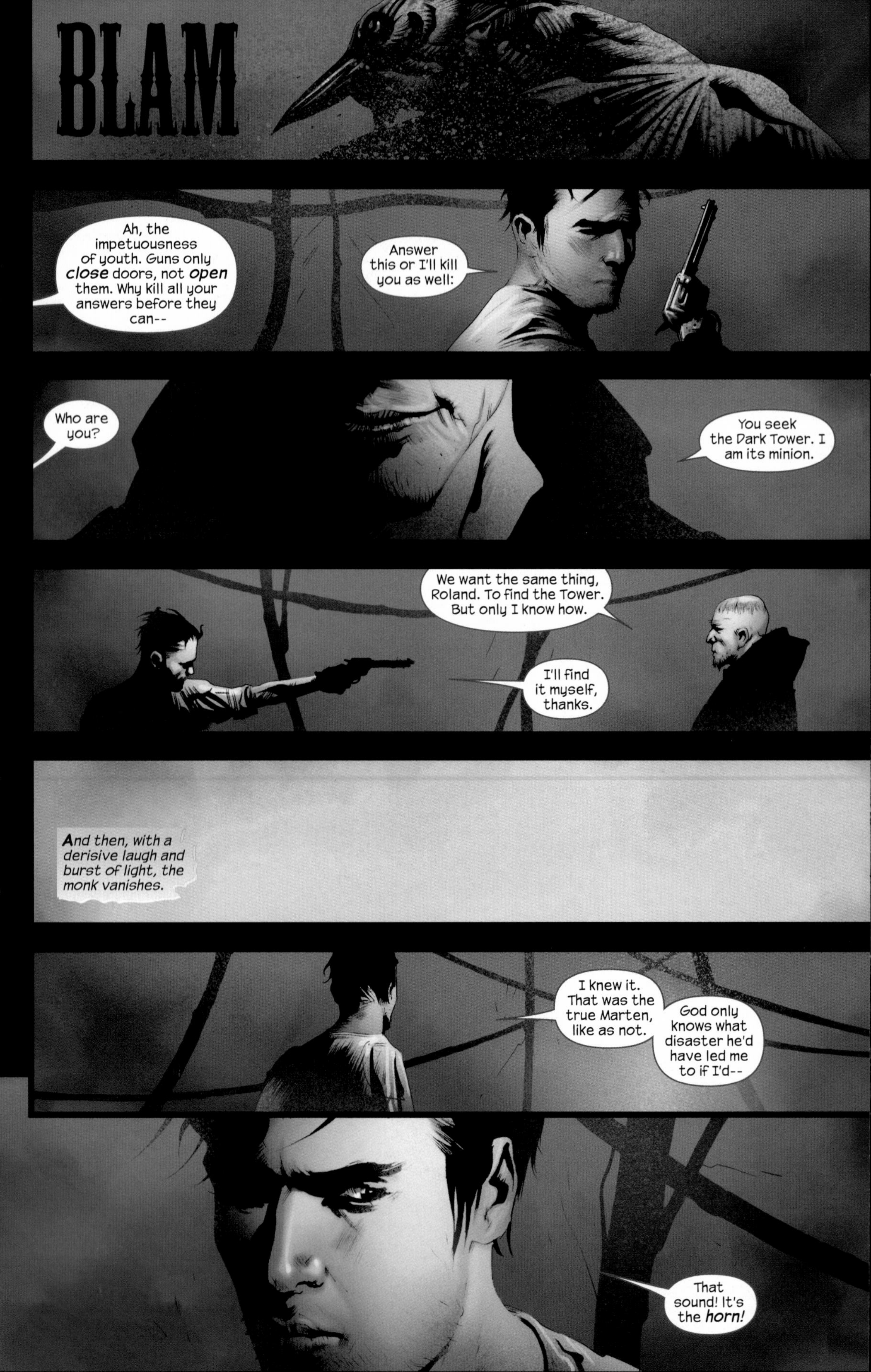
BLAM
Ah, the impetuousness of youth. Guns only *close* doors, not *open* them. Why kill all your answers before they can--
Answer this or I'll kill you as well:
Who are you?
You seek the Dark Tower. I am its minion.
We want the same thing, Roland. To find the Tower. But only I know how.
I'll find it myself, thanks.
And then, with a derisive laugh and burst of light, the monk vanishes.
I knew it. That was the true Marten, like as not.
God only knows what disaster he'd have led me to if I'd--
That sound! It's the *horn!*

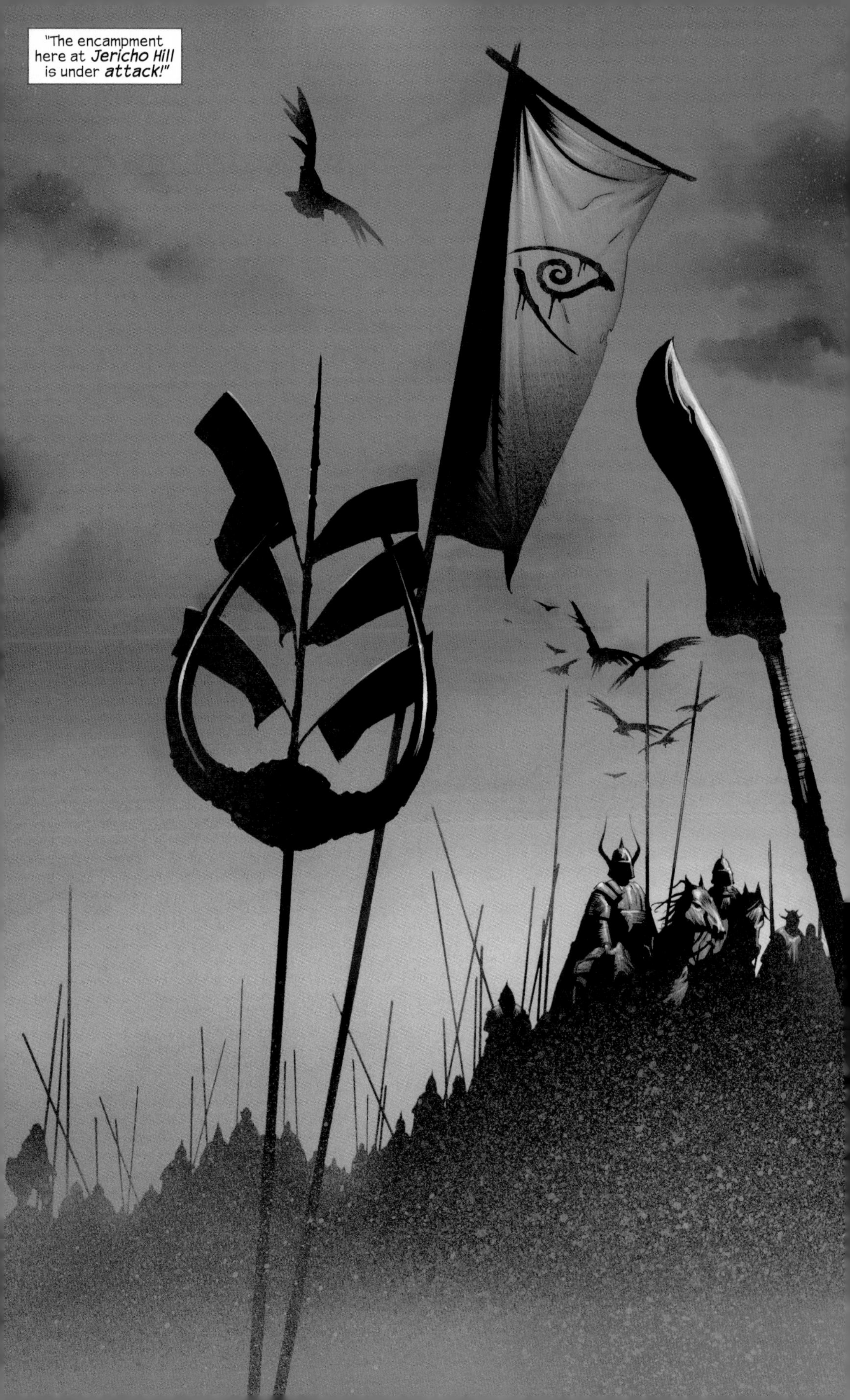
"The encampment here at *Jericho Hill* is under ***attack!***"

STEPHEN KING

THE DARK TOWER

BATTLE OF JERICHO HILL

CHAPTER FIVE

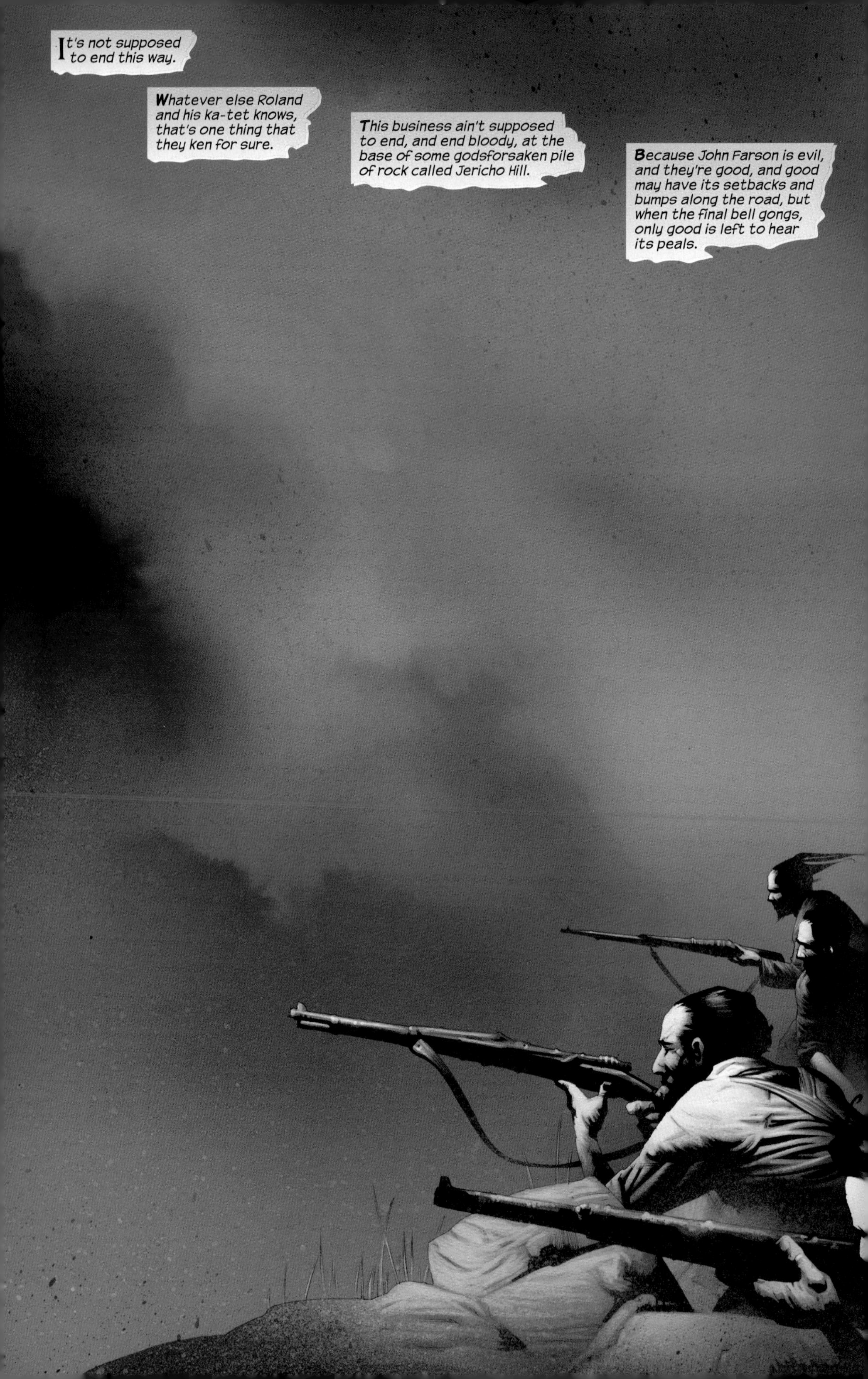
It's not supposed to end this way.
Whatever else Roland and his ka-tet knows, that's one thing that they ken for sure.
This business ain't supposed to end, and end bloody, at the base of some godsforsaken pile of rock called Jericho Hill.
Because John Farson is evil, and they're good, and good may have its setbacks and bumps along the road, but when the final bell gongs, only good is left to hear its peals.

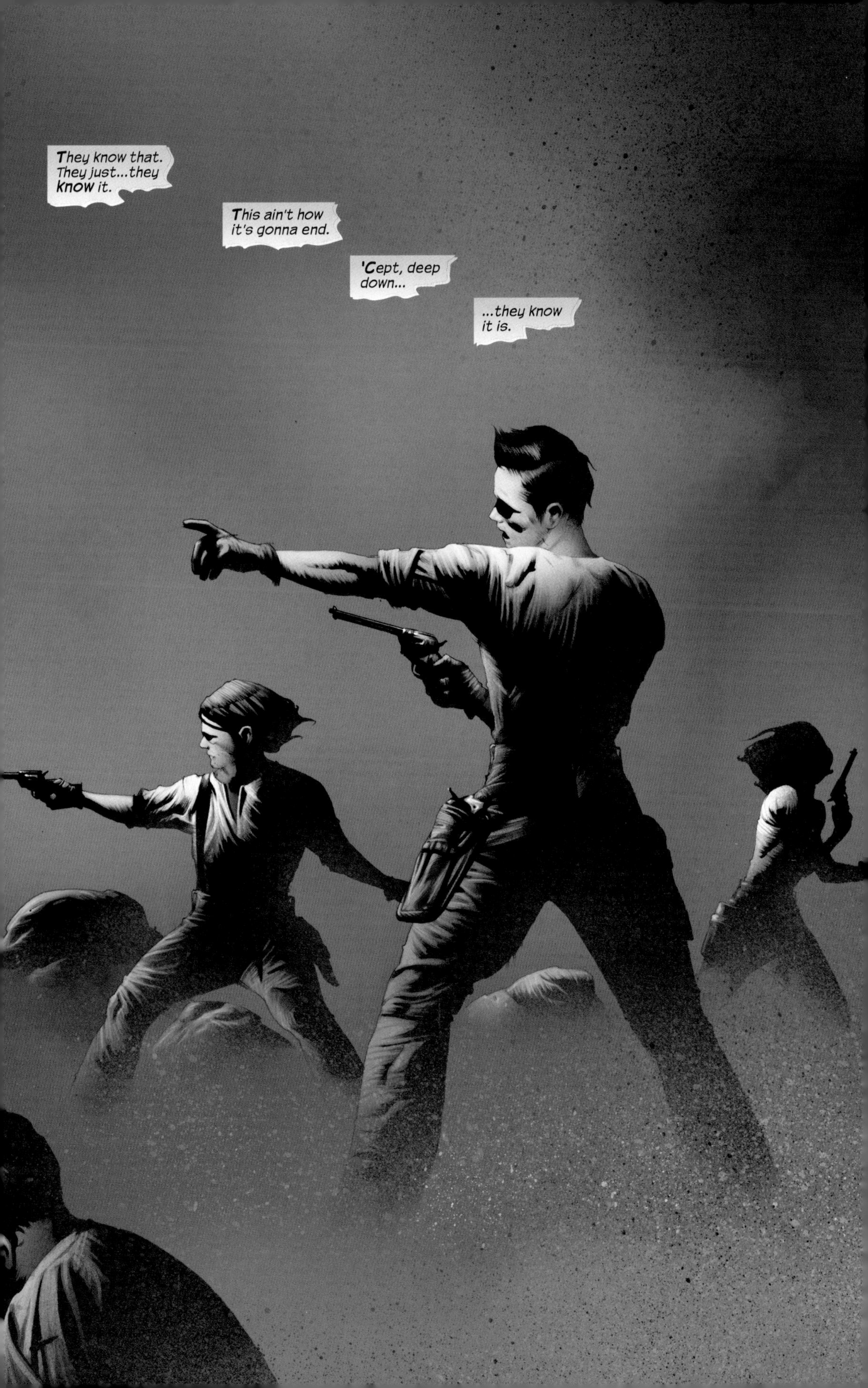
They know that. They just...they know it.
This ain't how it's gonna end.
'Cept, deep down...
...they know it is.

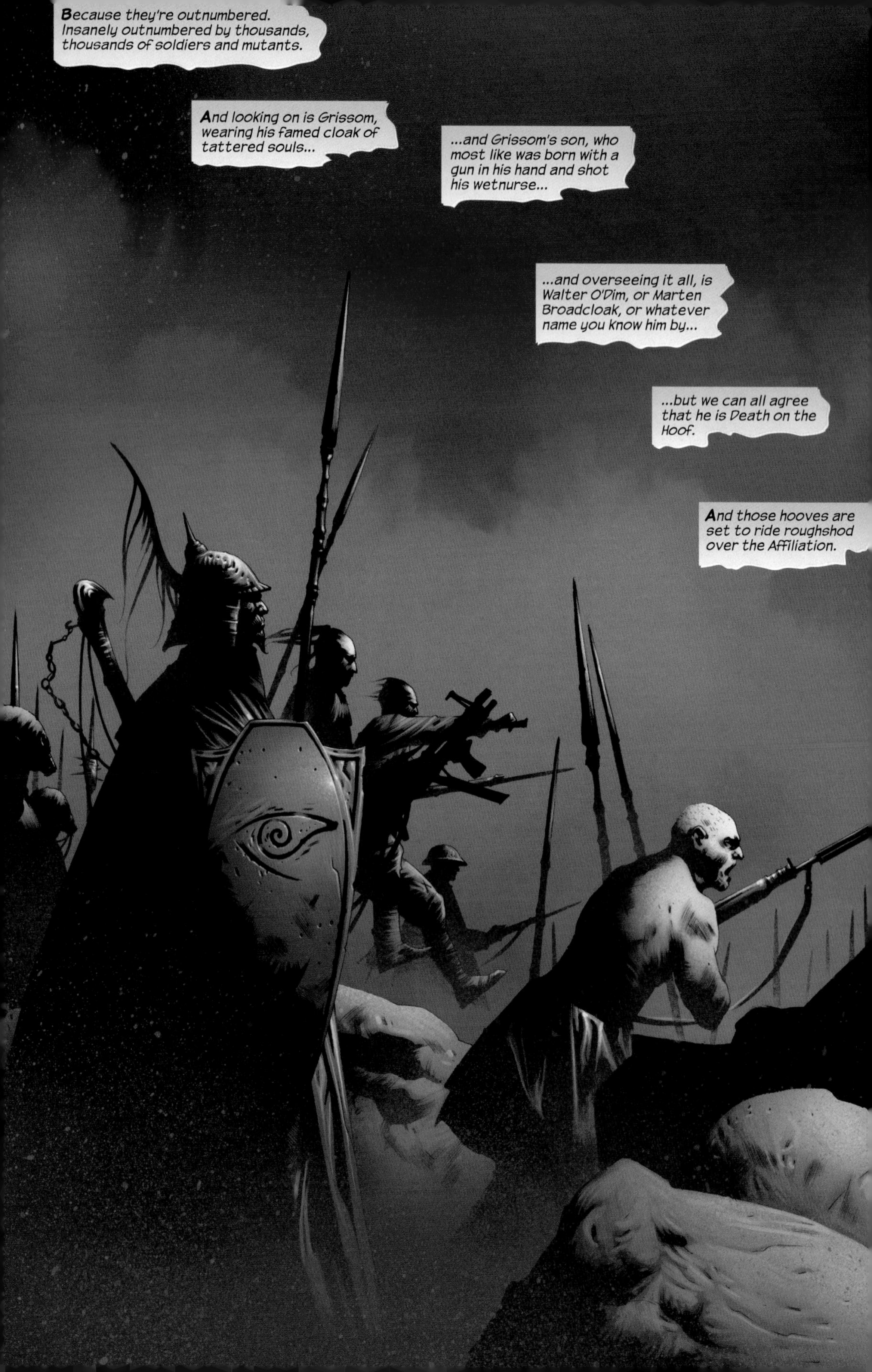
Because they're outnumbered. Insanely outnumbered by thousands, thousands of soldiers and mutants.
And looking on is Grissom, wearing his famed cloak of tattered souls...
...and Grissom's son, who most like was born with a gun in his hand and shot his wetnurse...
...and overseeing it all, is Walter O'Dim, or Marten Broadcloak, or whatever name you know him by...
...but we can all agree that he is Death on the Hoof.
And those hooves are set to ride roughshod over the Affiliation.

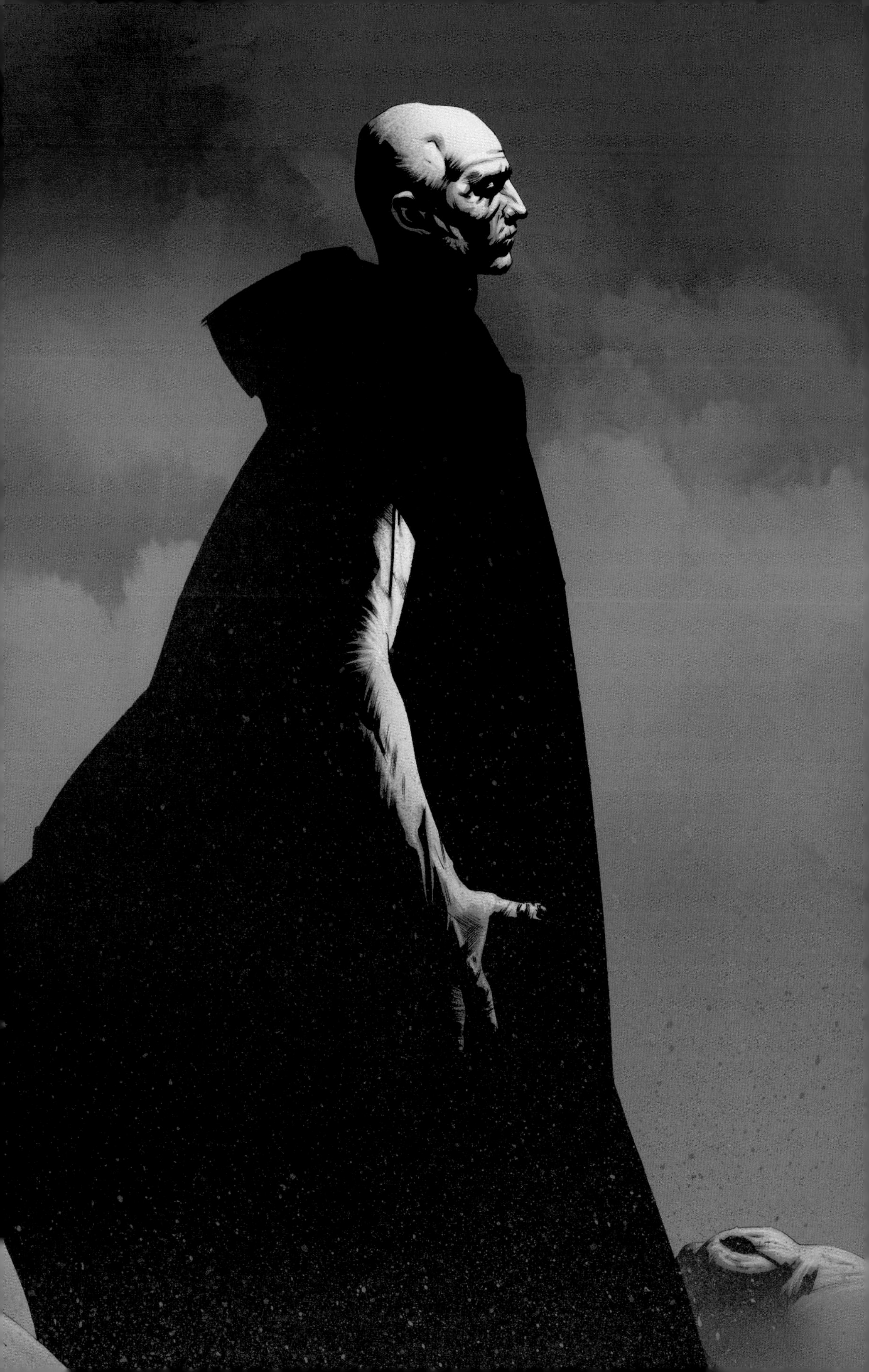

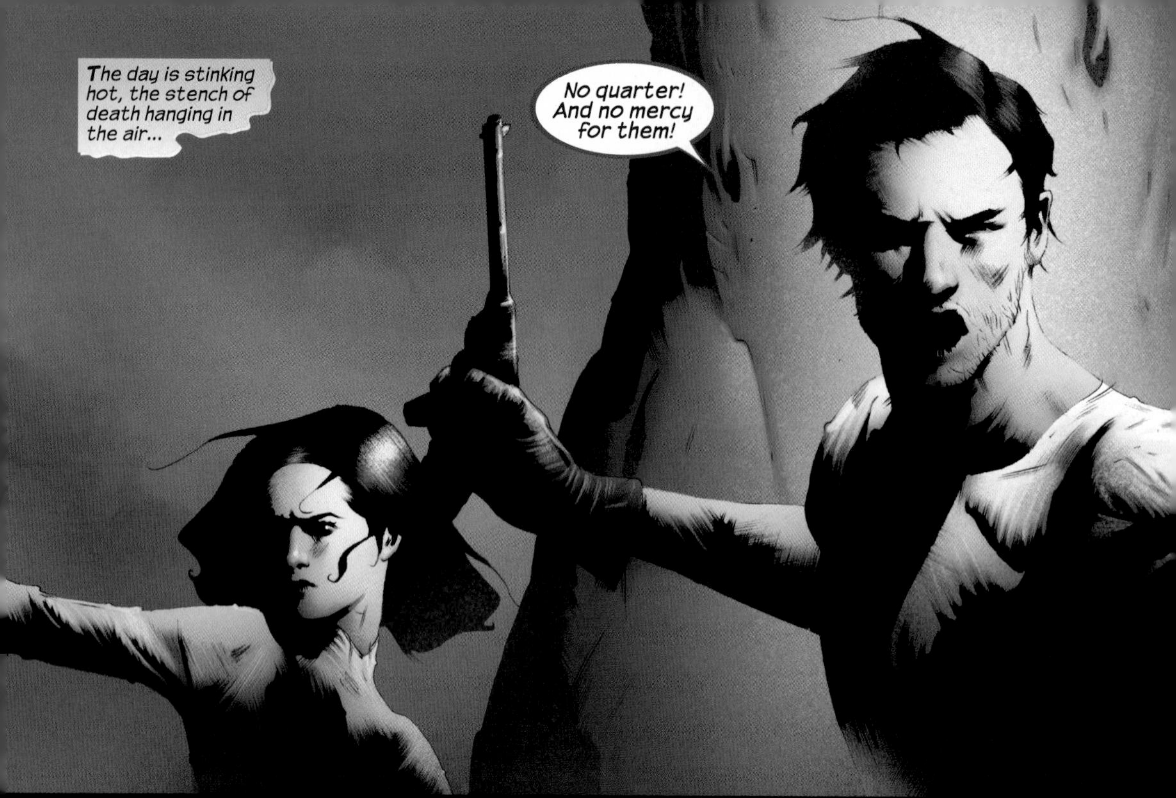
The day is stinking hot, the stench of death hanging in the air...
No quarter! And no mercy for them!

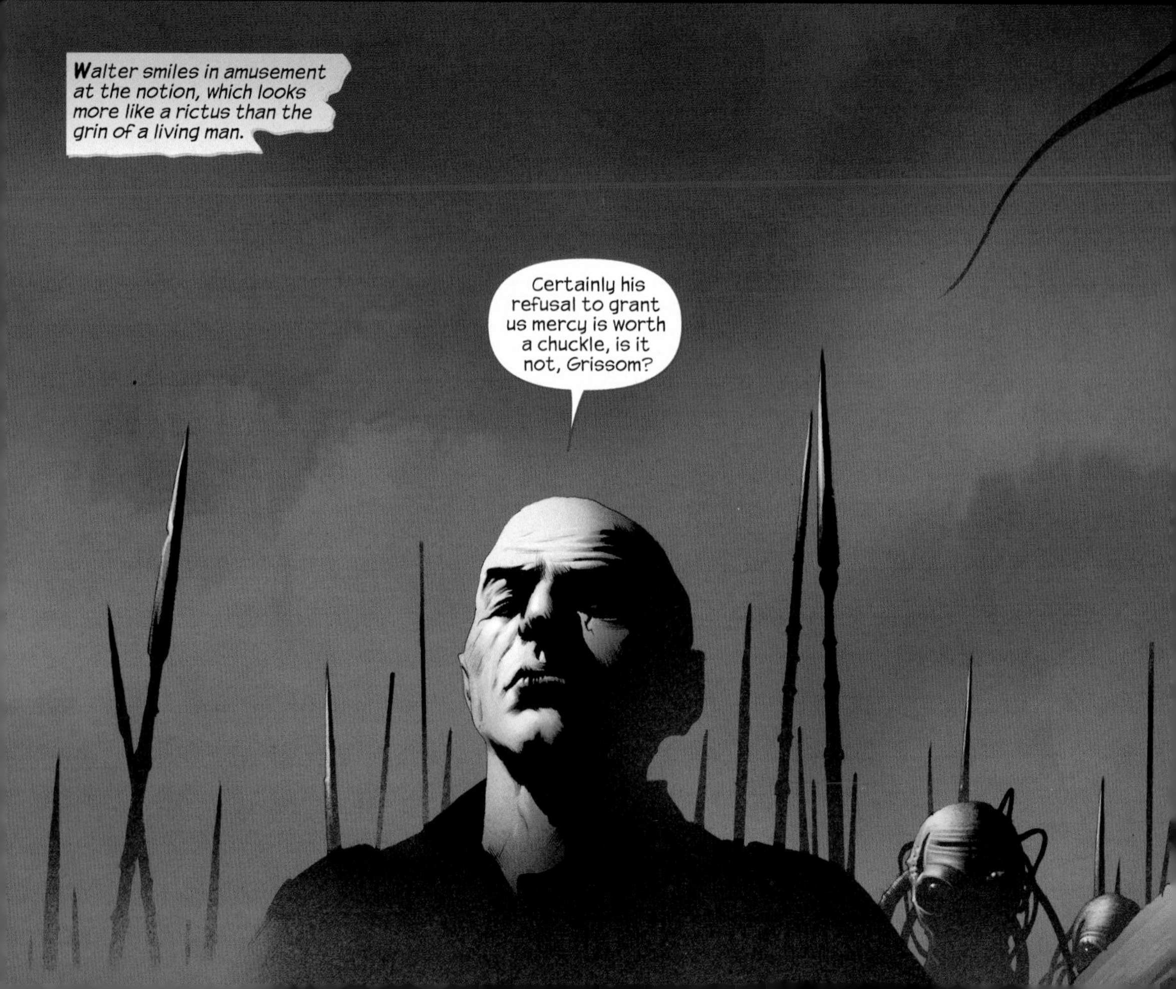
Walter smiles in amusement at the notion, which looks more like a rictus than the grin of a living man.
Certainly his refusal to grant us mercy is worth a chuckle, is it not, Grissom?

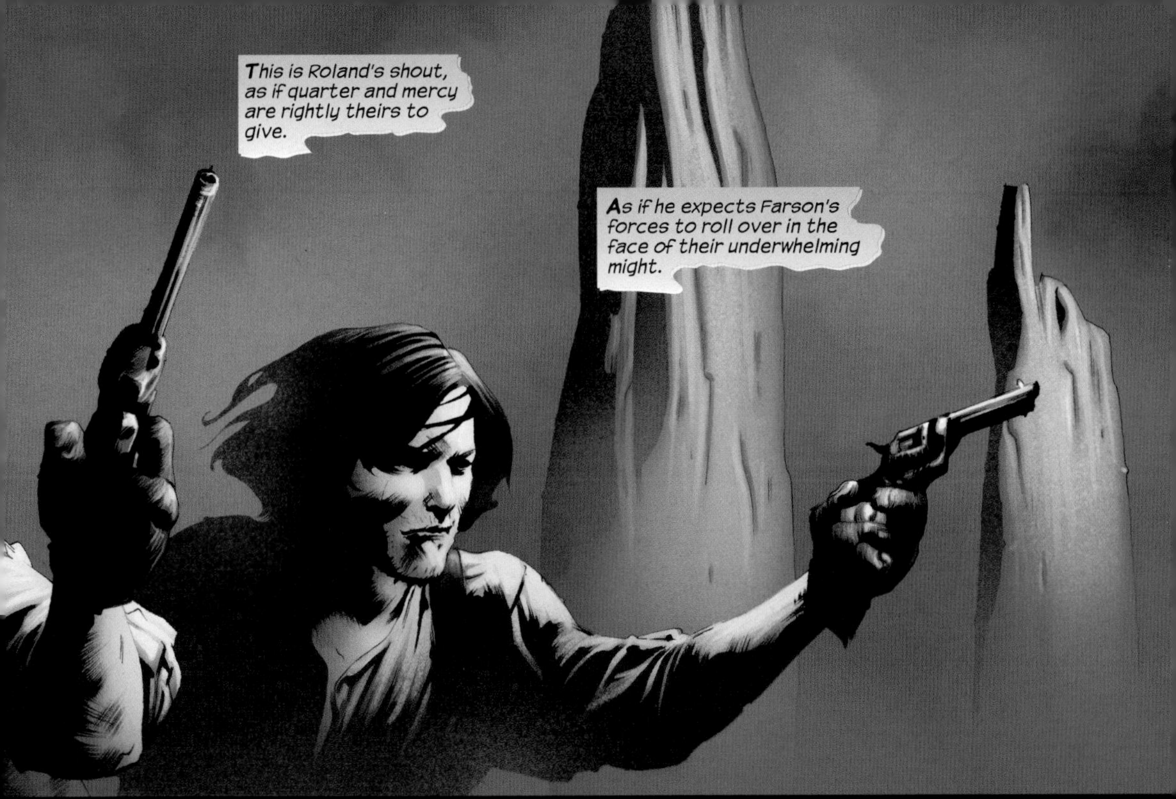
This is Roland's shout, as if quarter and mercy are rightly theirs to give.
As if he expects Farson's forces to roll over in the face of their underwhelming might.

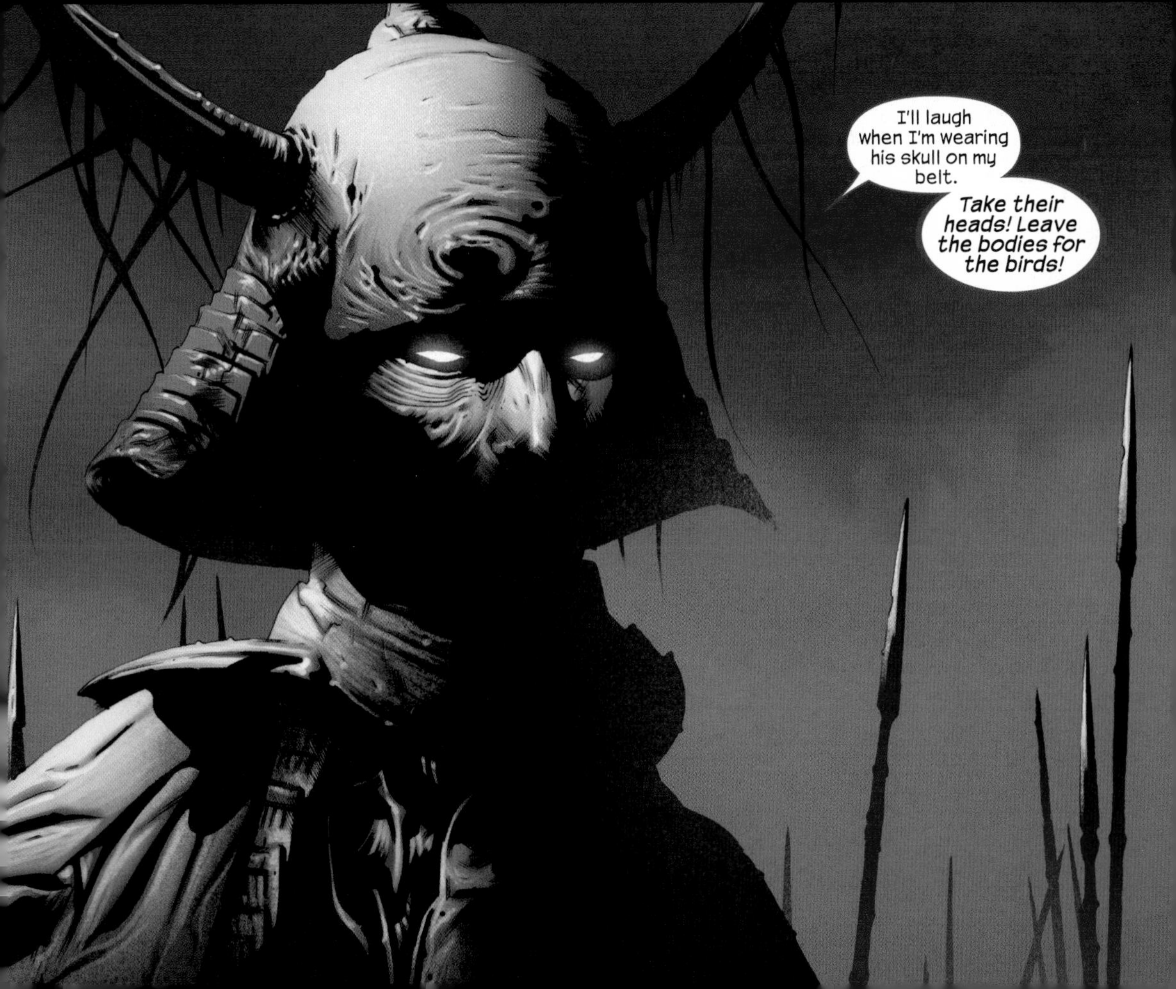
I'll laugh when I'm wearing his skull on my belt.
Take their heads! Leave the bodies for the birds!

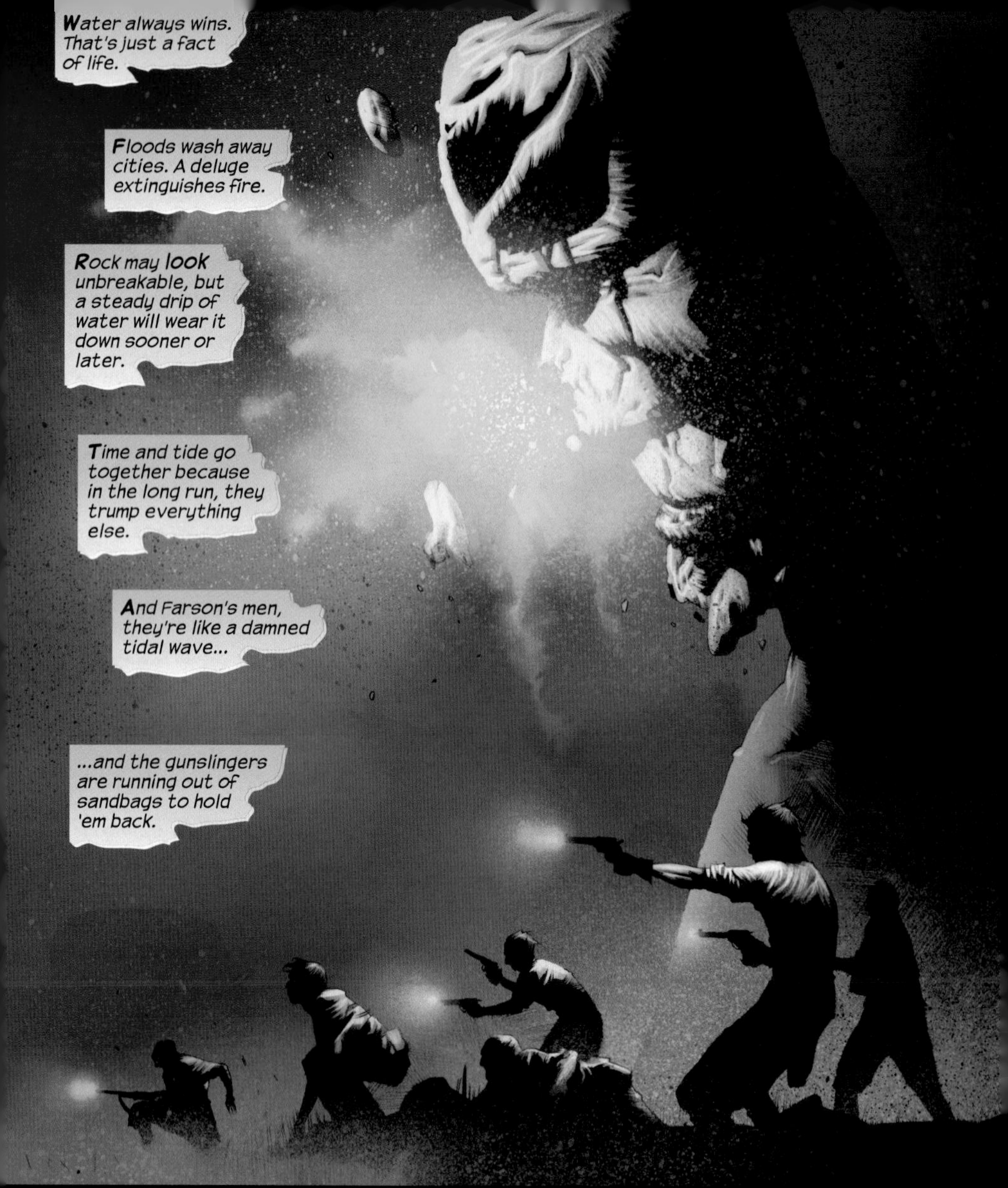
Water always wins. That's just a fact of life.
Floods wash away cities. A deluge extinguishes fire.
Rock may look unbreakable, but a steady drip of water will wear it down sooner or later.
Time and tide go together because in the long run, they trump everything else.
And Farson's men, they're like a damned tidal wave...
...and the gunslingers are running out of sandbags to hold 'em back.

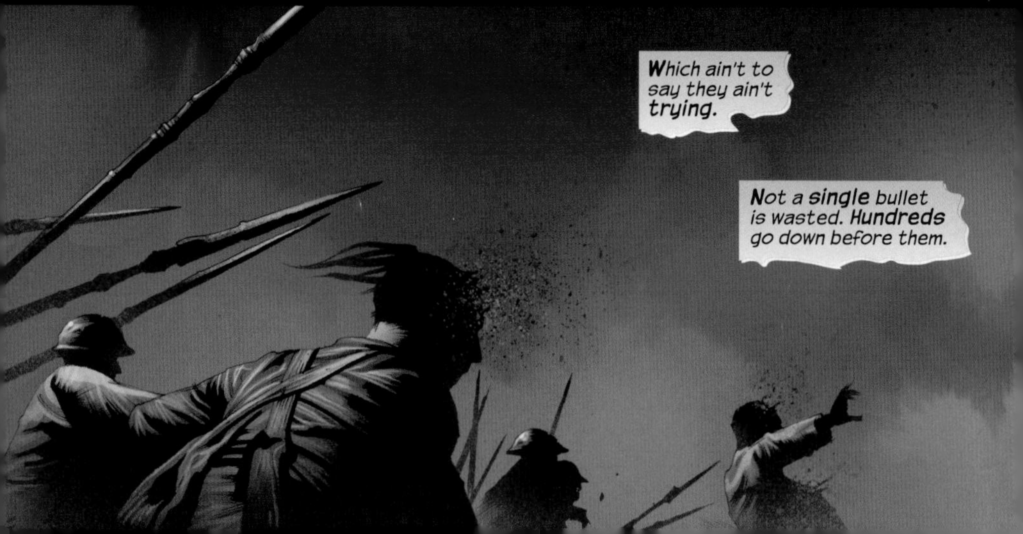
Which ain't to say they ain't trying.
Not a single bullet is wasted. Hundreds go down before them.

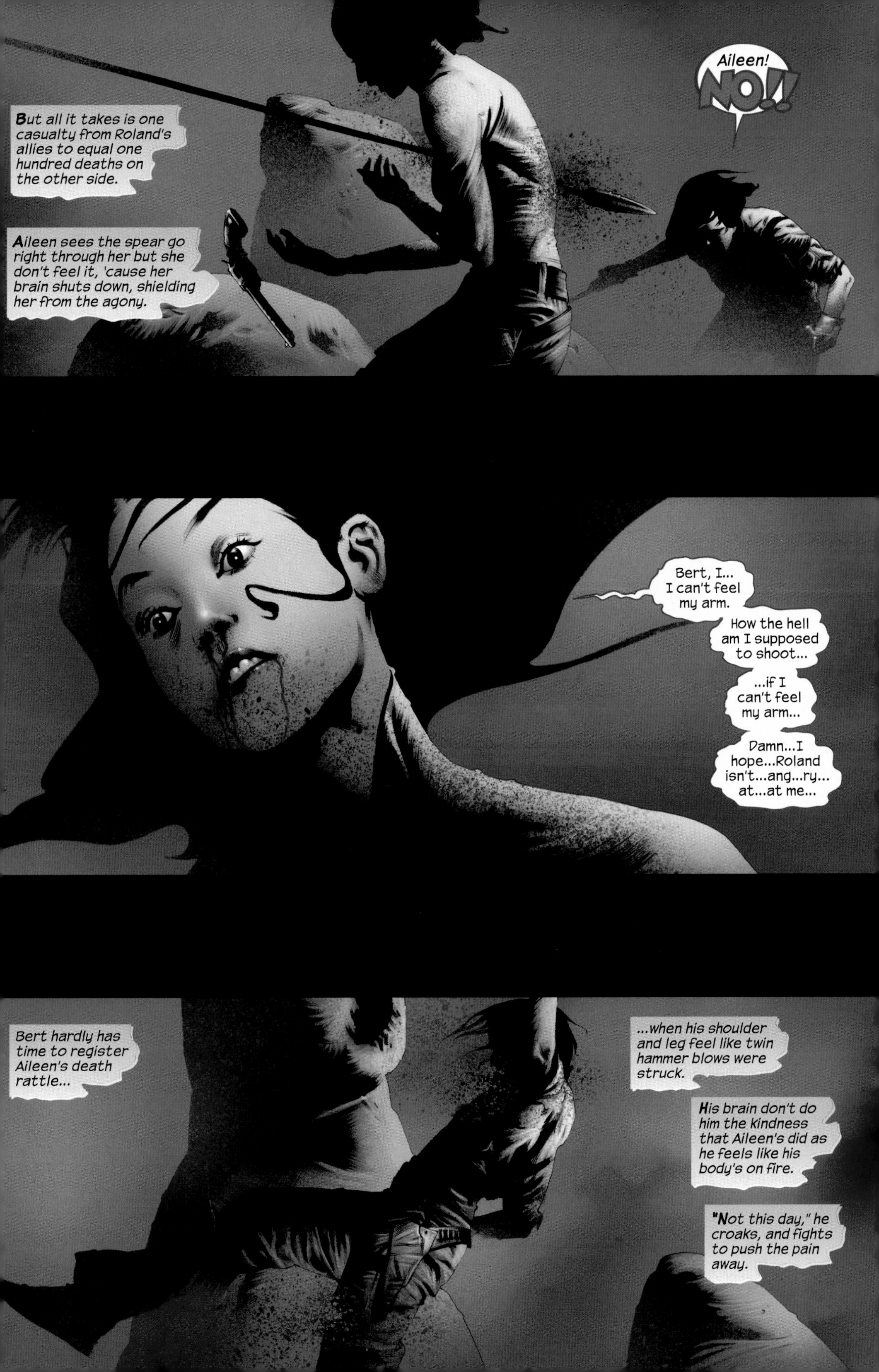
But all it takes is one casualty from Roland's allies to equal one hundred deaths on the other side.
Aileen! NO!!
Aileen sees the spear go right through her but she don't feel it, 'cause her brain shuts down, shielding her from the agony.
Bert, I... I can't feel my arm.
How the hell am I supposed to shoot...
...if I can't feel my arm...
Damn...I hope...Roland isn't...ang...ry... at...at me...
Bert hardly has time to register Aileen's death rattle...
...when his shoulder and leg feel like twin hammer blows were struck.
His brain don't do him the kindness that Aileen's did as he feels like his body's on fire.
"Not this day," he croaks, and fights to push the pain away.

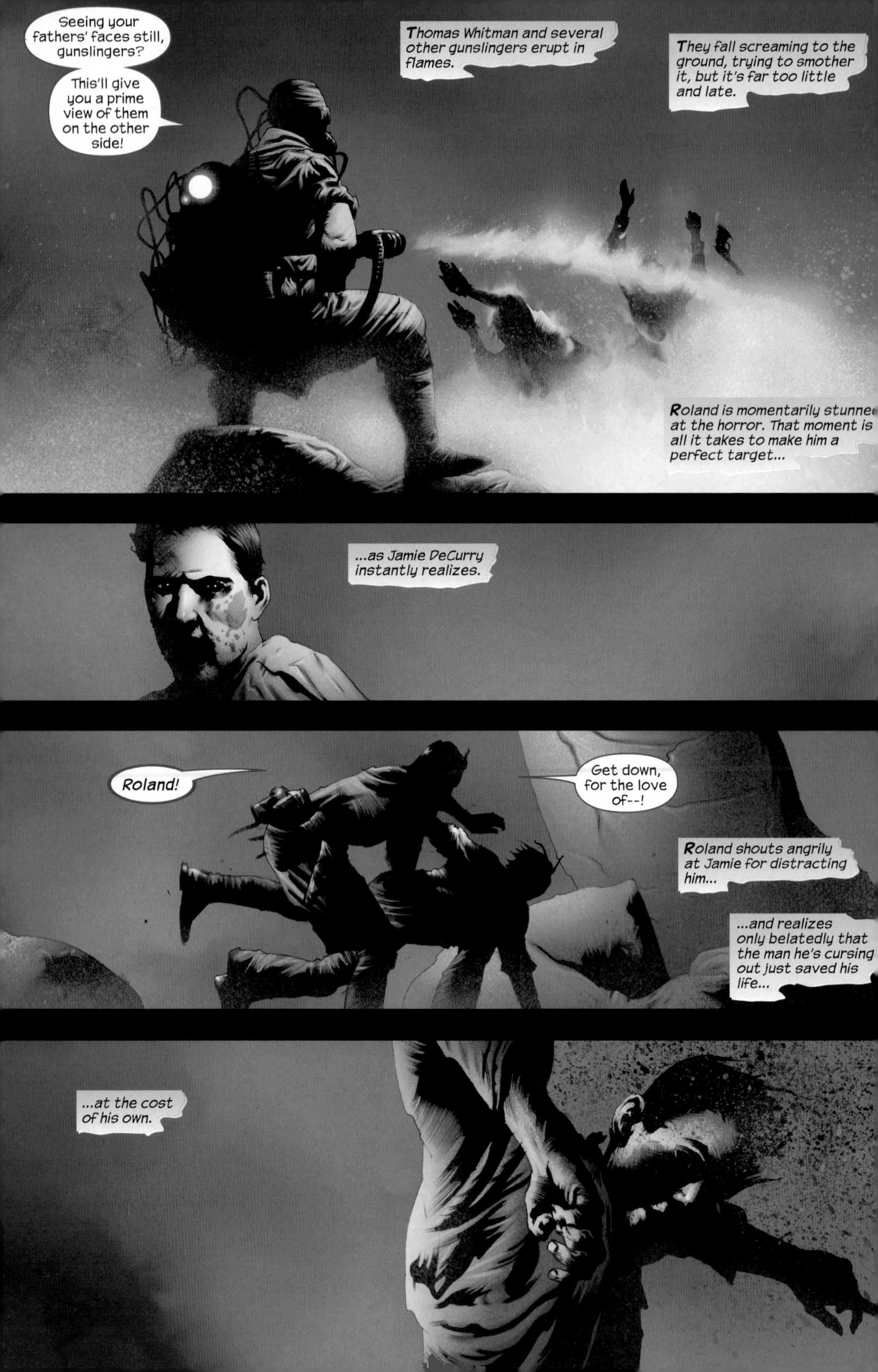
Seeing your fathers' faces still, gunslingers?
This'll give you a prime view of them on the other side!
Thomas Whitman and several other gunslingers erupt in flames.
They fall screaming to the ground, trying to smother it, but it's far too little and late.
Roland is momentarily stunne at the horror. That moment is all it takes to make him a perfect target...
...as Jamie DeCurry instantly realizes.
Roland!
Get down, for the love of--!
Roland shouts angrily at Jamie for distracting him...
...and realizes only belatedly that the man he's cursing out just saved his life...
...at the cost of his own.

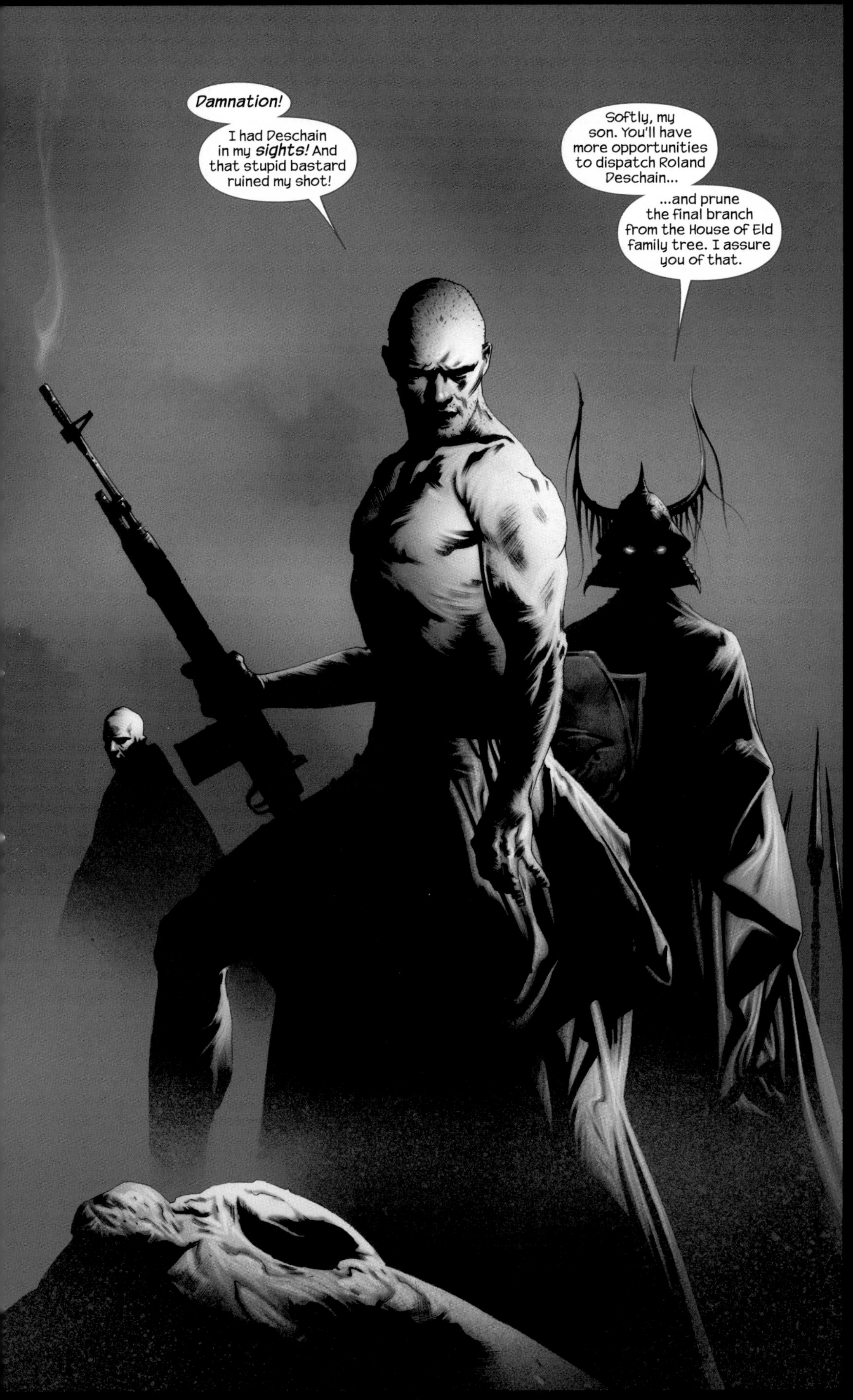
Damnation!
I had Deschain in my *sights!* And that stupid bastard ruined my shot!
Softly, my son. You'll have more opportunities to dispatch Roland Deschain...
...and prune the final branch from the House of Eld family tree. I assure you of that.

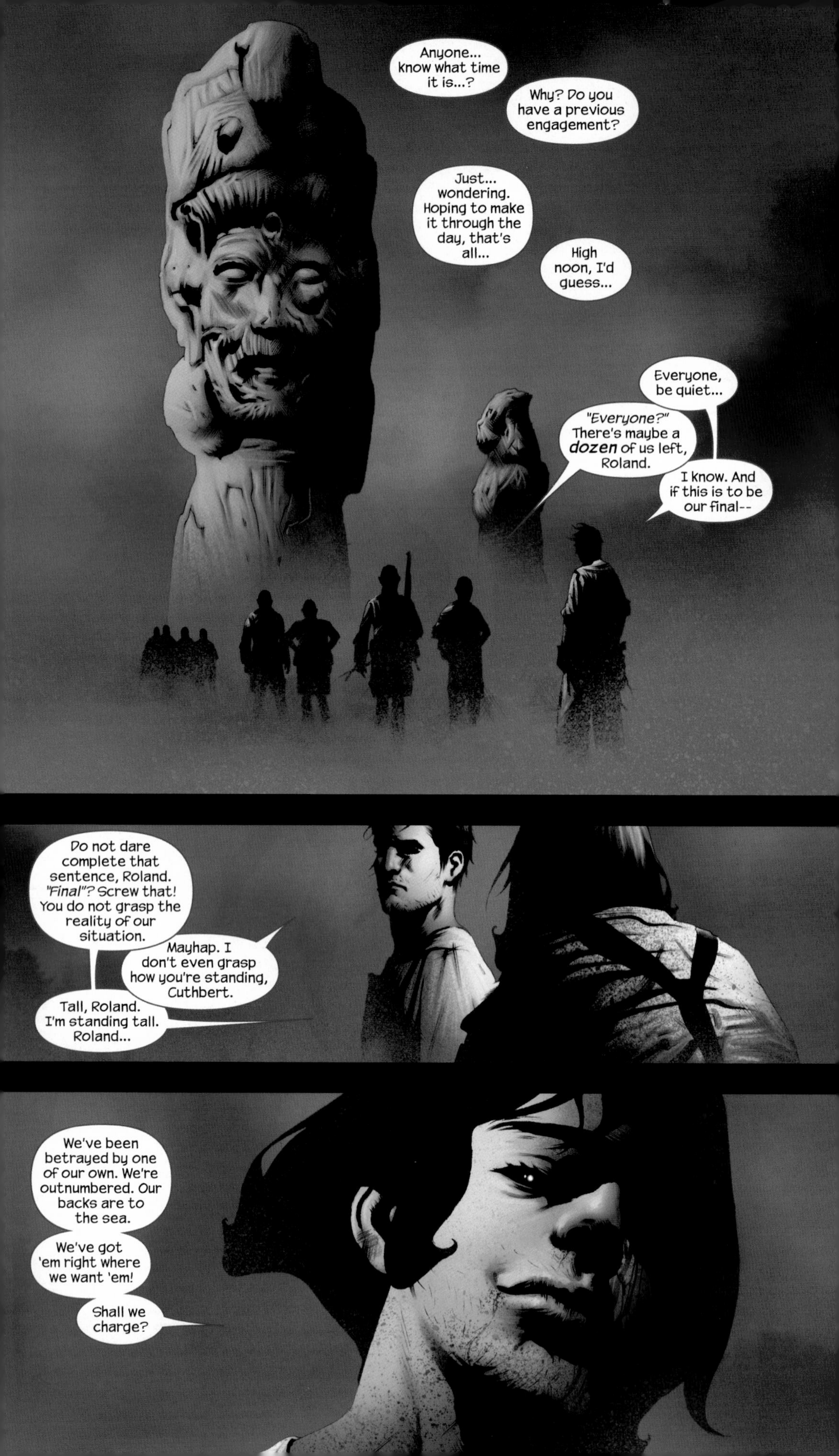

Anyone... know what time it is...?
Why? Do you have a previous engagement?
Just... wondering. Hoping to make it through the day, that's all...
High noon, I'd guess...
Everyone, be quiet...
"Everyone?" There's maybe a **dozen** of us left, Roland.
I know. And if this is to be our final--
Do not dare complete that sentence, Roland. *"Final"?* Screw that! You do not grasp the reality of our situation.
Mayhap. I don't even grasp how you're standing, Cuthbert.
Tall, Roland. I'm standing tall. Roland...
We've been betrayed by one of our own. We're outnumbered. Our backs are to the sea.
We've got 'em right where we want 'em!
Shall we charge?

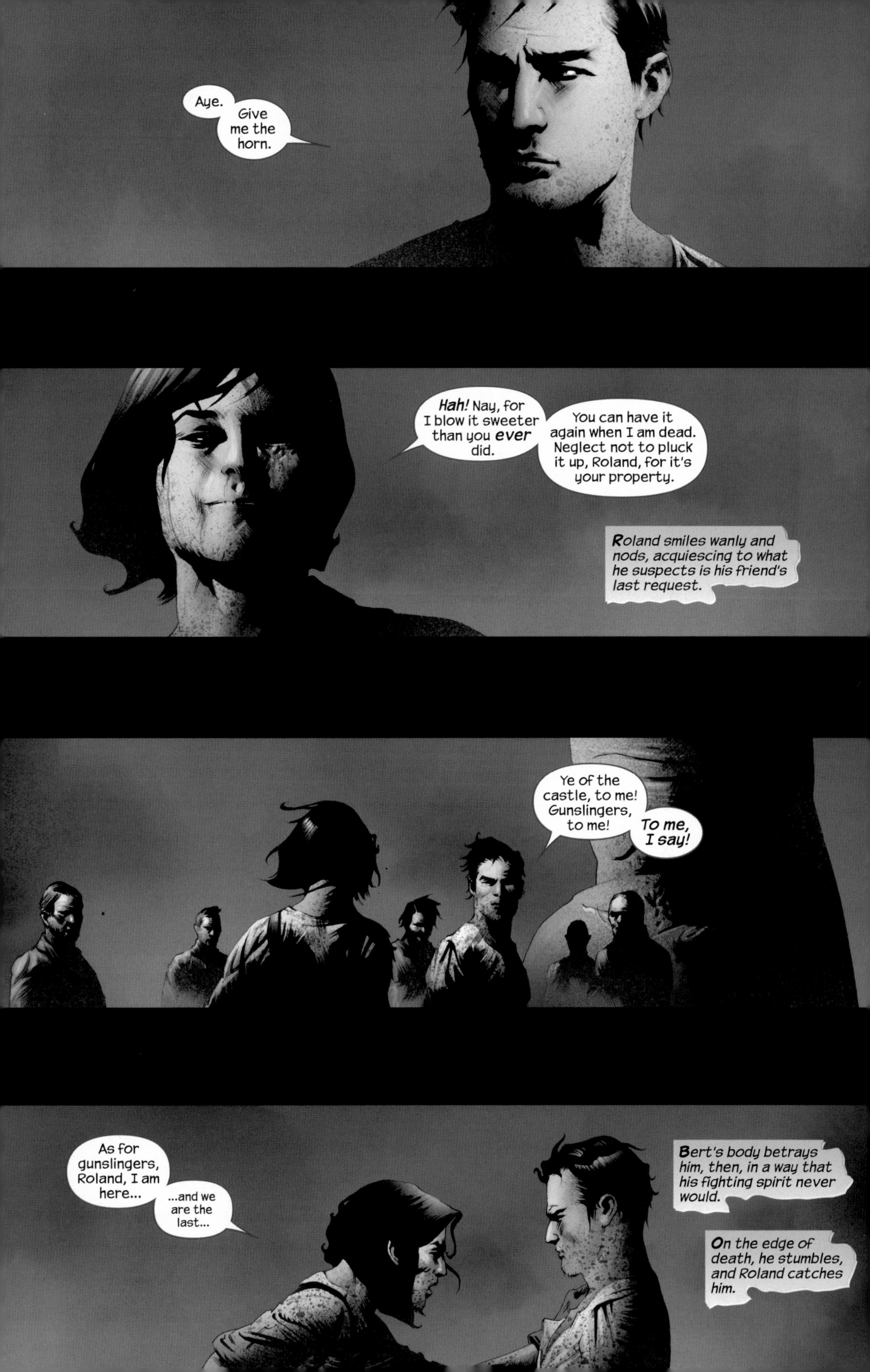

Aye. Give me the horn.
Hah! Nay, for I blow it sweeter than you ever did.
You can have it again when I am dead. Neglect not to pluck it up, Roland, for it's your property.
Roland smiles wanly and nods, acquiescing to what he suspects is his friend's last request.
Ye of the castle, to me! Gunslingers, to me!
To me, I say!
As for gunslingers, Roland, I am here...
...and we are the last...
Bert's body betrays him, then, in a way that his fighting spirit never would.
On the edge of death, he stumbles, and Roland catches him.

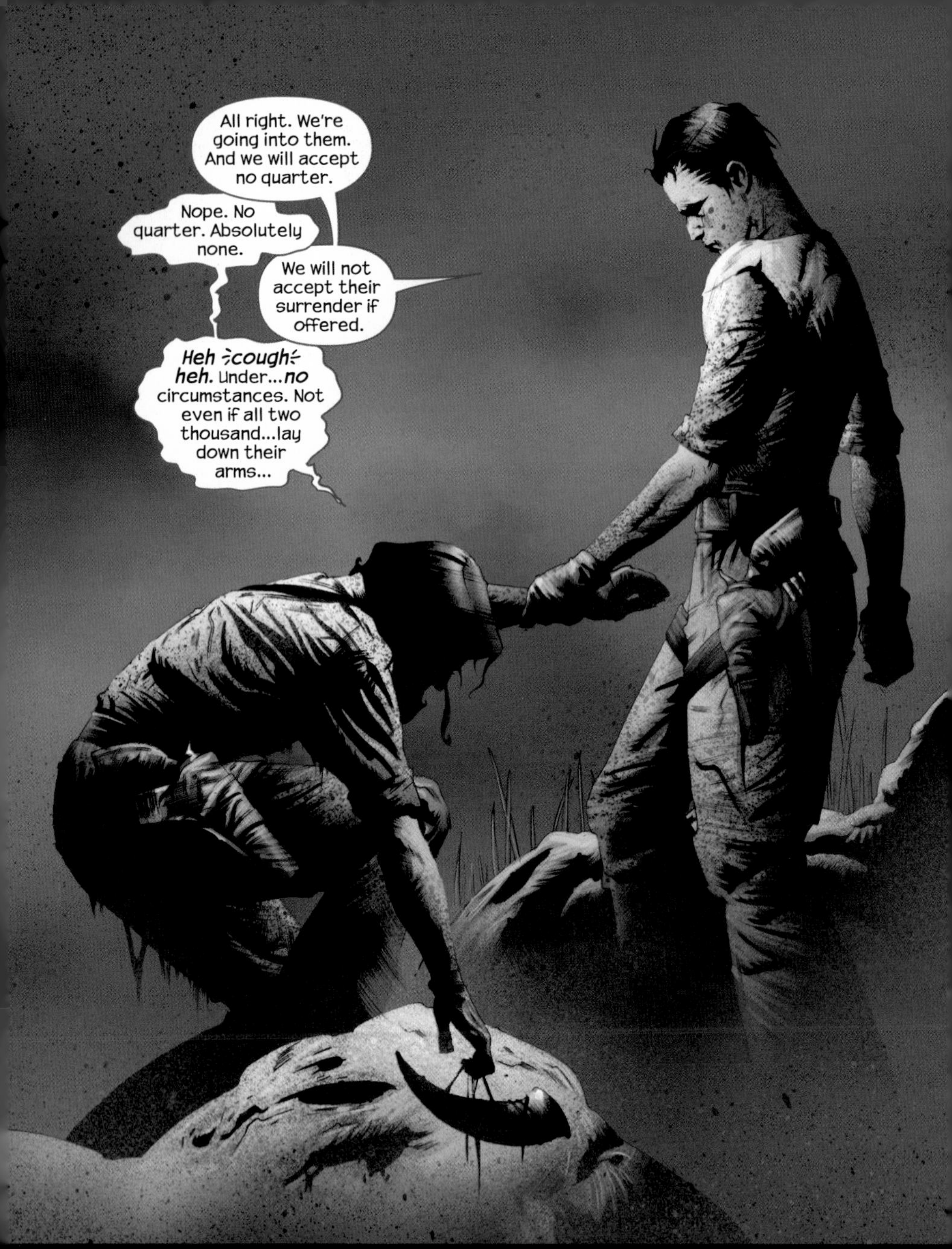
All right. We're going into them. And we will accept no quarter.
Nope. No quarter. Absolutely none.
We will not accept their surrender if offered.
Heh ⁼cough⁼ heh. Under...no circumstances. Not even if all two thousand...lay down their arms...

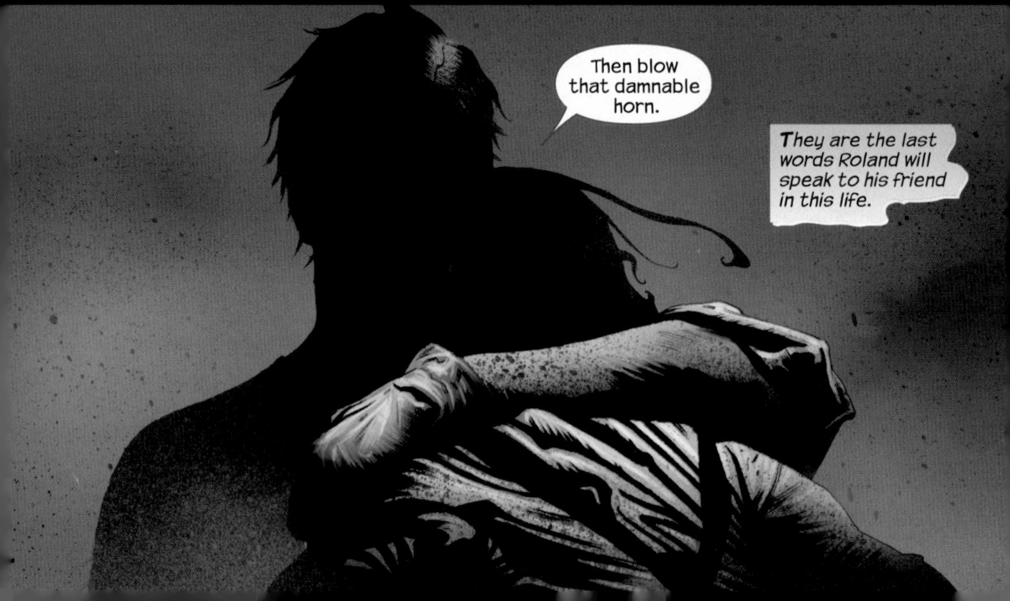
Then blow that damnable horn.
They are the last words Roland will speak to his friend in this life.

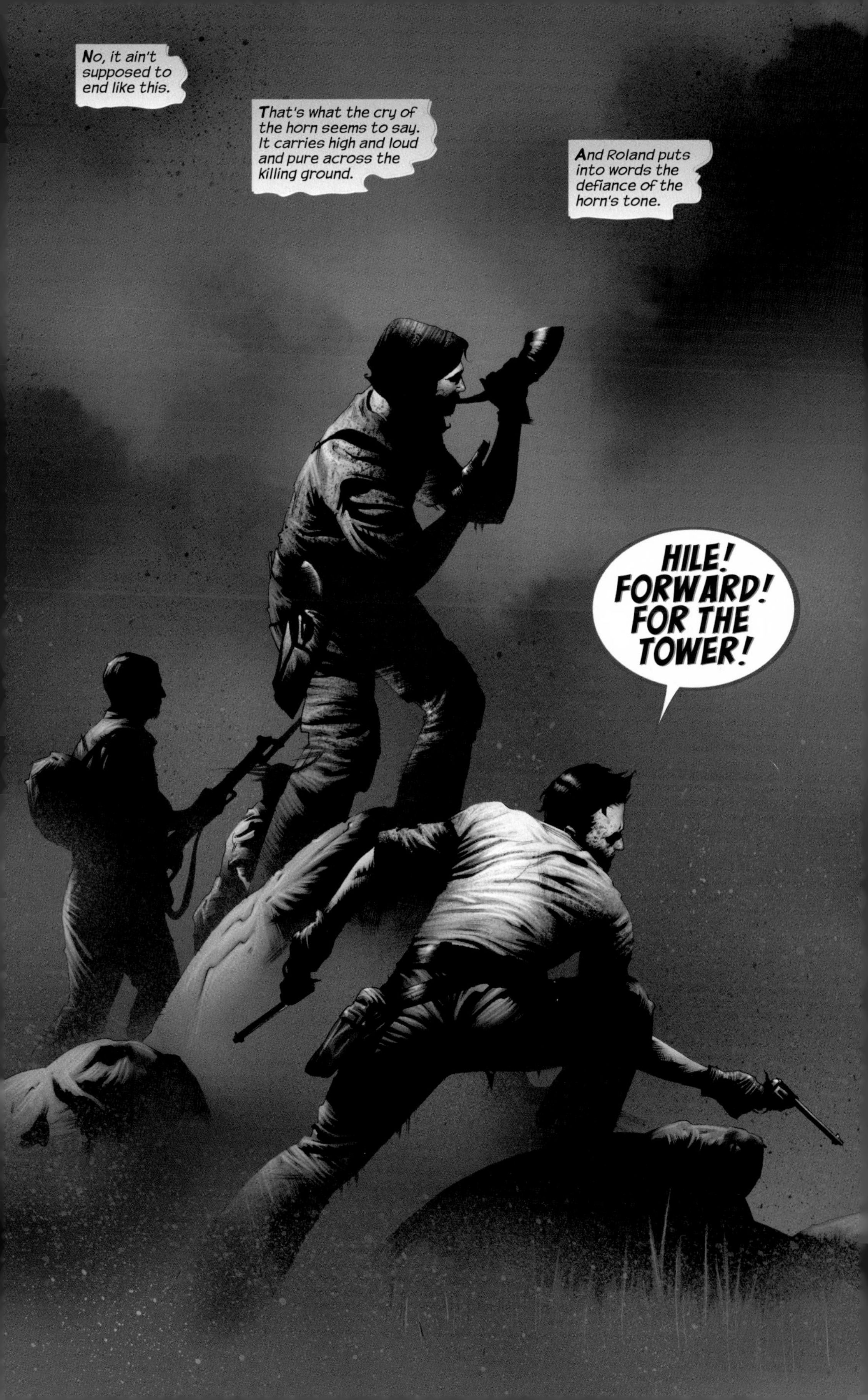
No, it ain't supposed to end like this.
That's what the cry of the horn seems to say. It carries high and loud and pure across the killing ground.
And Roland puts into words the defiance of the horn's tone.
HILE! FORWARD! FOR THE TOWER!

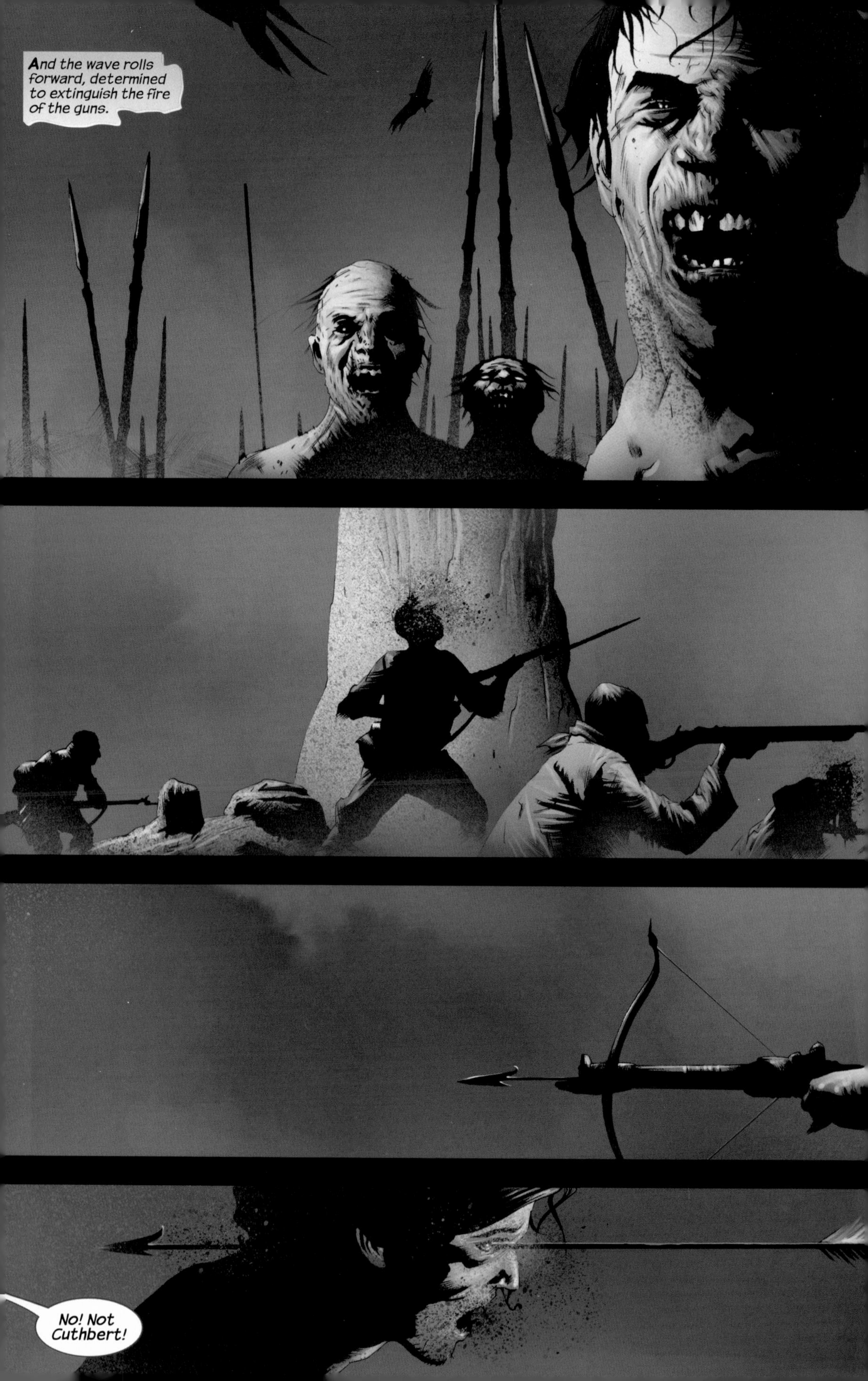
And the wave rolls forward, determined to extinguish the fire of the guns.
No! Not Cuthbert!

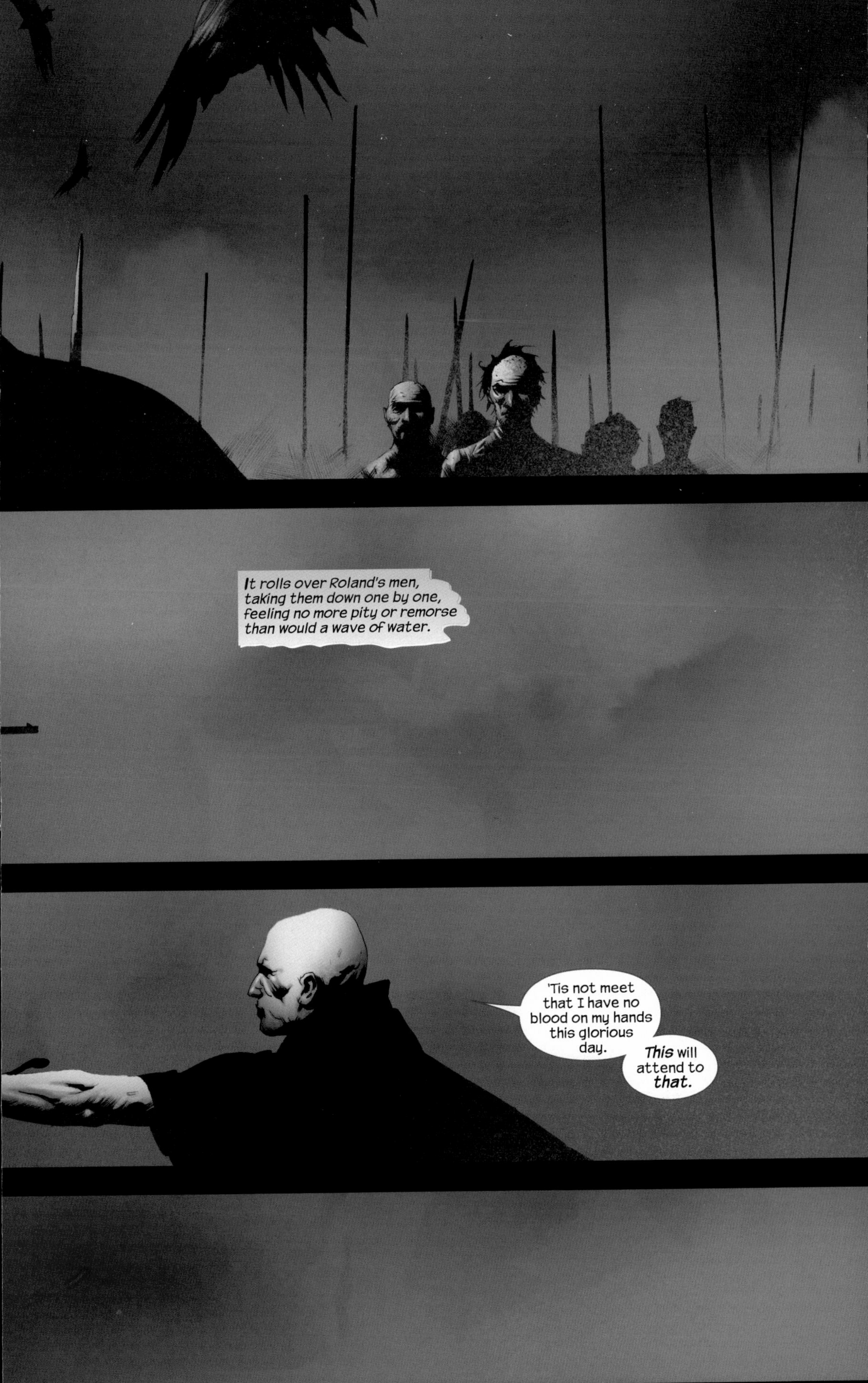
It rolls over Roland's men, taking them down one by one, feeling no more pity or remorse than would a wave of water.
'Tis not meet that I have no blood on my hands this glorious day.
This will attend to *that.*

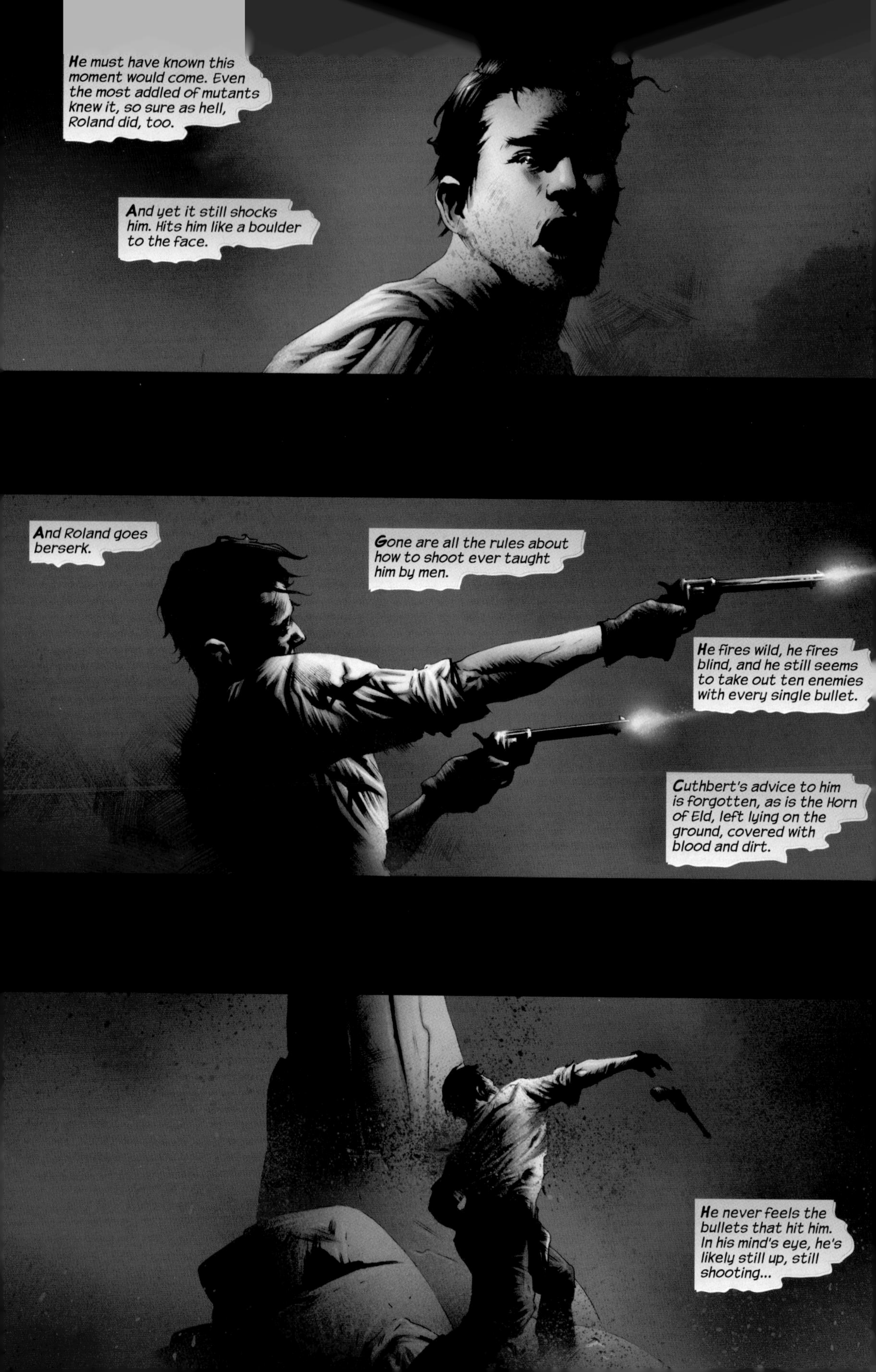
He must have known this moment would come. Even the most addled of mutants knew it, so sure as hell, Roland did, too.
And yet it still shocks him. Hits him like a boulder to the face.
And Roland goes berserk.
Gone are all the rules about how to shoot ever taught him by men.
He fires wild, he fires blind, and he still seems to take out ten enemies with every single bullet.
Cuthbert's advice to him is forgotten, as is the Horn of Eld, left lying on the ground, covered with blood and dirt.
He never feels the bullets that hit him. In his mind's eye, he's likely still up, still shooting...

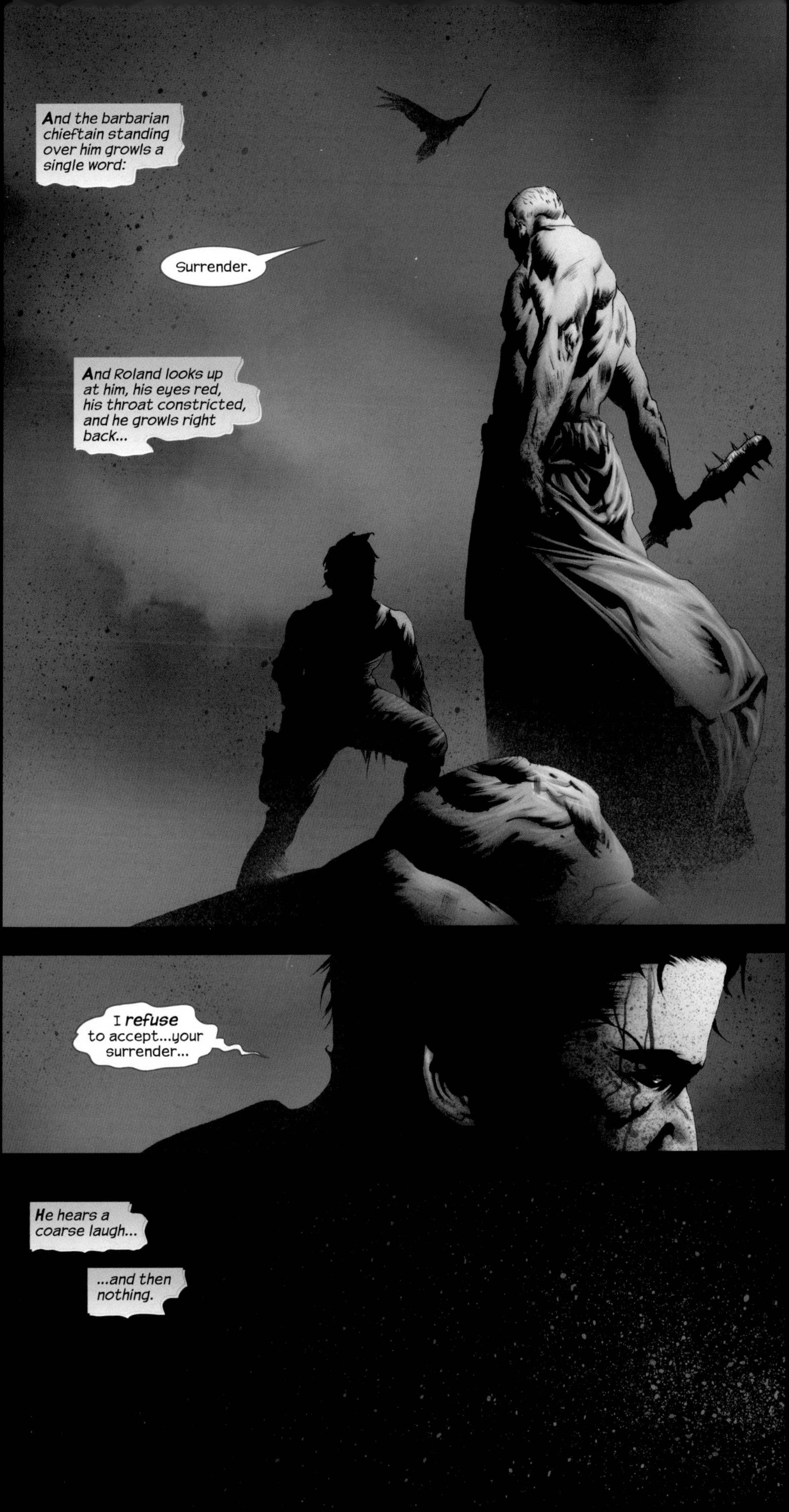
And the barbarian chieftain standing over him growls a single word:
Surrender.
And Roland looks up at him, his eyes red, his throat constricted, and he growls right back...
I *refuse* to accept...your surrender...
He hears a coarse laugh...
...and then nothing.

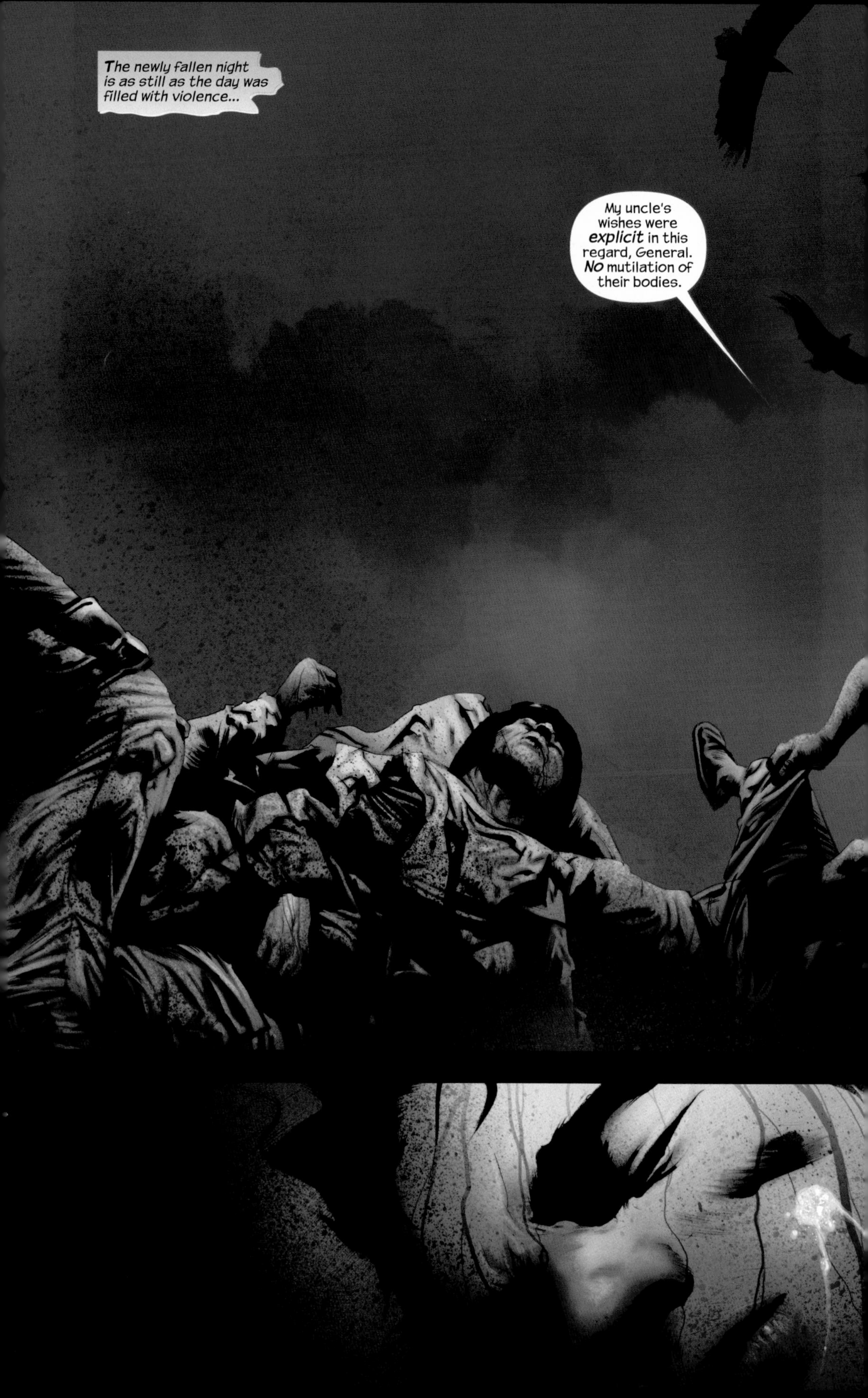
The newly fallen night is as still as the day was filled with violence...
My uncle's wishes were explicit in this regard, General. NO mutilation of their bodies.

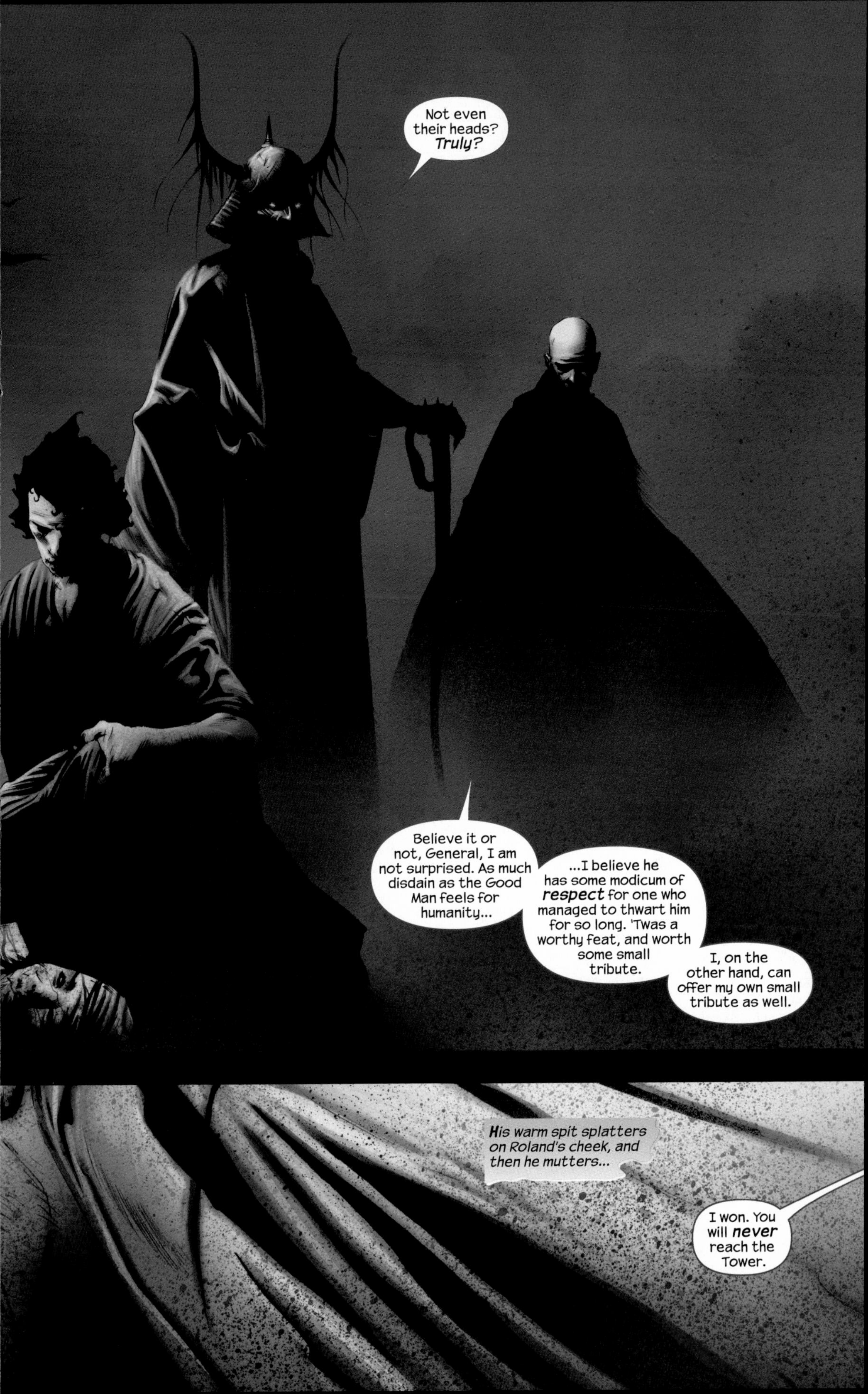

Not even their heads? *Truly?*
Believe it or not, General, I am not surprised. As much disdain as the Good Man feels for humanity...
...I believe he has some modicum of **respect** for one who managed to thwart him for so long. 'Twas a worthy feat, and worth some small tribute.
I, on the other hand, can offer my own small tribute as well.
His warm spit splatters on Roland's cheek, and then he mutters...
I won. You will **never** reach the Tower.

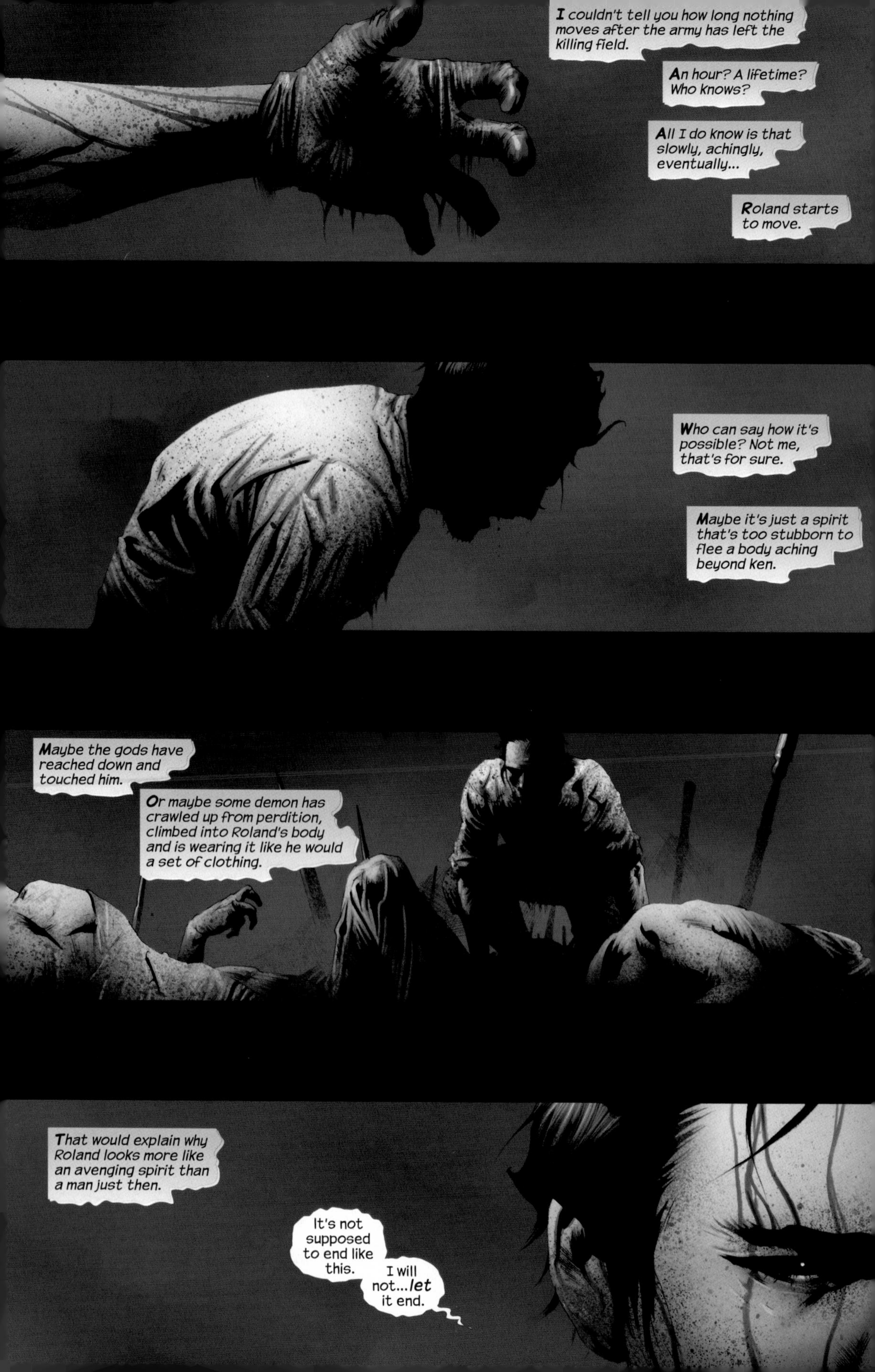

I couldn't tell you how long nothing moves after the army has left the killing field.
An hour? A lifetime? Who knows?
All I do know is that slowly, achingly, eventually...
Roland starts to move.
Who can say how it's possible? Not me, that's for sure.
Maybe it's just a spirit that's too stubborn to flee a body aching beyond ken.
Maybe the gods have reached down and touched him.
Or maybe some demon has crawled up from perdition, climbed into Roland's body and is wearing it like he would a set of clothing.
That would explain why Roland looks more like an avenging spirit than a man just then.
It's not supposed to end like this.
I will not...let it end.

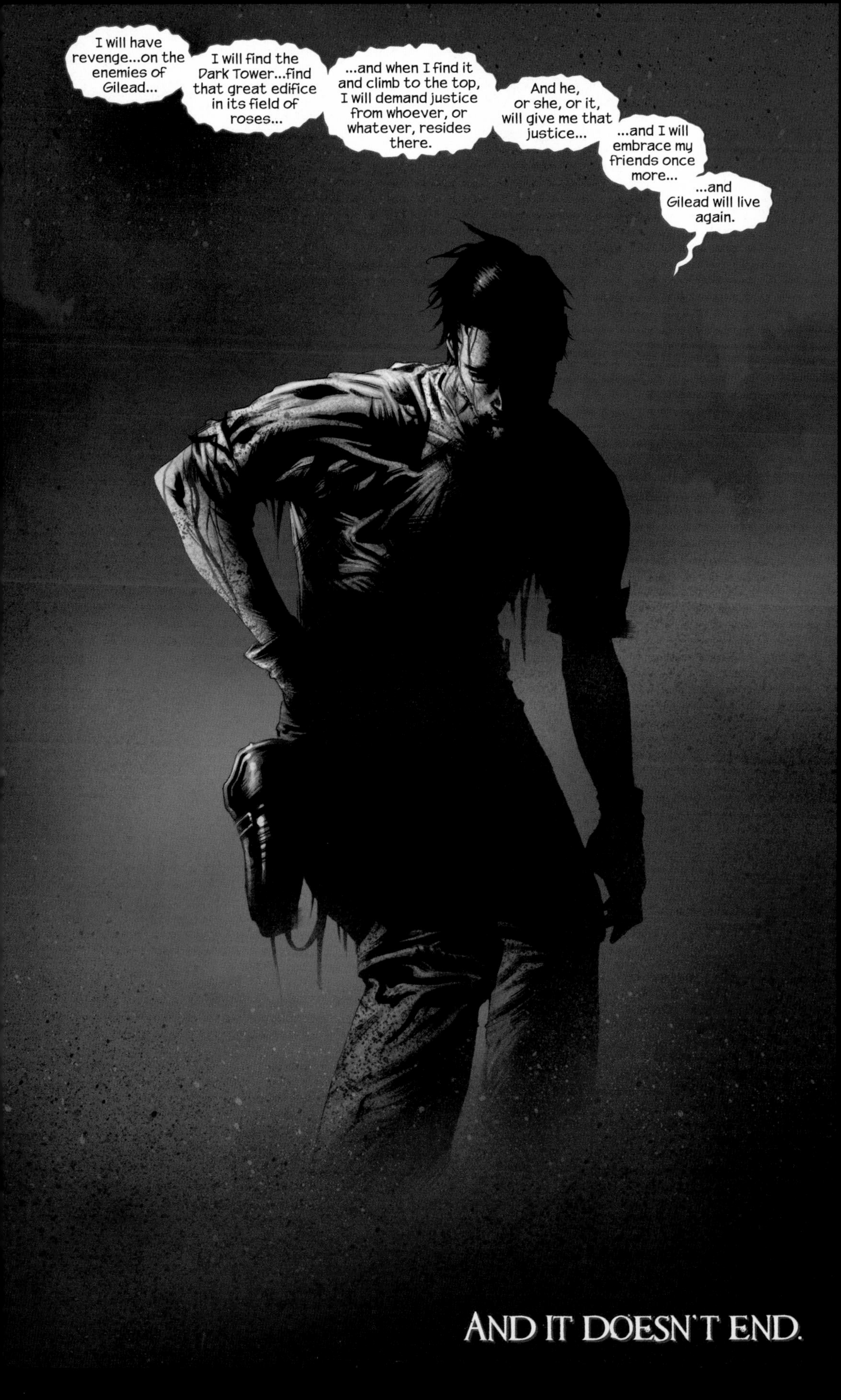

I will have revenge...on the enemies of Gilead...
I will find the Dark Tower...find that great edifice in its field of roses...
...and when I find it and climb to the top, I will demand justice from whoever, or whatever, resides there.
And he, or she, or it, will give me that justice...
...and I will embrace my friends once more...
...and Gilead will live again.
AND IT DOESN'T END.

The story continues in...

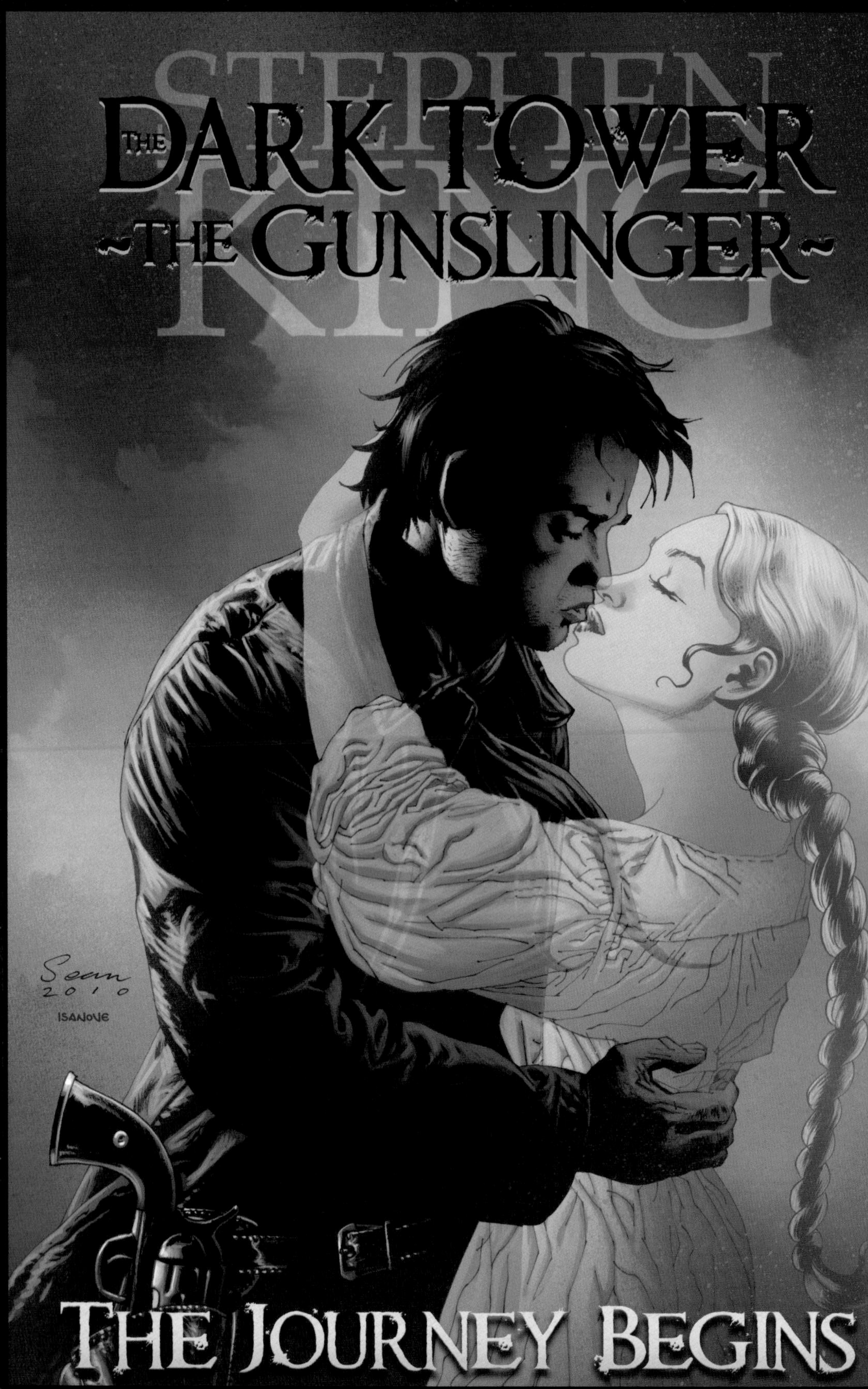
STEPHEN KING
THE DARK TOWER
~THE GUNSLINGER~
Sean 2010
ISANOVE
THE JOURNEY BEGINS

THE DARK TOWER READING CHRONOLOGY

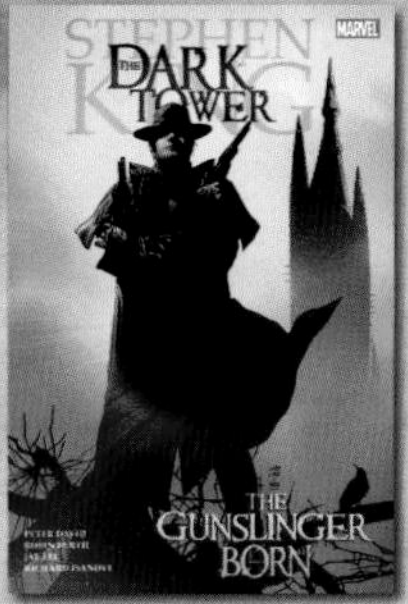
STEPHEN KING
DARK TOWER
MARVEL
THE GUNSLINGER BORN

BOOK 1

THE DARK TOWER THE GUNSLINGER BORN

ISBN: 978 0 7851 2144 2

A man's quest begins with a boy's test.

The world of Roland Deschain — the world of the Dark Tower — has been a thirty-year obsession for Stephen King. And now, King carries his masterwork of fantasy to Marvel, bringing stunning new textures to his epic story!

The Gunslinger Born seamlessly integrates the wonder of Mid-World and the story of its hard-bitten cast of characters into the finest Marvel Comics storytelling tradition.

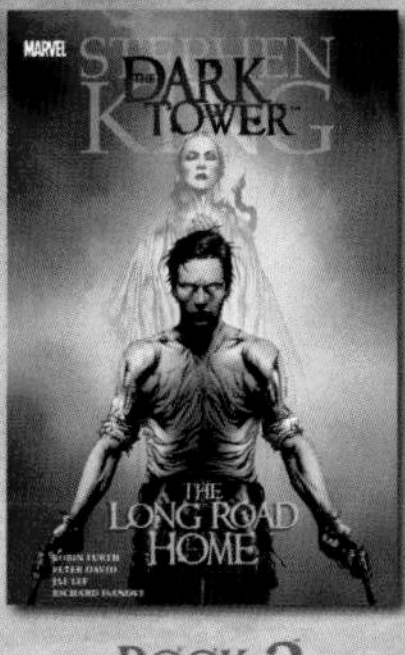
MARVEL
STEPHEN KING
DARK TOWER
THE LONG ROAD HOME

BOOK 2

THE DARK TOWER THE LONG ROAD HOME

ISBN: 978 0 7851 2709 3

The gunslinger is born into a harsh world of mystery and violence.

Susan Delgado is dead. Clay Reynolds and the vestiges of the Big Coffin Hunters are in pursuit. The ka-tet fragments as evil abounds. It will be a long road home. With Roland seemingly lost inside the haunted world of Maerlyn's Grapefruit, and the dark forces therein tugging at his soul, it will take all the courage of his ka-tet to get him out of Hambry and back home. But as the Dogan stirs, portending an evil of which Roland and his ka-tet have no ken, it may very well be that the gunslinger born walks a long road home to death.

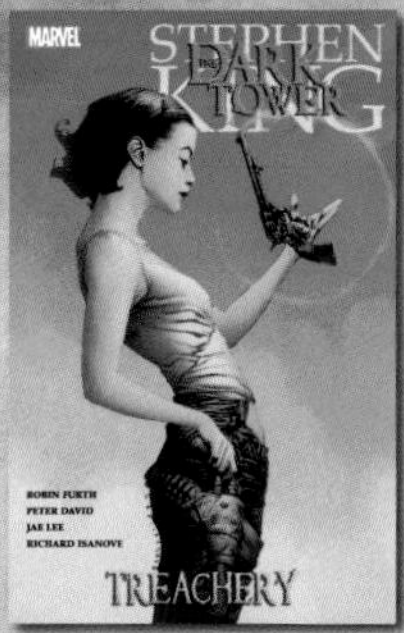
MARVEL
STEPHEN KING
DARK TOWER
ROBIN FURTH
PETER DAVID
JAE LEE
RICHARD ISANOVE
TREACHERY

BOOK 3

THE DARK TOWER TREACHERY

ISBN: 978 0 7851 3574 6

From the creative team that brought Roland's early adventures to life in *Dark Tower: The Gunslinger Born* and *Dark Tower: The Long Road Home* comes the third chapter of this dark saga of friendship, betrayal and a cosmic quest as conceived by master storyteller Stephen King.

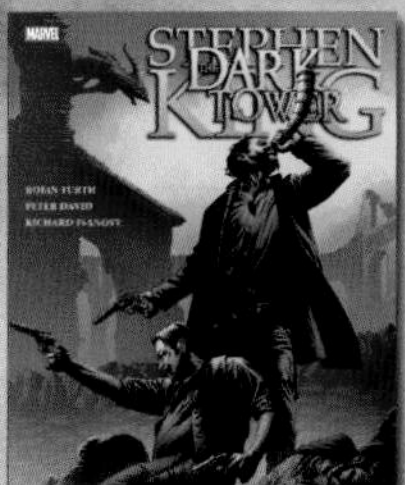
MARVEL
STEPHEN KING
DARK TOWER
FALL OF GILEAD

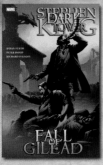

BOOK 4

THE DARK TOWER FALL OF GILEAD

ISBN: 978 0 7851 2951 6

How could you have done it, Roland? How could you have killed your own mother? That's what everyone in Gilead's asking — even your grieving father. But you know the answer: Marten Broadcloak and one of them evil grapefruits. That's how. And while you rot in jail, the plot your matricide was only one small part of is wrapping its bloody and black tendrils around Gilead. Your town — the home of the Gunslingers — is the prize possession of the great enemy of the land, John Farson. And he means to have it.

Gilead will fall, it will. And it will fall to the death of a thousand cuts. It started with your mother, yes, but it won't end there.

Dark Tower: Battle of Jericho Hill #1 **Cover by Jae Lee & Richard Isanove**

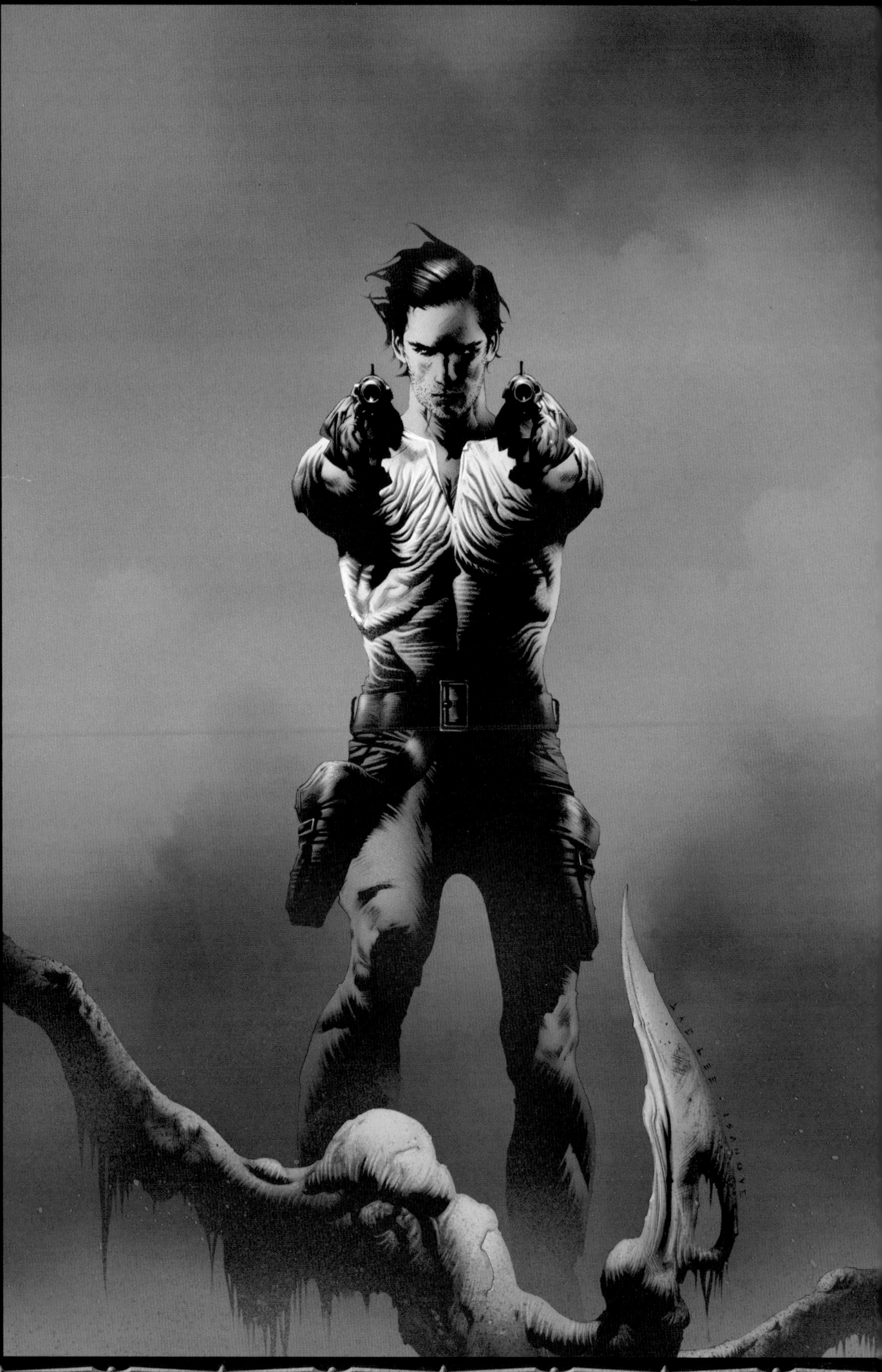

Dark Tower: Battle of Jericho Hill #1 **Variant Cover by Brandon Peterson**

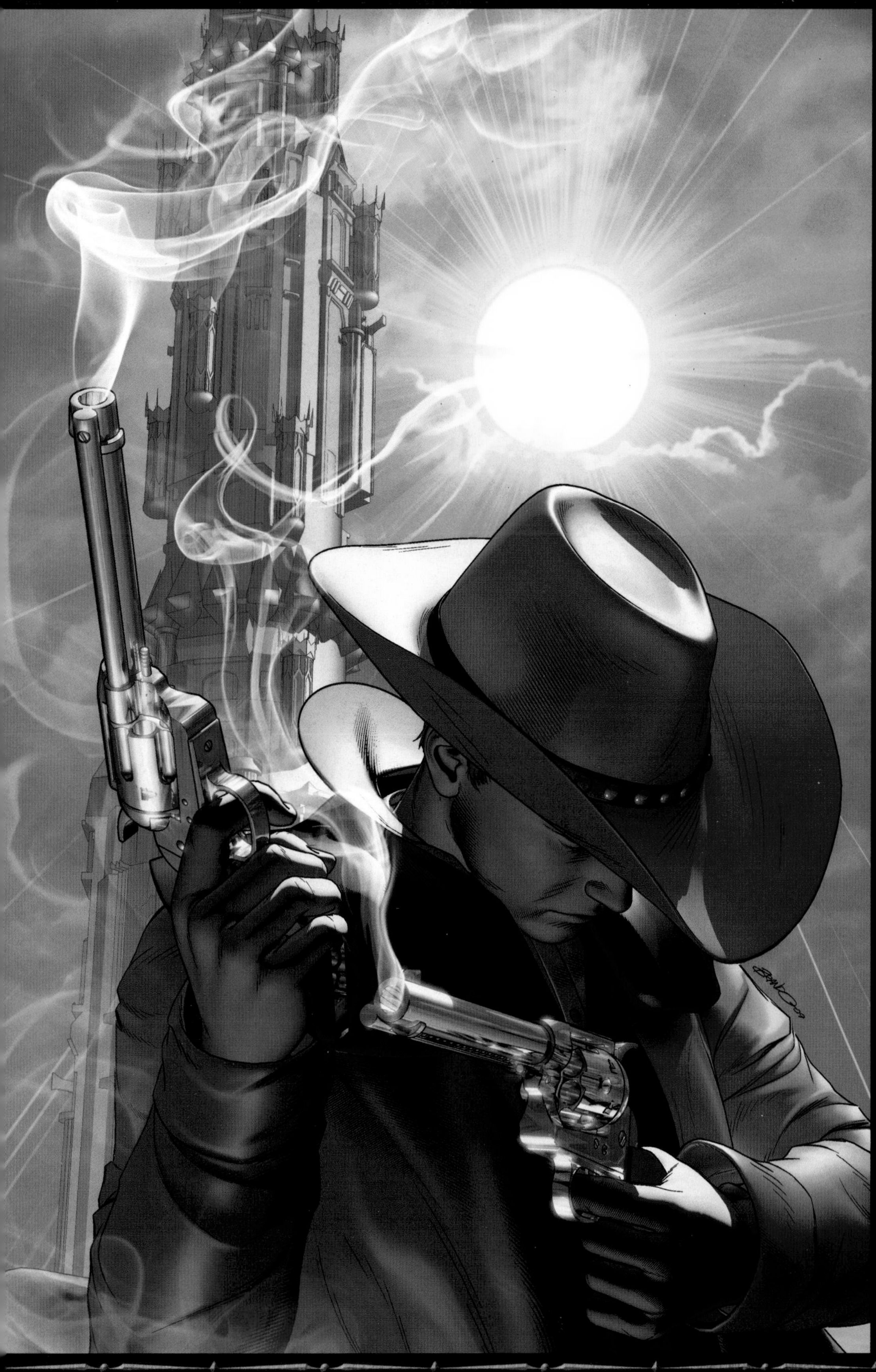

Dark Tower: Battle of Jericho Hill #2 **Cover by Jae Lee & Richard Isanove**

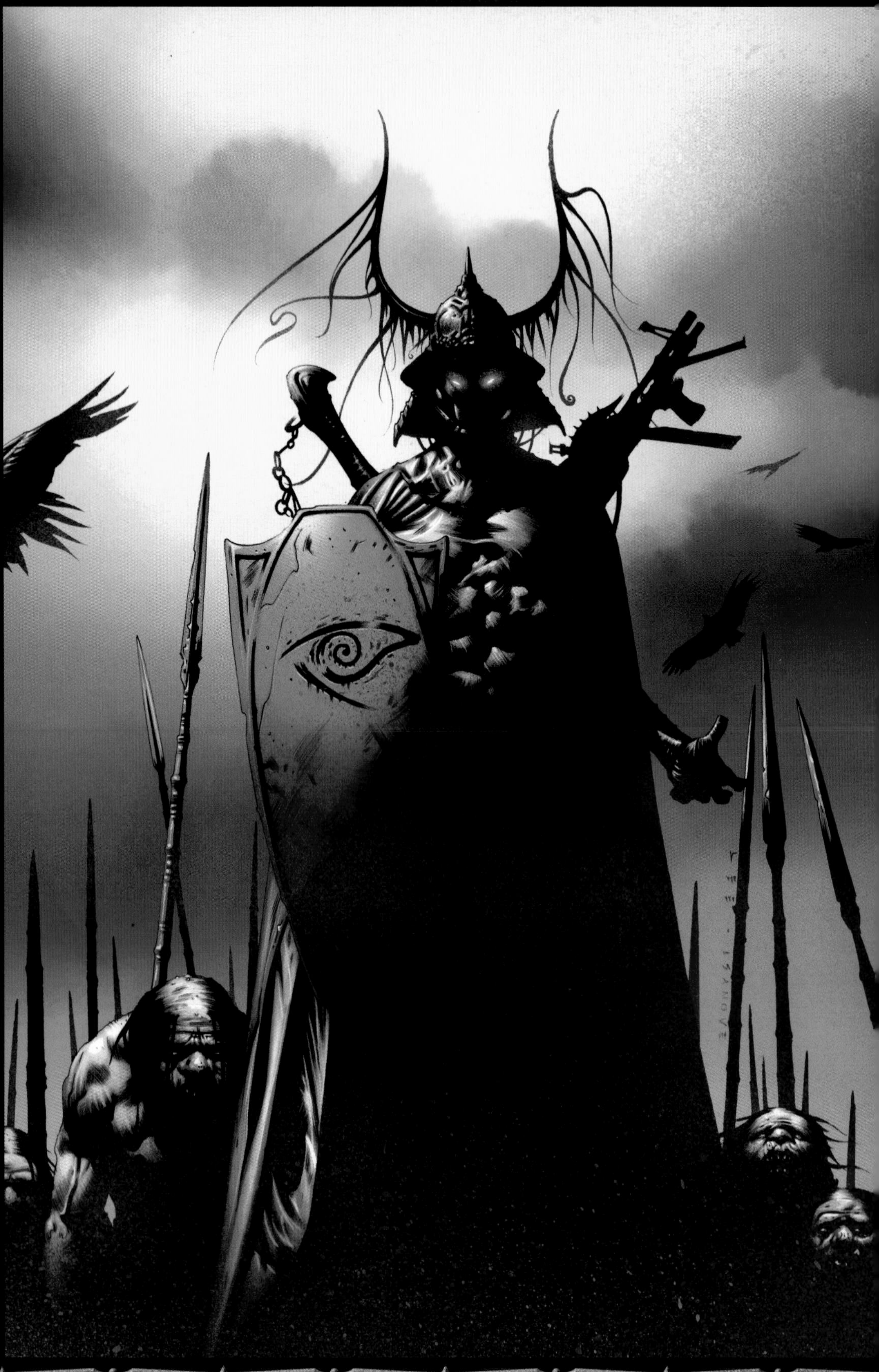

Dark Tower: Battle of Jericho Hill #2 **Variant Cover by Leonardo Manco & Jay David Ramos**

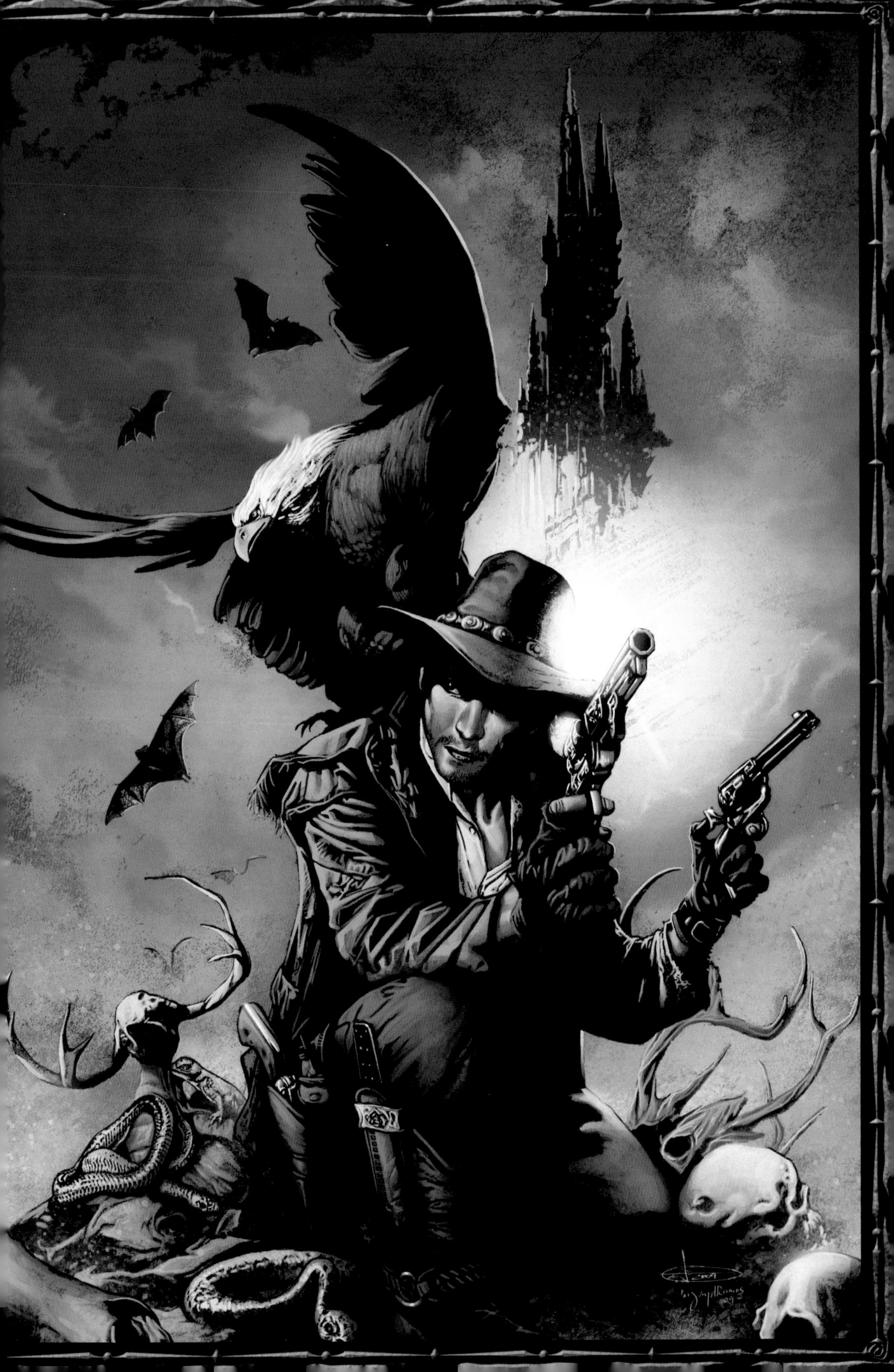

Dark Tower: Battle of Jericho Hill #3 **Cover by Jae Lee & Richard Isanove**

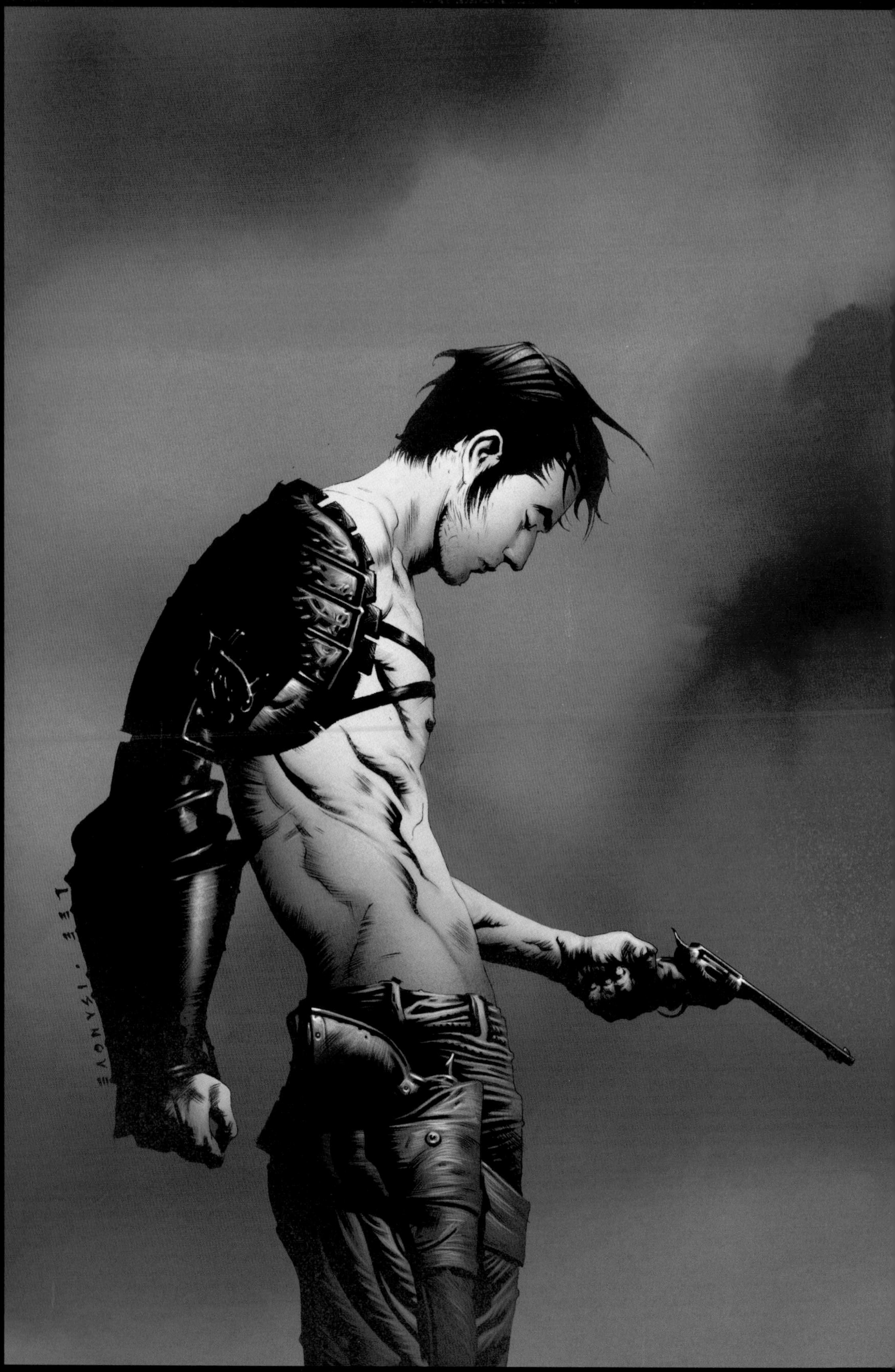

Dark Tower: Battle of Jericho Hill #3 **Variant Cover by Patrick Zircher & June Chung**

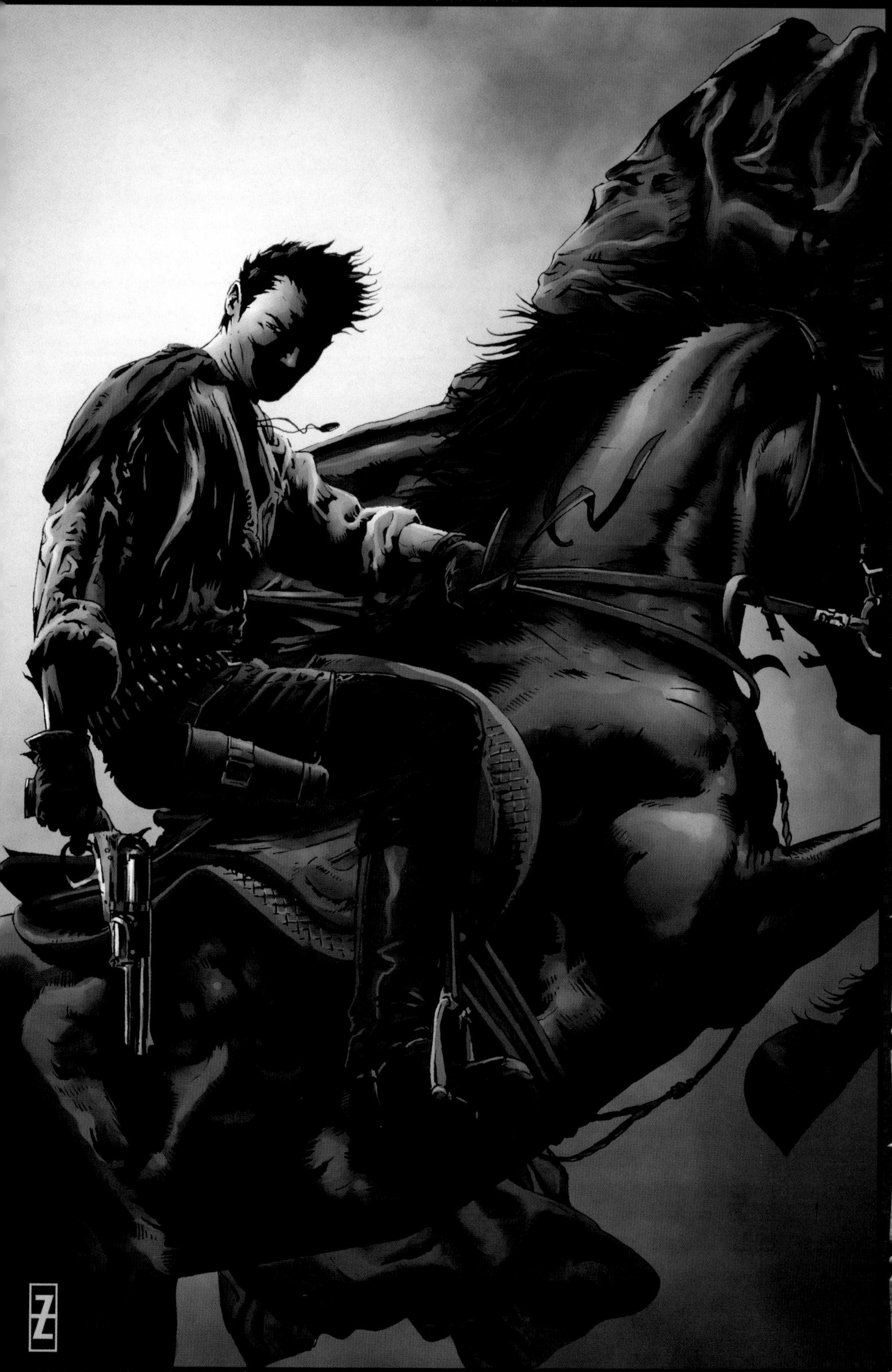

Dark Tower: Battle of Jericho Hill #4 **Cover by Jae Lee & Richard Isanove**

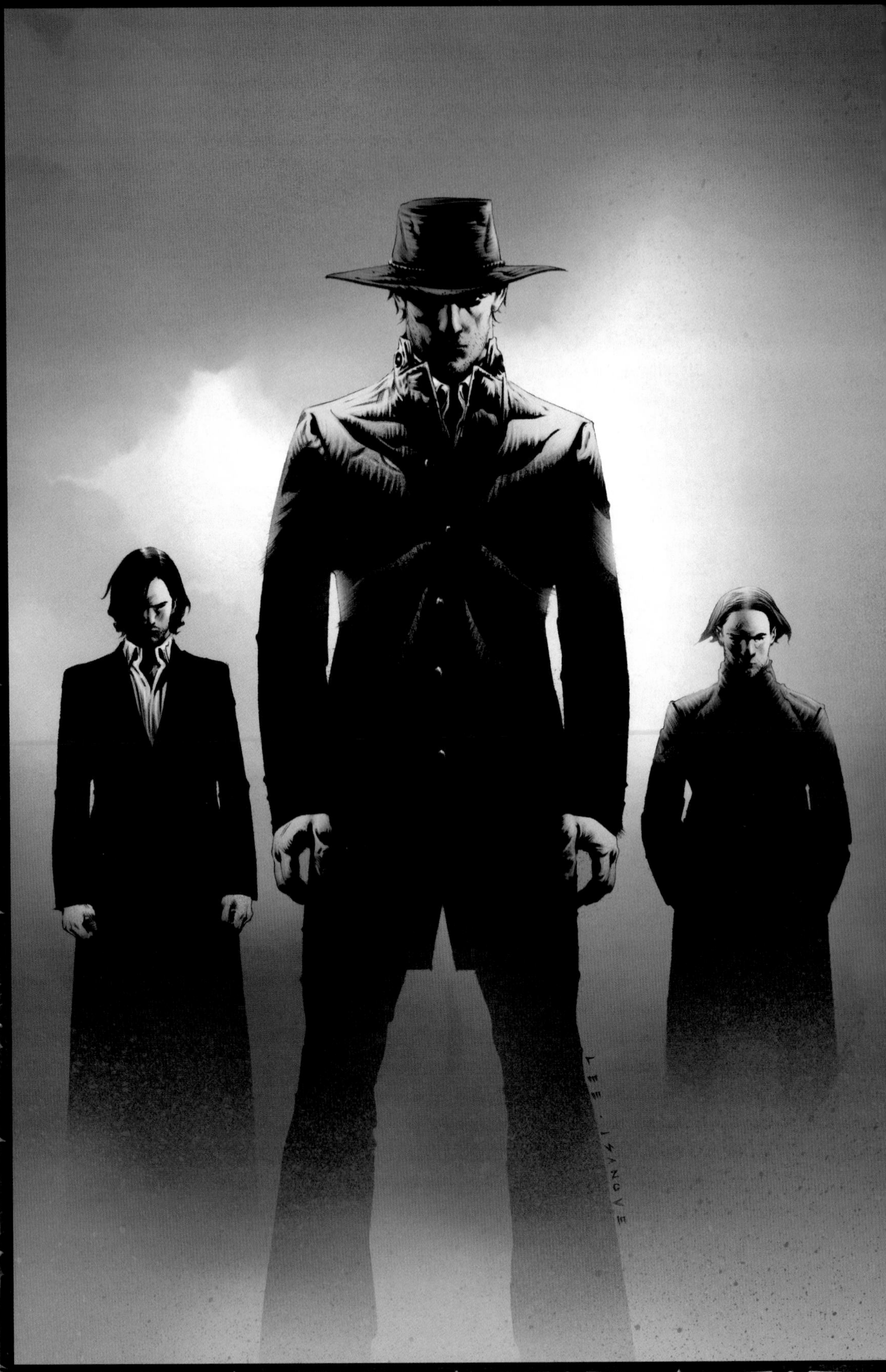

Dark Tower: Battle of Jericho Hill #4 **Variant Cover by Steve Kurth with Kai Spannuth**

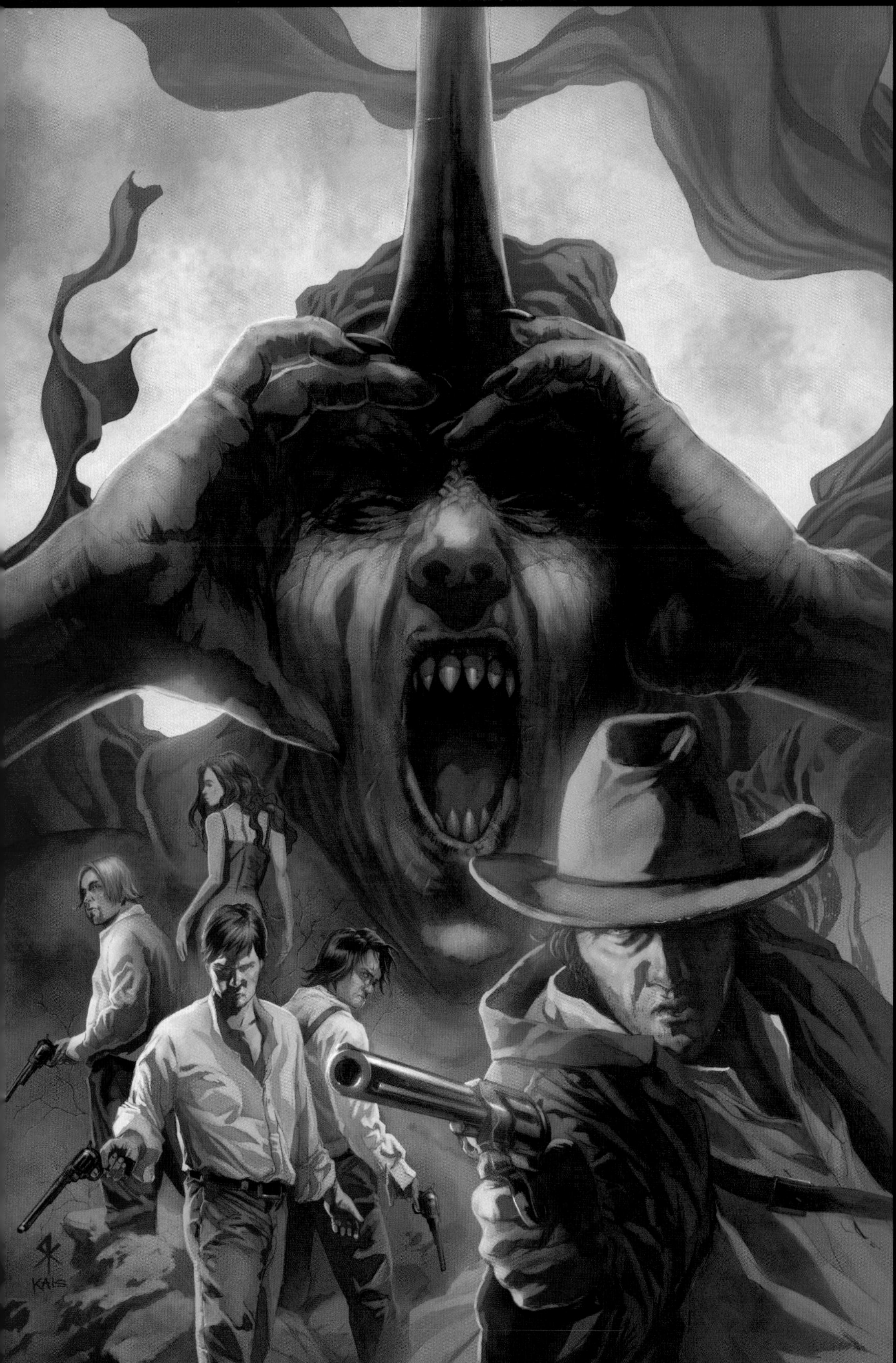

Dark Tower: Battle of Jericho Hill #5 **Cover by Jae Lee & Richard Isanove**

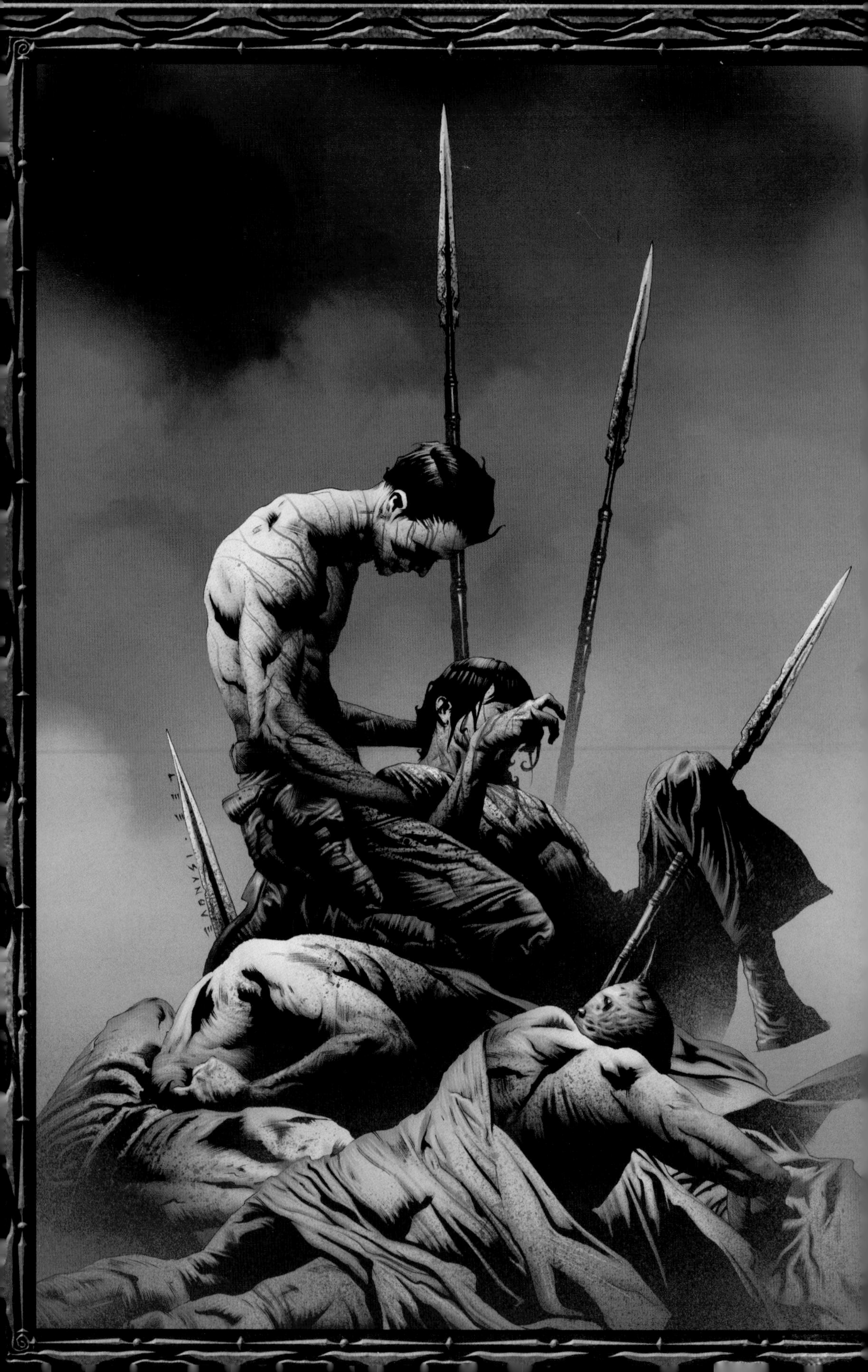

Dark Tower: Battle of Jericho Hill #5 **Variant Cover by Cary Nord & Christina Strain**

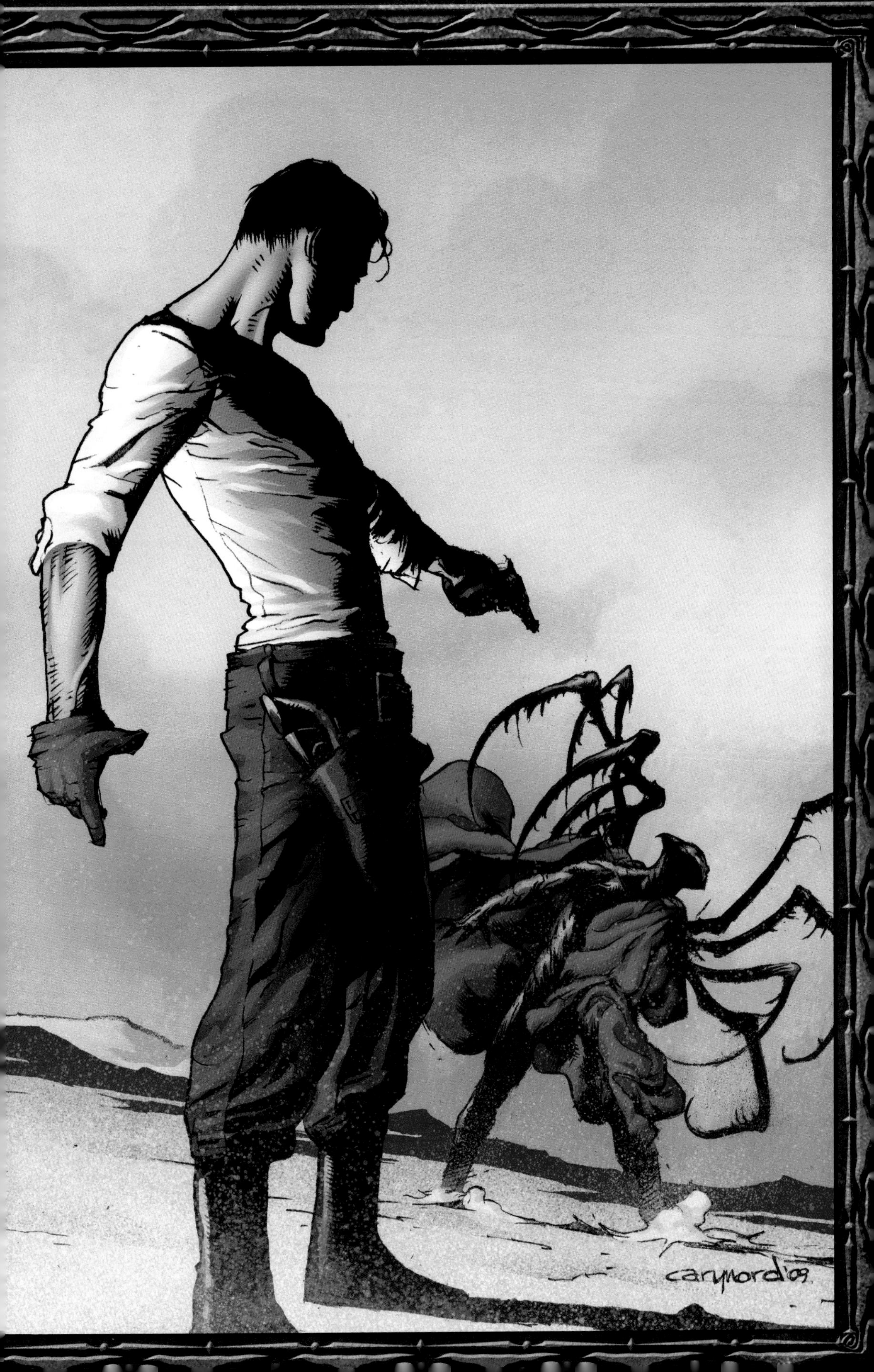

Jae Lee's unused layouts for issue 1.

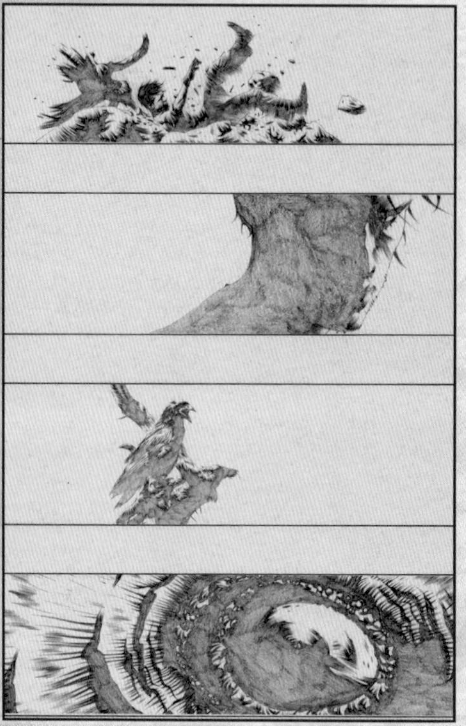

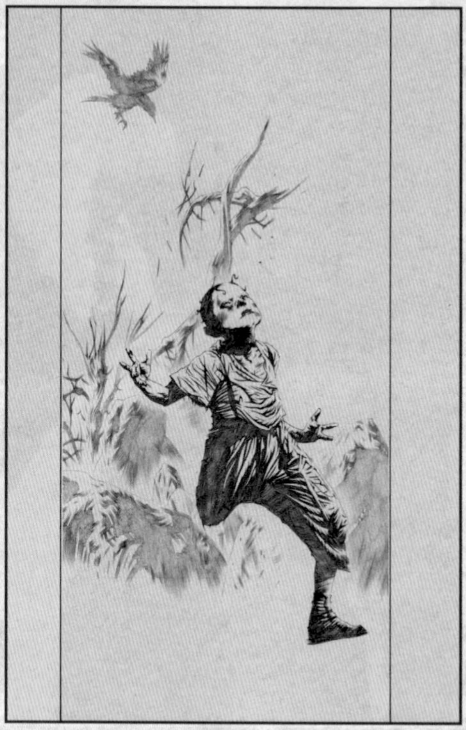

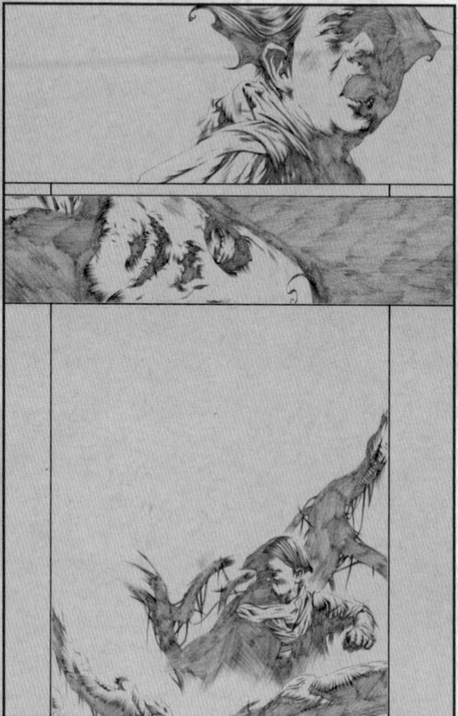

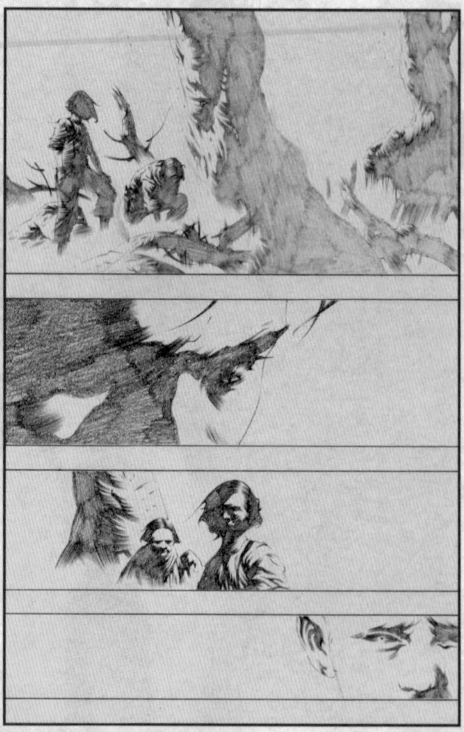

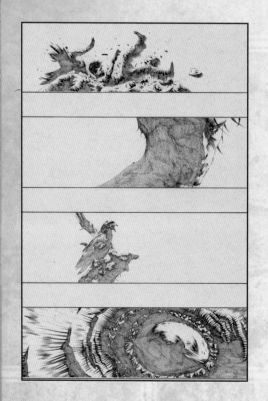

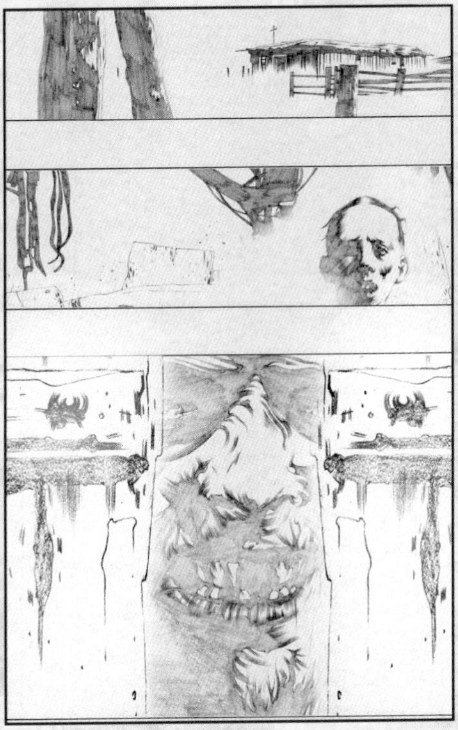

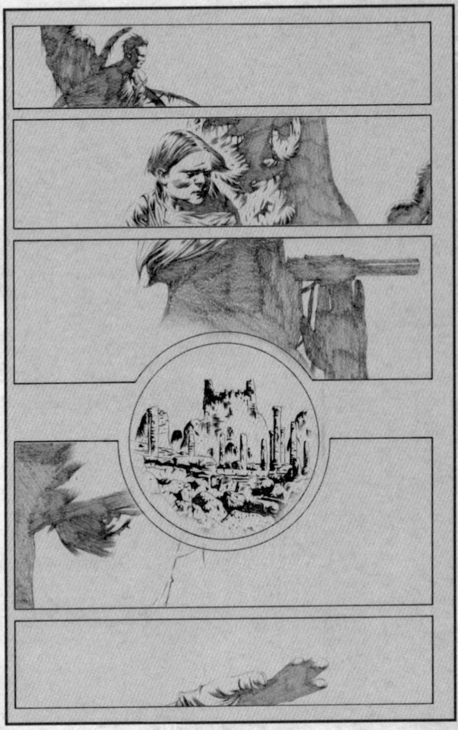

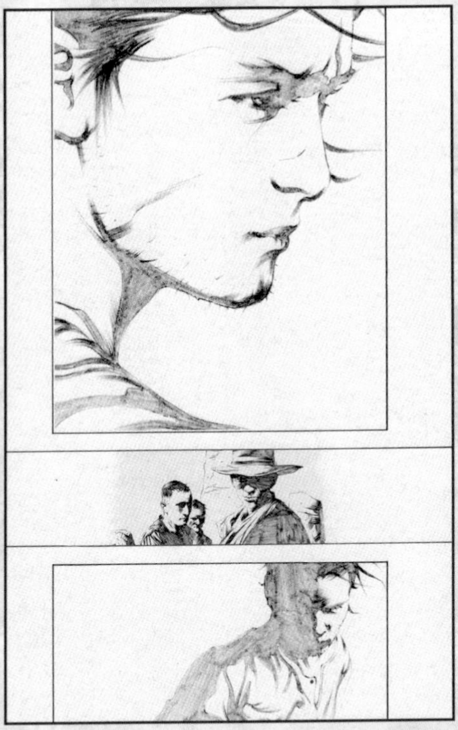

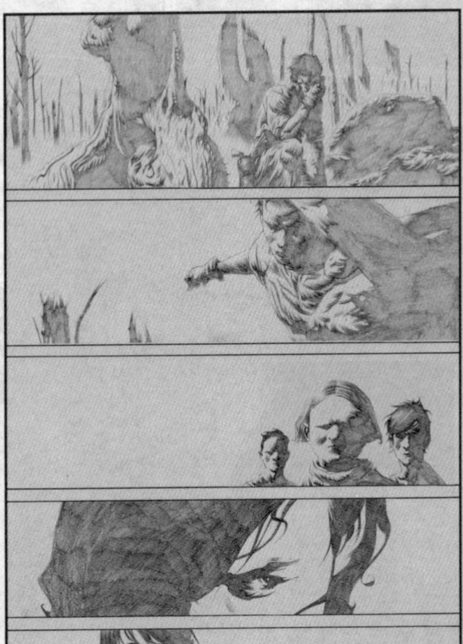

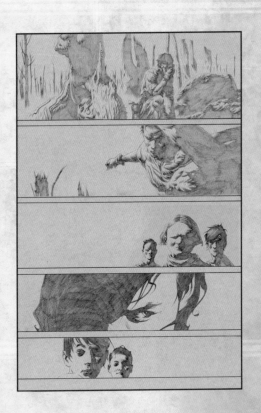

JAE LEE'S ORIGINAL PAGE LAYOUTS FOR ISSUE 2.

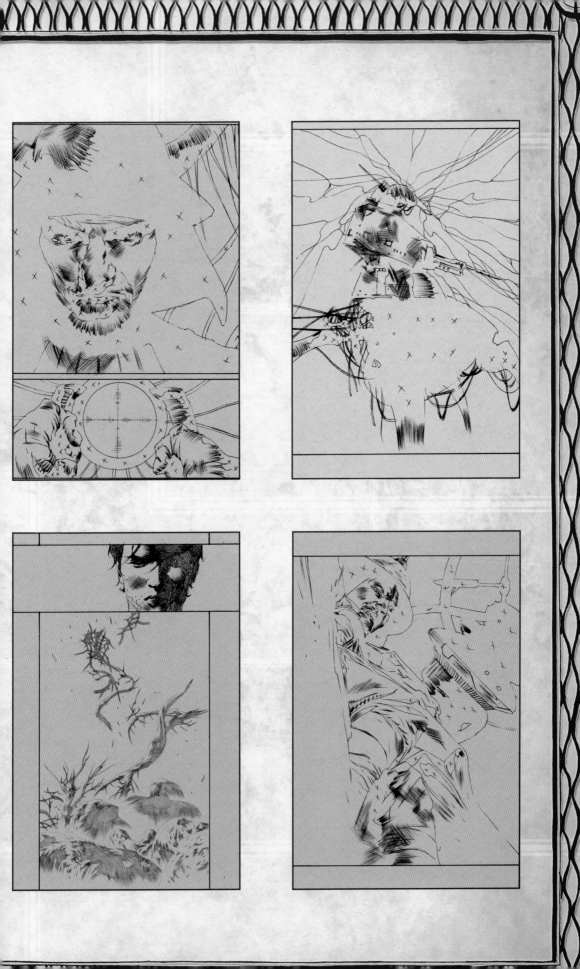

Jae Lee's original page layouts for issue 5's opening spread.

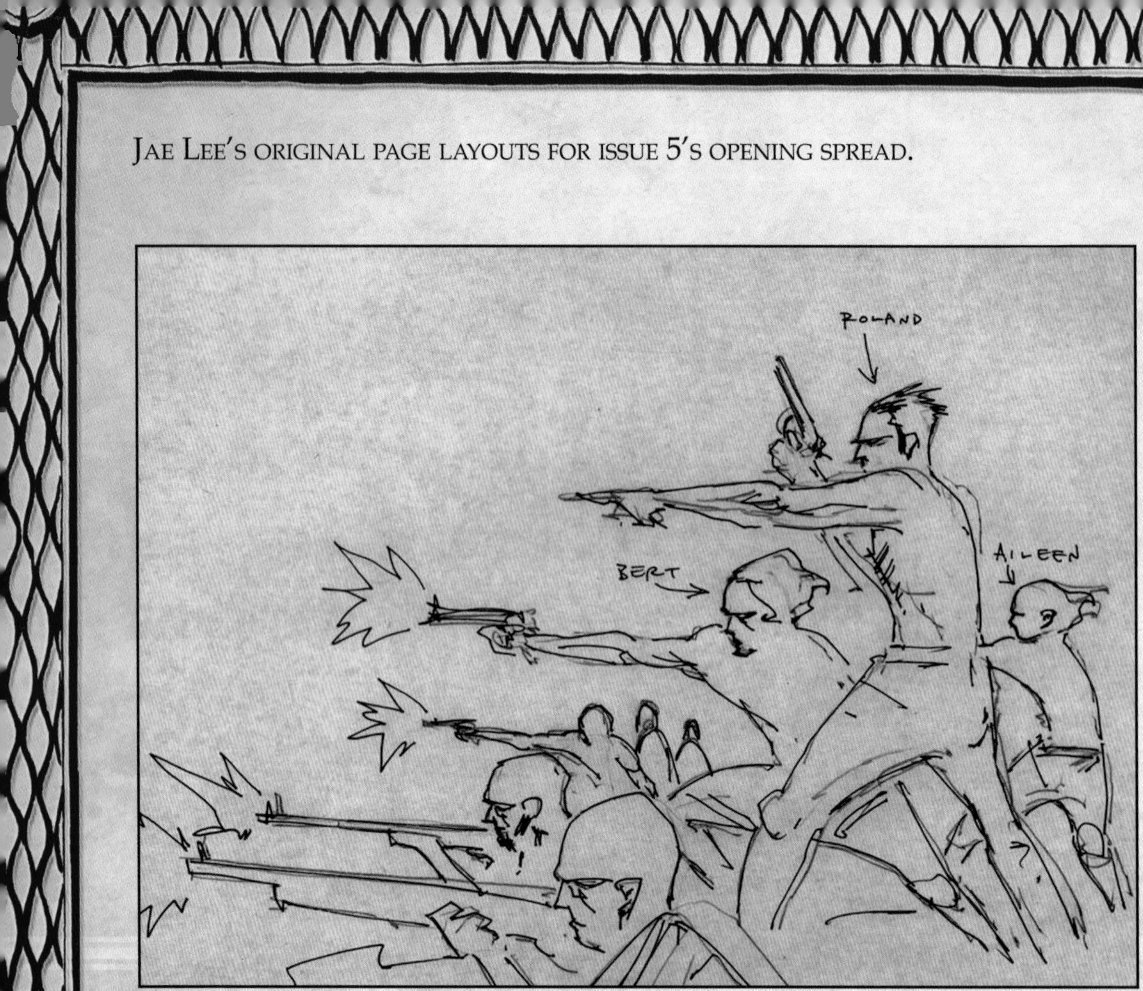
ROLAND
BERT
AILEEN

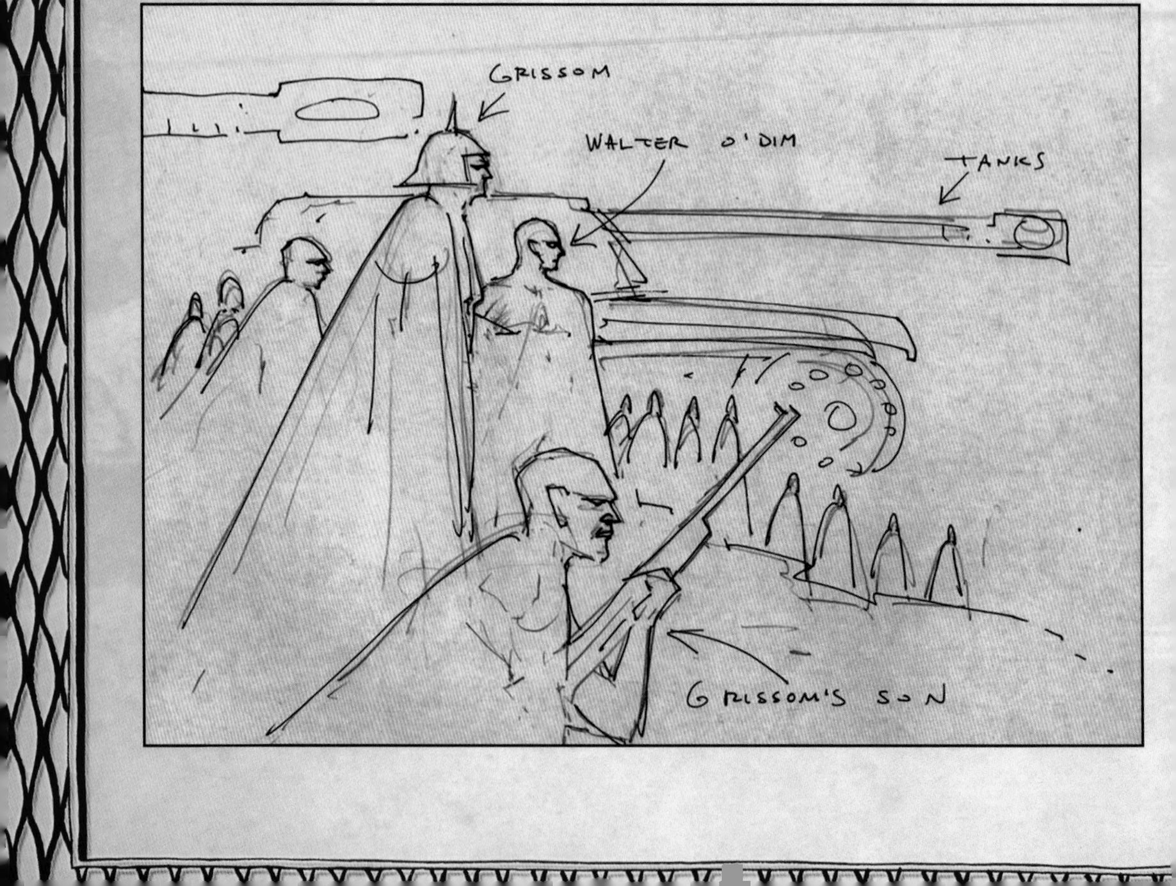
GRISSOM
WALTER O'DIM
TANKS
GRISSOM'S SON

ROLAND GUNS BLAZING
AILEEN
BERT
JAMIE
THOMAS
GRISSOM
WALTER O'DIM
GRISSOM'S MEN CHARGING UP THE HILL GETTING ALL SHOT UP.
BERT
ROLAND
ROLAND'S MEN GET SHOT DOWN.
CROSSBOW
WALTER TAKES AIM
BERT SHOT THROUGH THE EYE

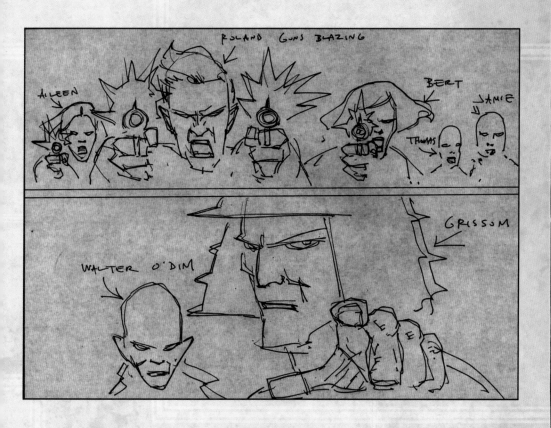

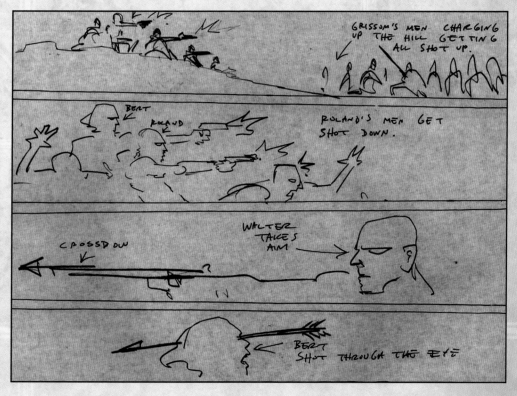

A DEVOTED KING FAN, RISING MARVEL SUPERSTAR STEVE KURTH (ULTIMATE COMICS ARMOR WARS, NEWUNIVERSAL) SUMMARIZED THE HORROR AND MAJESTY OF STEPHEN'S MID-WORLD WITH HIS STUNNING COLLAGE COVER. SEEN HERE ARE HIS INITIAL COVER CONCEPTS.